Dreaming of Wolves

The howls of wolves break the mountain stillness and send chills down his spine. Thus begins the adventure of Alan Sparks and his human "pack," tracking and relating to the wild wolves of Eastern Europe.

Woven into this great tale of adventure are the personal stories, sights, sounds, and insights of a multi-layered experience that proved to be much deeper than Alan had ever imagined.

The legacy of the wolf and the honoring of nature and life itself have been enriched by the author's compassionate and thought-provoking story, and we are all privileged to share in the journey.

— PHILIP RUBINOV JACOBSON, artist, author, educator, and traveler
www.rubinovs-lightning.com
www.myspace.com/oldmastersnewvisions

Dreaming of Wolves is an entertaining and truly inspirational story describing one's decision to leave corporate America behind and pursue new dreams and goals. Alan Sparks teaches us to not settle for the status quo, and to live life as an adventure!

— DON STRANKOWSKI, nationally recognized motivational speaker,
president of Ascend Career and Life Strategies (www.ascendcareers.net), and author
of *Get Hired! 10 Simple Steps for Winning the Job You Desire in Any Economy*

Dreaming of Wolves

ADVENTURES IN THE
CARPATHIAN MOUNTAINS OF TRANSYLVANIA

ALAN E. SPARKS

hancock
house

ISBN 978-0-88839-663-1
Copyright © 2010 Alan E. Sparks

Cataloging in Publication Data

Sparks, Alan E. (Alan Edward), 1956–
    Dreaming of wolves : adventures in the Carpathian Mountains of Transylvania / Alan E. Sparks.

Includes bibliographical references and index.
Issued also in electronic format.
ISBN 978-0-88839-663-1

    1. Wolves—Romania—Transylvanian Alps. 2. Sparks, Alan E. (Alan Edward), 1956– —Travel. 3. Transylvania (Romania)—Description and travel. I. Title.

QL737.C22S66 2009   599.773'094984   C2009-901507-2

Printed in South Korea — PACOM

Editor: Theresa Laviolette
Production: Ingrid Luters
Cover design: Mia Hancock
Cover Wolf photo: © StettenLeiprecht/Froggypress.de
Photography: © as credited

Published simultaneously in Canada and the United States by

HANCOCK HOUSE PUBLISHERS LTD.
19313 Zero Avenue, Surrey, B.C. Canada V3S 9R9
(604) 538-1114 Fax (604) 538-2262

HANCOCK HOUSE PUBLISHERS
1431 Harrison Avenue, Blaine, WA U.S.A. 98230-5005
(604) 538-1114 Fax (604) 538-2262

Website: **www.hancockhouse.com**
Email: **sales@hancockhouse.com**

Contents

Prelude: To Catch a Dream / 9

The Wolves of Transylvania / 31

Epilog / 232

Postscript / 234

Notes / 235

Acknowledgements / 246

References / 248

Resources / 250

Index / 251

For Puffy and Inca.
Their lives taught me how to love.
Their deaths taught me how to live.

The Way of the Wolf Expedition

Prelude: To Catch a Dream

Friday, April 1, 2005

Why didn't I realize I would need better hiking boots? Certainly I've had enough experience in these rugged mountains of Transylvania to know I would need something more waterproof, especially in early April, when cold winter meets wet spring in this wild and remote corner of the world. Yet, recalling the excited rush of packing back in my comfortable home in the States, I suppose I shouldn't be too hard on myself. Trying to consider all the contingencies for a four-month expedition along the length of the Carpathian Mountain chain from Romania to Germany — some 1700 miles — can be overwhelming. Not that *I* was going to hike the entire distance; only "The Way of the Wolf" expedition leader, Peter Sürth, intended to do that. I would primarily serve on the support team. Nevertheless, between picking up groups of eco-volunteers at airports and train stations, procuring food, water, and supplies, and locating and setting up campsites along the way, I anticipated ample trekking opportunities in these lush and spectacular mountains. Accustomed to the relatively dry conditions of Colorado, I guess it slipped my mind that my old, reliable, leather hiking boots wouldn't suffice. But I should have known better, and my soggy, frozen feet wouldn't let me escape self-reproach as we faced the prospect of an unplanned night on the steep, snowy slopes near the end of this, our first day out.

Our elation at finding fresh wolf tracks and scat in the deep snow on top of the ridge faded with the late afternoon light as we realized we were still far from our planned rendezvous with the support team. The hiking team this day — Peter, from Germany;

Thilo, a photojournalist also from Germany; Marcus, an eco-volunteer from Switzerland; Ana, a local member of our team while we were in Romania; and I — stood catching our breath and evaluating our options. We were soaked, both from the meter-deep wet snow through which we had trudged and climbed and slid all afternoon, and from the sweat of exertion as we lugged and pushed and dragged the heavy, awkward wagon full of Thilo's photography equipment up and down the steep slopes, frantically quickening our pace as darkness and cold approached.

We had planned to meet the support team where they were to prepare a camp somewhere far down the densely forested slopes, somewhere along a rough track accessible by the project's Land Rover. But we had no cell phone connection to receive their GPS coordinates, so we didn't know exactly where they were. Peter, who knows this confusing jumble of forested mountains as well as anyone, having tracked wolves here for seven years, scanned the slopes, looking for some channel of light through the dark wood that might reveal a path, or at least for some recognized undulation of the landscape. He had expected a trail leading down from the ridge, but the one we were following near the top had abandoned us, gradually fading into nothing other than narrow passages wandering aimlessly between the trees of the chaotic forest.

In the enthusiasm of that early morning, before the festive send-off in Zarnesti Gorge by local dignitaries, school children, and media from Romania and Germany at the official start of the expedition, we had packed our sleeping bags and pads into our backpacks in order to help condition us for the rigors we expected during the months ahead. But we hadn't packed our tents or tarps, and now there was not a flat or dry spot in sight. We had already struggled several times back up the slopes after attempts to descend had brought us to dead ends created by cliffs or steep thickets impassable with the wagon. If we didn't find a way down before dark we were in for a long, uncomfortable night — and possibly frostbite.

Had we lingered too long at Cabanna Lupului (the Wolf Cabin) where we had stopped in the late afternoon for more formalities and media interviews? I discreetly searched Peter's face for some hint of confidence. It was obvious that four months of this would be impossible, and all my suppressed doubts about the wisdom of this unusual endeavor resurfaced. Meanwhile, the here and now demanded a change in strategy. We wouldn't make it out before dark to the relative comfort of a camp — to something resembling the images of dry tents and warm food that were beginning to invade my imagination — if we kept descending blindly into dead ends.

At least avalanches were of no concern. Unlike the open conditions typical in the familiar dry forests of the Rocky Mountain West, here in the Carpathians the density of trees not only limits sight, but also locks the snow securely to the slopes. If it wasn't for the wagon, which I admit rolled nicely along the rough but flat dirt roads during the first fifteen cheerful and sunny kilometers of our trek, we could slip and slide down about anything (excepting the cliffs), and although soaked and freezing, we'd likely make it out.

"Should we ditch it?"

My companions looked at me with puzzled expressions.

"What?"

[Sorry. I had been trying to avoid idioms, but this one slipped.]

"The wagon…should we leave it here? We could climb back up and get it tomorrow."

I avoided Thilo's gaze, already figuring he wouldn't be pleased with the suggestion of leaving his entire net worth at some uncharted, lonely spot in this wilderness, even if just for a night. And a sour glance from Peter, who is never loquacious, acknowledged the response I already expected. Losing a day to retrieve the wagon would seriously hamper his ambitious — some might say *extremely* ambitious — schedule of trekking nearly twenty-five kilometers a day, six days a week, over the difficult mountainous terrain of the Carpathians, much of it trackless wilderness.

Noticing the concerned expressions around me, it was natural to wonder: had anyone before ever traversed on foot the length of this fabled mountain chain? We can never know whether some unknown nomad unwittingly accomplished the epic feat sometime in the distant past while on an extended hunting expedition, or a forced migration, or merely some protracted aimless wander; but given the physical hurdles, the paucity of motivating factors, and the fact that the region has been perpetually cut by numerous and usually conflicting tribal, cultural, and political divisions, it is safe to doubt it. During their reign of terror in the Middle Ages, marauding bands of Tartars on raids from their Crimean base into Central

Europe for slaves and booty would have covered much of the general route, but to ensure the swift passage of their small horses they would likely have kept to the steppes and lowlands along the mountains' feet.

During most of the last century, when the idea of hiking for the sake of hiking — hiking for recreation — first arose in the human psyche, brutal invasions, insurgencies, counter-insurgencies, and intimidating national borders would have made it highly improbable. Even today there is no single trail, no chain of campgrounds, no established potable water supplies, no accommodations or conveniences of the kind that most modern trekkers have come to expect. I suppose it could be compared to hiking the Appalachian Trail before there was an Appalachian trail, with the added complication that one must pass through a multiplicity of cultures, languages, and nations.

To make the enterprise at least marginally feasible, Peter had found sponsors to provide camping and backpacking gear, and he assembled a support team to handle the day-to-day logistics: Jürgen, a forty-nine year old ex-high-tech worker from Germany, and me, a forty-nine year old ex-high-tech worker from America. We would be joined along the way by "eco-volunteers" who would fund the expedition by paying 300 Euros a week for the privilege of hiking and camping in the mountainous wilds of Eastern and Central Europe and helping us to find signs of wolf, bear, and lynx — the large carnivores of the Carpathians. We were expected to arrive as special guests for the festivities of "Wolf Day" in Rietschen, Germany, some sixteen weeks later, on July 20, and then to give presentations hosted by one of our primary equipment sponsors, Marmot, at a large outdoor equipment expo in southern Germany. We desperately needed a good start in order to believe in our entire plan and preparations for the next four months. To lose the first day wouldn't be it.

After twenty-one years of employment as a software engineer in the intense but staid (and office-bound) world of telecommunications research and development, how did I find myself stuck on a cold and snowy hillside on the trail of wolves in the heart of the Carpathian Mountains of Eastern Europe?

The story began four years earlier with events that led to my first sojourn in Romania, working as a volunteer for a wolf research and conservation project. These are the chronicles of those events — and of my initial adventures with the wolves of Transylvania.

In 2001, the tech bubble burst, and suddenly I found myself "free." True, I was luckier than most of the tens of thousands of other professionals who also got slammed by the unexpected downturn. At forty-five and with almost twenty years at one of the largest telecommunications firms in the world, I just squeaked by in qualifying for an early retirement package. The package was "voluntary," but along with the offer came the sage advice that if we were thinking of not accepting the gracious proposal, we had better think again. Benefits for all subsequent retirees were being drastically reduced, and, more significantly to me, there was no guarantee of continued employment — which really meant, in the euphemistic corporate lingo always designed not to offend, anyone not accepting the offer would likely be "terminated" anyway.

Like most American males, and perhaps especially most boomer American males, I had defined myself by my career, and prior to that by years of arduous studies, without a break, really, since that wondrous day in my childhood when, accompanied and encouraged by my two older brothers, I walked tentatively the one half mile of sleepy streets to the local elementary school in Westbrook, Maine to attend my very first day of school. Still, I was not concerned. I was confident in my abilities and prospects as an engineer. Unlike many others working at the stodgy corporate giant, I had been fortunate to work on exploratory projects utilizing and developing the latest technology, so I knew my skills were current. I had no doubt that prospective employers would recognize my professional talents.

Nevertheless, there I was in July 2001, for the first time in my conscious memory, directionless: unemployed, and not a student. "No problem," I continued to reassure my startled ego. I'd take a little time off to unwind from forty years of continual effort and stress. I'd do some projects around the house, enjoy the companionship of my dogs, spend more time with my parents, siblings, nieces, and nephews back east, and re-evaluate my career goals. Then, after a few months, surely I'd move on to the next job in the long line of jobs that would occupy most of my waking hours, presumably until my retirement, or my death, whichever came first. Meanwhile I'd be supported by the small pension I had been awarded by my generous former employer.

October 8, 2001: The younger of my two dogs, twelve-year old Inca, dies from a debilitating respiratory disease after a painful three-week struggle. Puffy, my other canine friend of fifteen years, trembles as he looks at me with questioning eyes.

May 17, 2002: I walk into the animal hospital room at midnight. I'm dazzled by the blazing, sterile white light. Puffy somehow manages to pull himself up from his seizures for one last look into my watery eyes. I don't know how he knows I've come to say my final goodbye, as he is basically deaf by now. He was never really the same after the passing of Inca, and this is the end of his agonizing three-day battle with kidney failure.

The world I inhabited held no longer my loyal companions, who during the years had waited patiently (or not) each day with their entire beings for me to return from work.

[*What am I to do now? And why?*]

No one depended on me, not even an employer, so what should be my role in the world? For what had I been striving all those years? Studying, taking tests, designing, defending, developing, evaluating, validating, training, promoting, continually facing the pressure of deadlines — allegedly for my always yet-to-be family, for which I never had the time, or the social skills — or, could it be, the inclination — to create. And at forty-six it didn't seem likely I would. So why return to high-pressure high-tech, where it is a full time job simply keeping up with what is always becoming. And where, in any case, the future seemed to be moving east...Far East.

A few months lost, a few months adrift... eventually I knew I needed an anchor, and I felt I should be productive once again. But not as an engineer. That was over. I wanted a completely new experience. I had never had what I considered to be a "fun" job, which I imagined involved performing various low-stress but not-too-mundane tasks while enjoying the camaraderie of fellow workers. During my college years, instead of flipping burgers, or teaching kids how to shoot hoops at summer camp, or making sure people didn't drown in the municipal pool, I had worked summers in a paper mill. The pay was good, but the work was hard, hot, noisy, and dirty, and definitely not fun. Now I was sure I had missed something. I wanted to work with people instead of computers.

[Maybe I can sell things. Seems simple enough, and all the people working in those clean, comfortable stores seem happy enough.]

Since I love books, the choice of venue was obvious, and once I latched onto the idea of working in a bookstore, I imagined fascinating evenings filled with conversation about the relative merits of the latest hot writers, about whether the depth and richness of classical writing would sell today, about whether fiction or nonfiction can more effectively express the truths of human existence. I began visiting all the bookstores in town, but prospects were bleak. I was too late for the holiday hiring. Feeling a bit dejected while driving home one evening from my last visit to a bookstore, I noticed a "Help Wanted" sign at a video store.

[Why not? Movies are just another form of media.]

I stopped in and asked the young clerk how to apply. Barely looking up from his screen, he shoved an application in my direction. I didn't think my master's degree in electrical engineering and my experiences designing telecommunications applications were all that pertinent, but I dutifully scribbled down the requested information, and handed the form back to the clerk. He poked it down a sharp-tipped metal rod onto a large stack of crumpled papers.

The next day the manager called and asked me to come in for an interview.

"What's your favorite movie?"

"I don't know. I like *2001: A Space Odyssey*[1] quite a bit."

"Oh…well, we're looking for someone who really loves movies. Someone who can talk to people about movies."

"Well, actually, I don't watch movies all that much. I like books a lot."

"Well, we're looking for some mature folks so we can establish a rapport with the adults of the neighborhood. Not just kids."

"I guess I'm mature."

"Yeah, you're perfect. We pay seven dollars an hour."

"That's not very much."

"Well, that's just to start. There are opportunities for advancement."

[I don't want advancement. I don't want stress. Like that Spacey character...what was the movie? American Beauty?[2] *He wanted the least responsibility possible, flipping burgers. Hmmm, maybe I know something about movies after all.]*

"Ok, when do I start?"

My first day on the job, I looked for the kindly face and slouched figure of the amiable but harried, middle-aged man who hired me. Instead, a tall, serious young woman of about twenty-seven curtly greeted me and directed me to a computerized register.

"Where is..."

"He's gone. I'm the new manager."

She had come from another store and this was a promotion for her. She seemed competent enough, but I didn't have time to contemplate this management change as customers lined up and impatiently waited for service while I tried to figure out the register. Accounts had to be found, IDs had to be verified, late fees had to be assessed for unhappy customers, people wanted to know where *Attack of the Killer Tomatoes*[3] was located. As I struggled to keep up, I gained a new respect for all those fresh, smiling faces behind the cash registers of America.

My second day on the job, the computer system was down. The lines of huffing and shuffling customers rapidly grew. The district manager happened to be in the store, and I could hear her on the phone with tech support as I stood behind the counter alongside my young manager frantically jotting down people's names, the movies they were renting or returning, swiping credit cards (thankfully that still worked), and collecting cash. I sensed the district manager wasn't making much progress.

"I happen to know something about computers. Maybe I can help."

"You do? That would be great. Do you know what a router is?"

"Yes."

"Think you can find it?"

"Yeah, I think so."

"Here, take the phone."

After a few minutes on the phone with technical support, the computers were up. The store manager continued reassuring customers while we stood around the glowing screen of her re-booting register.

"Wow. Thank you! This is wonderful!" raved the district manager. "How long have you been working here?"

"This is my second day."

"Wow. You know, there are many opportunities to advance here. We need people like you."

The young manager began ringing people up at her register.

My third day on the job, the manager came in and warmly greeted the boy working next to me and asked the young woman stocking the shelves how was her day; for me, not a word. I needed additional training, but whenever I asked her a question, she was too busy to respond. Over the next couple of weeks I had to cop the training I needed from co-workers. Finally I asked the manager if she had a problem with me.

"No, no problem."

"Well, you don't say much to me."

"I'm busy."

"Well, if a problem should come up, please tell me so we can talk about it."

"Ok."

After three weeks, I had had enough. Seven dollars per hour to be shunned by my manager was not the experience I had hoped for. I resigned, and my second career was over.

"What about the Peace Corps?" I suppose this question eventually hits most directionless Americans who are seeking meaning in their lives, although perhaps more typically at an earlier age. Yet I'd heard of a few older people doing it. Didn't Jimmy Carter's mom do it at who knows what age? And if not meaning, it certainly would add excitement to my life — a completely novel experience, to embed in another part of the world, another culture. Maybe I'd even hit it off with a pretty, idealistic fellow volunteer. Once I thought of it, there seemed no alternative: it was the perfect solution. I'd found a vehicle; now I only needed a destination.

I'll resist the urge to say there are two kinds of people in the world; I am convinced there are almost seven billion. Nevertheless, within this vast field of individuality, there are those who love the cold and snow of winter, and those who do not. You can easily distinguish the former. They include your friends who can't wait to send you an email or a text message, or maybe even make a phone call, to inform you they've just seen falling the first white flake of the season. Of course, they won't put it that way, they'll simply declare, "It's snowing!!!" And, while everyone else is congratulating themselves on the "nice weather" when it is twenty degrees above average in January, the lovers of winter fall silent, and furtively glance around to see if anyone shares their depression.

Count me among the lovers of winter. The colder and snowier, the better. In winter the stark beauty of frozen nature lingers, allowing the soul to clutch existence in protracted, crystalline moments. I'm sure I first became hooked as I walked home from school one day while the falling whiteness gradually calmed and silenced an enchanting world. And now I recall with nostalgia the frosty winter scenes while growing up in Maine in the sixties: the snow banks towering far above my head, forming dazzling white tunnels with infinitely high blue-sky canopies; the raging blizzards, in which I could become lost to the world and could imagine trudging through the stinging wind and the blinding snow on some knight's errand to save a pretty maiden; the festive, multi-colored Christmas lights forming luminescent orbs in the snow; the walks through early evening twilight with my young friends to the skating pond, where we would glide over the ice until our hearts were exhausted and our feet were frozen; the amber light from warm, cozy homes spilling through frost-glazed windows into the immense, cold, blue-black night. Winter was magical, and its approach an impending, mystical shift in the world, an exciting alteration that seemed to last forever.

The Peace Corps doesn't allow you to pick a country. You can only specify a preference for a region, and the only region not in warm, equatorial climes was that of Eastern Europe and Central Asia. In addition to winter, I also long for the cover of forests. When you grow up in Maine, unless in the midst of one of its few small cities, you grow up in the forest. And not just any forest, but a forest that, during the summers at least, is largely impenetrable. Not only the dense trunks and branches of trees and the sticks and thorns of brush, but the uneven and slippery footing of logs and muck and moss-covered rock, and the cobwebs of spiders, and the buzzes and bites of mosquitoes and flies and things you can't see hinder your path. And to one so formed — to one reared at the edges of those living, swaying green walls — landscapes without forests seem to hold no mystery. Of course this isn't true. There is no landscape without mystery. But in forests things are explicitly concealed. It's no coincidence, I think, that Stephen King grew up in Maine and writes what he writes. Surely something wild, possibly dangerous, and, just maybe, something evil, lurks in those shadowy domains — something unknown and unknowable.

Thus, hoping for the cold of winter and the mysteries of forests, I chose the Peace Corp's Eastern Europe/Central Asia region, solicited letters of recommendation, and marched through the application process.

"What about language?" I asked the Peace Corps agent at my interview in a downtown Denver high-rise.

"You'll have three months of language training before you go. That's why it's twenty-seven months. Three months language, two years abroad."

"Can I really learn a language in three months, enough to teach in a classroom or help formulate business development plans?"

"You can't do those, you don't qualify. You'll do agricultural work."

"I qualify for agricultural work? What do I know about agriculture? I'm going to teach farmers how to farm?"

"Don't worry, we'll teach you."

By early January I was in, waiting only to schedule the required medical exam. But I soon discovered they wouldn't tell me to which country I'd be assigned until just a few weeks prior to departure. I preferred the forests of Eastern Europe to the steppes of Central Asia, but they didn't want people joining the Peace Corps just to get to a particular place. They wanted people dedicated to *service*, not to travel. I understood that, but I was beginning to see that I'd have to do things this way and that way, follow the rules. I had received an opportunity, finally, to live an unplanned existence. I hadn't gotten to that point of my life to follow more rules, other than the ones in my own heart. Maybe the Peace Corps wasn't the thing.

Colossal machines creep relentlessly over the American landscape like giant termites and locusts and dung beetles, knocking down trees and plowing up the earth to make room for more roads, houses, gas stations, and strip malls. In the East, much of the destruction is hidden by small groves of trees that are left standing amongst and between the developments, to give people the sense they have their private place in the forest. But in the drier and more open West, the "taming" of the land is on full display, and leaves one wondering whether any places will be left truly wild, whether any places will be left as refuges for non-human beings to live out their lives. A few parks are scattered here and there, and a few tracts of land too rugged or desiccated to be economically useful (thus far), but are these islands enough to sustain something essentially free, something truly untamed and tangled, as buildings and manicured landscapes and roads and parking lots surround and isolate them?

Does it matter? As we rush about our busy days, getting educated and earning money and going to movies and eating at restaurants, does it matter whether salamanders and possums and deer have dark, quiet forests in which to crawl and climb and walk, and snakes and field mice and prairie dogs have rough, buzzing meadows in which to slither and scamper and dig, and foxes and fishers and hawks have ample, wild expanses in which to run and prowl and soar? One can enumerate the various practical benefits of maintaining biodiversity in the world, some minimum level of which is presumed necessary for the long-term viability of the biosphere. But what about the *quality* of being in the world? Isn't wilderness necessary for the contentment of the human soul? Millions of harried Americans swarm to forests and mountains and parks each year to "get away," to enjoy the aesthetic quality of wildness — an absence of human dominion, a negation of human power — as though our innate sense of beauty is a recognition that our existence springs from and depends upon that which is beyond us, and is a reminder that there is more to our being than what goes on in our heads. "In wilderness is the preservation of the world", Thoreau wrote. Isn't also in wilderness the beauty and serenity of the world? Yet, soon will come the time when no large mammal will be capable of living its life in something like its natural habitat unless it be by the intentional allowance of humans.

The degree to which an ecosystem is wild and sustainable is measured by the viability of the animals at the top of the food chain. Predators, particularly the large and "dangerous" predators, have come to symbolize what little of the world remains wild and free. Like many lovers of wilderness, I've always had an appreciation for these animals, for their beauty, intelligence, and strength, and I've always been especially fascinated by wolves, which happen to share with my domesticated canine friends a relatively recent ancestry.

For countless millennia, wolves were an integral feature of northern ecosystems. Populations of the adaptable canine spanned all the great landmasses encircling the Arctic Sea. In North America, they roamed the frozen tundra and boreal forests of Alaska and northern Canada, the mountains of the west as far south as the arid uplands of Mexico, the open expanses of the central plains, and the lush deciduous forests of the east. Across the Bering Strait, wolves inhabited lands of similar features and climes: the frozen Siberian tundra, the taiga of Russia, the vast steppes of central Asia, the temperate forests that span the middle latitudes and blanket most of Europe, and ranging south into the deserts of the Middle East and the jungles of India. Yet, while robust populations of wolves still exist in Russia, Canada, and Alaska, and scattered remnants linger elsewhere, during the last century and a half the wolf has been forced to relinquish most of its former domain.

Wolves long shared the diverse landscape of the northern third of the planet with another intelligent, social, and adaptable predator — one that walks upright on two legs. Wolves and early human hunter-gatherers not only shared the land, they also shared an ecological niche, competing for essentially the same prey. Given that the two species faced such similar dynamics of nature — the same landscape, the same climes, and the same prey — it may be no coincidence that the size and organization of their social structures and methods of hunting in cooperative groups were also remarkably similar. But the competing species were bound to conflict, and by medieval times human attitudes about wolves had descended into dark depths of imagination and fear, as the wolf came to personify evil in the myths and legends of Europe. Among the early Europeans who migrated to North America, these beliefs, along with a general desire to subdue all things wild, led to a ruthless campaign to completely eradicate wolves from the landscape. The last wolves in New England were exterminated by the mid nineteenth century, around the same time that Bram Stoker penned *Dracula*, the popular horror novel that helped to foster a mythological image of the Romanian province of Transylvania as a frightening abode of evil — and, not coincidently, a land of marauding creatures somewhat resembling wolves. By the early 1900s, the eradication of wolves was essentially complete in the lower forty-eight states of the United States, except for a small population that survived in northern Minnesota. (Today, with legal protection, reintroduction programs, and natural migration, wolves are making a comeback in the United States — in the Northern Rockies, the Upper Midwest, marginally in the Southwest, and possibly in the Northeast.[4])

Yet, wherever there is much in common, cooperation is also possible, and apparently at least one truce was made: all dogs living today descend from wolves that somehow formed a symbiotic relationship with humans. Perhaps after driving off or killing wolves and raiding their dens, a sympathetic soul took to rescuing and raising the pups. Or, as the other leading theory puts it, perhaps a few scavenging wolves became habituated to feeding from human refuse dumps, and those less fearful of and aggressive towards humans were better able to survive and propagate, not running off from the reliable food supply and not getting killed by defensive humans, until over some generations, animals with a tame disposition evolved. In any case, at some point (or points)[5] some humans took in some wolves, and those best adapted to living in close proximity with people — the least antagonistic and the best at begging for food — were more likely to survive and reproduce. As time passed, people naturally favored those animals with the most desirable traits: the best guardians, the best hunting companions, the best friends — and dogs eventually evolved. While there are obvious morphological and behavioral differences, nevertheless dogs are classified as *Canis lupus familiaris*,[6] a subspecies of wolf, and genetically the two animals are nearly identical.[7]

I stepped back, stepped away from my failed retail career and the Peace Corps, and assessed my proclivities: winter, snow, deep forests, wilderness, wolves — and suddenly I recognized a dream I didn't realize I had: wolf research. For me, could anything surpass tracking wolves in the thick forests and deep snow of the northlands, in the wilderness somewhere away from all the high-tech drudgery, the congested traffic and sprawling suburbs, the bustling rush to nowhere? Working to comprehend a different world, a wild world, and maybe helping to protect it as well. Wouldn't it be a fitting tribute to my departed canine friends? Certainly there were people who actually did that kind of thing. I'd read numerous books about it. But I knew wolves were "in," I wasn't a trained biologist, and opportunities would be hard to come by.

I looked on the web to see what I could find. A website for eco-volunteering led me to the website of something called the Carpathian Large Carnivore Project (CLCP). I was astounded: shepherds tending flocks on rolling meadows surrounded by lush green forests and spectacular snow-capped mountains; rustic wooden carts being pulled along quiet rural roads by handsome, red-tasseled horses; idyllic farms and quaint villages. It looked like nineteenth century New England with a Rocky Mountain backdrop. And what's more, there were wolves and bears and lynx!

Tracking wolves *there*? If anything was ideal for me, that was surely it. But *Romania*? What did I know about Romania? I was pretty sure I could find it on a map, but all I really knew of Romania was that it was recently behind the Iron Curtain and seemed to produce a lot of children with world-class gymnastic aptitude. Could I really pull off going to Romania by myself to live for months (hopefully) in who knows what conditions, amidst an unknown culture with an unfamiliar language?

Anyway, I was getting way ahead of myself. What were the chances there would be an opportunity for me at the Carpathian

Large Carnivore Project? The website offered jobs for eco-volunteers, people who are willing to shell out a fair number of bucks for the privilege of working — perhaps at some rather mundane tasks (being untrained) — during a few short weeks of their vacation time. I was looking for something more embedded, a longer-term commitment; I wanted to immerse myself in the experience for at least a year.

EMAIL January 6, 2003:

Hello,

I am writing to inquire about volunteer opportunities with the Carpathian Large Carnivore Project. I know there are opportunities for participating for a few weeks through the eco-volunteer program that requires a fee, but I am wondering if it is possible to volunteer for a more extended time, such as about 12 months, where a fee would not be required for this much participation.

I have a strong love of nature, and of animals, and forests, and believe that the health of an ecosystem is best measured by the health of the carnivore population. Although I am 46, I am very physically fit and am experienced in traveling in forests (hiking, skiing, snow shoeing). I have a strong back and am willing to work hard at any tasks that may be helpful, whether helping to set up electric fences, following tracks in the forests, counting deer pellets, or helping to increase public awareness in the United States, including raising funds or establishing relationships with travel agencies (I believe there could be significant eco-tourism interest in the CLCP from the United States).

Although I speak only English (and a little French), I would try to learn the Romanian language as much as possible, and in general I would have great respect and sensitivity for the local culture and local interests. I understand well the issues identified in your annual report and the importance of having local support for the program. Thank you for your time. I am happy to learn there is a program like the CLCP, and I wish you the best success in your work. If you believe that I could help with the program as a long-term volunteer, please contact me...

Sincerely,
Alan Sparks

As I continued to peruse the CLCP website I became more and more enamored with the idea, and my hopes fell proportionally. I thought that such a project in such an enchanting locale must receive innumerable requests like mine. Well, I had given it a try. Meanwhile I kept my Peace Corps option open and continued searching for other opportunities.

Two days later I received a reply from Christoph Promberger, the founder and leader of the Carpathian Large Carnivore Project. He felt I could "actively contribute to the success of the CLCP" and he wanted me to come to Romania! It happened that the research activities of the project were ending in late March, but they were beginning to design a Large Carnivore Information Centre and perhaps my technical skills would be useful. I could also help with fundraising, particularly from potential US sources. Christoph added that he hoped my goal in volunteering for a conservation project wasn't to "escape technology only to end up in front of a computer again," but, in any case, if I were to come around the first of March, I could work in the field for the final month of the CLCP's research program and then take it from there.

In an email explaining the reasons for the termination of the ten-year research program, Christoph provided a brief history of the CLCP. He founded it in 1993 as a wolf research project affili-ated with a private research and consulting institute. He began to raise funds from governmental and non-governmental organiza-tions[8] and put together a staff. During the ensuing years the project grew and expanded its research to include the two other large car-nivores of the region, brown bears and lynx, and then began to promote the conservation of Romania's unique natural heritage:

> Romania is a country in transition, where the new technologies hit almost medieval rural communities. As well, a small part of the population has become very rich, whereas half of the people live below poverty level. This all, together with the political and socio-economic changes, creates new and important threats for the con-servation of large carnivores and their habitat.
>
> Consequently, we (the project staff grew to about 10 full employed staff and approximately 5 volunteers) started to develop activities in three other fields: Conservation and management, rural development and public awareness. The first field of activities was

supposed to directly mitigate conflicts (e.g. the electric fences), the rural development was to create the economic basis for conservation and sustainable development, and public awareness was to support the other components.

Now, after ten years, we believe that the CLCP should come to an end, we believe in creating sustainable structures and not in institutionalizing ourselves. Things have worked out very well and, although there is still much to do in terms of research, we think we understand the basic elements necessary for wildlife management. At the same time, also funding for research has decreased considerably, since we told our donors from the beginning we wanted a 10-year project and to create sustainable structures.

As a last important step, we believe the area needs a tourist attraction to secure sustainability and this Large Carnivore Centre would also contribute to the education of national and international visitors with respect to large carnivores.

"Be careful what you wish for, because you might get it." Romania? In a "primitive" cabin in the middle of winter without electricity and running water? I assumed I'd be the only one there, at least at that time of year. I thought this was what I wanted, but was this *really* what I wanted? How would I get there? This outfit was obviously not the handholding, don't-worry-we'll-take-care-of-everything type. I was told only to fly to Bucharest, take a train to Brasov (pronounced "Brashof"), and from there they'd get me to Zarnesti (pronounced "Zarneshte") somehow.

"Where is Zarnesti?" I queried in another email.

"It's a small town some thirty kilometers from Brasov, where the project is headquartered."

A bit of research suggested that getting from the Bucharest airport to the appropriate train station, "Gara Nord" (the North train station) could be daunting. Something about illegitimate and unscrupulous taxi drivers and hoards of thieves and other unsavory types just waiting to prey upon naïve travelers. But surely other people had gone to Romania to work as volunteers for the CLCP and survived. And anyway, having already lost my two best friends and my job, I didn't think I had much else to lose. Adventure was exactly what I was seeking.

Adventure yes, but informed adventure, so my research continued. More travel information websites contained warnings about the hazards of traveling and living in Romania: diseases (lots of diseases, especially for travelers visiting rural areas or "spending a lot of time outdoors or with animals": tuberculosis, tick-borne encephalitis, lyme borreliosis, hepatitis, typhoid, rabies); pick-pockets; lawless bands of roaming mafia-types; thugs disguised as police who'll pull you over and ask for your passport and wallet, which you'll never see again; thugs not disguised as police who'll ram your car and ask for your passport and wallet, which you'll never see again.

But isn't American society one of the most violent on the planet? Seems I had heard as much somewhere. I read about a few teenagers in nearby Fort Collins, Colorado who had recently been driving along roads knocking people off bicycles with baseball bats. I wondered if such purposeless, random violence is common in more traditional and less consumption-driven societies, and I suspected that in spite of the warnings, I was likely heading towards a place of relative amicability.[9]

But what if I get injured? Surely not a negligible risk while traipsing through the wilderness tracking large carnivores, not only wolves, but maybe also European brown bears, the same species as the North American grizzly bear. What kind of medical treatment could I expect in Romania? A report issued by a travel immunization clinic was not reassuring: "Medical care is substandard throughout the country…Adequate evacuation procedures for all travelers is a high priority…every effort should be made to go to Western Europe…Hospital accommodations are inadequate throughout the country…Shortages of routine medications and supplies may be encountered."[10]

While my fears and reassurances thus ebbed and flowed, I resolved to take a few precautions. I confirmed that my tetanus was current, scheduled a hepatitis A vaccination, and in my next message to Christoph I asked if I should get a rabies inoculation, recommended if one is going to be around animals in Romania.

"Don't worry about it," was Christoph's terse reply.

The travel advisory websites having duly instilled in me sufficient paranoia about traveling to Romania, I decided to put a lid on the research and turned to less timorous matters.

"What about a visa?"

"You don't need one for less than ninety days. If you stay longer, we'll get you one."

"What about language?" I certainly wanted to be able to communicate. In addition to the practical aspects, I knew it would provide a richer experience, and I considered it a matter of respect for the culture and people who would be hosting me. Apparently Romanian language instruction materials are not in high demand in America, so it took a bit of searching, but Amazon came through and I managed to find a small introductory language instruction booklet and a phrase book with a CD. As if I needed further proof of my ignorance, I was surprised to learn that Romanian is a Romance language. Since I knew Romania lies far to the east of the countries typically associated with this language group, I had assumed Romanian was a Slavic tongue. (Upon some further thought, I wasn't so surprised — after all it is called ROMANia).

With about two weeks to go before my departure I diligently began studying the little book and the CD, with results that I knew were quite inadequate. Then, a fortuitous event: a friend of a friend had a friend from Romania who might be willing to help. Thus I was introduced to Maria. In her late fifties, or so I guessed when I met her, Maria is a fascinating woman with a mysterious history that I gathered from bits and pieces is extraordinary. She had left Romania sometime in the 1960s after having been persecuted as a political prisoner by the ruthless communist regime. I could only imagine what that might mean, and she didn't offer to elaborate. She was proud that her family had been aristocratic and powerful before the communist takeover, and was sad over what had been lost. After somehow getting out of prison and the country, she traveled and lived in several European countries before arriving in the United States.

Maria is a brutally honest, quick-to-the-point veterinarian and lover of animals, which, as she observed, is an anomaly in Romania. On visits back to the old country after the fall of the Iron Curtain, she amazed and confounded relatives with antics such as stopping and jumping out of a car to care for one of the countless stray dogs that roam the streets. Apparently she utilized unusual methods in her veterinarian practice — homeopathy and other techniques sworn as effective by her long-time clients, who, however, had been naturally and gradually falling off as time went by. She refused to participate in the high-powered marketing efforts of her competitors, many who are financed by the deep pockets of veterinary franchise chains that are springing up like dandelions. She also admitted that some people just didn't like her. I could see why some people could be put off by her direct and abrupt style, but I found her honesty refreshing. And I sensed an inner strength, forged, no doubt, by some horrendous experiences.

After deflecting her initial skepticism — she wanted to know why someone from America would voluntarily go to Romania and especially why he'd want to make the effort to learn a language that will "surely die" — I began Maria's informal no-nonsense language instruction about ten days before my departure. Her critique of my novice efforts was severe, but the results were encouraging, at least compared to using a book. I seemed to be managing a few key words and phrases, such as "yes," "no," "thank you," and "I can't speak Romanian." With a couple of days left to go, as I was struggling with a twister particularly difficult for my American tongue, Maria lit a cigarette, took in a deep draught, let it slowly out, and abruptly asked in a scratchy voice, "How are you going to get from the airport to Gara Nord?"

"A taxi?"

With a quick, skeptical glance Maria assessed my naiveté and dismissed my chances. She picked up the phone, placed a call, and started an animated conversation in Romanian. The music of the language reminded me of Italian. She was speaking with her cousin "Nini" in Bucharest. It was quickly arranged: he would pick me up at the airport and transport me to the train station. Well, this was more than I expected, and to be honest I was not comfortable accepting such gracious favors from complete strangers in Romania.

"Buy them dinner if it makes you feel better. He is my cousin."

"Ok."

I can't deny that this development relieved one of my primary worries, and it seemed a good omen. The next occurred on the final, long leg of my flight to Bucharest, from New York. I was unexpectedly bumped up to business class due to overbooking.

Thus began my adventures with the wolves of Transylvania.

The Wolves of Transylvania

Monday, March 3, 2003

These last two or three weeks I've been clearing away eighteen years of dust as I packed and put my affairs in order. Since my life is about to change so drastically, I feel I'm experiencing its end, with all the associated angst. Attending several going-away celebrations with friends was a bit like attending my own funeral.

The suitcases are packed full and laying open on the living room floor. Daisy, my house-sitting friend's Pomeranian, has jumped up onto a suitcase and curled herself on top of my wool coat, putting her chin down and giving me a stare, as though declaring, "You're not to go!" Thanks… just the encouragement I need.

I suddenly realize I've led a charmed life and didn't know it. One of the great tragedies, really, to be happy and not to notice, wrapped up in this and that: my job, my worries, my entertainments and diversions. Well, if from this adventure I realize only this — to *notice* — before I have even stepped from the door, then I've already attained a great end.

Wednesday, March 5

I've arrived at "Cabanna Lupului," the Wolf Cabin.

My journey here went smoothly enough. But was it really just yesterday that I staggered off the plane and down the steps and through the cold mists to the terminal building at the Bucharest airport? Once inside I remember being interrogated by a bored and sullen customs agent who asked why I was here and where I was going. Sensing she'd be skeptical of the details, I mumbled something about "tourism" and "Zarnesti." It seemed to suffice.

Maria's cousin Nini and his wife Carmi were waiting outside the baggage claim, as we had planned. I recognized the couple looking for a man they didn't know, they recognized me looking for a couple I didn't know, and an exchange of tentative smiles confirmed our identities. They appeared to be in their forties — Nini a stocky, powerfully built man with thick dark hair just beginning to go gray, and Carmi a slender, perky woman with short blond hair. They greeted me warmly and enthusiastically, as though I was a long lost friend, and then introduced me to Christien, a young man who had been standing politely nearby. Christien spoke a little English, he explained, and had come along to translate, and was very enthusiastic about the opportunity.

As we left the building and walked through the parking lot I was slapped and finally roused by the stark, damp cold. A blanket of stale but eerily luminescent snow, slightly brighter and whiter than the gloomy gray sky, shrouded a foggy, unfamiliar world. We crammed my luggage and then ourselves into a tiny, beat-up, red car, and Nini drove us crisply from the airport and into the chaotic streets of the darkening city.

Nini and Carmi were putting me up for the night, so soon after our awkward exchange of pleasantries, haltingly translated by Christien, I got around to my plan of inviting them to dinner. They spared me the embarrassment of a protracted refusal — actually, of any refusal at all — and I wondered whether Maria had smoothed the way on this point. Taking us first to their flat, Nini navigated a dizzying maze of streets, eventually pulling into a dark parking lot in front of one of the countless, drab, communist-era apartment block buildings that surround and infiltrate the central districts of the city. As we unloaded my bags onto to the icy pavement, several scrawny, skittish dogs approached to investigate.

The interior of the flat was surprisingly cozy, albeit dimly lit. I focused my dwindling energy on being as sociable as possible, and asked a few questions about the heirlooms and books that were displayed on a large bookcase dominating the main living room. Carmi removed a few albums and the couple began showing me ancient family photos. As our chat warmed, I was surprised to learn that Nini was involved as some kind of director with a national mountain rescue organization. He took frequent trips to the mountains and knew of "Cabanna Lupului," where I would be staying.

After placing the albums back on the shelves my hosts exchanged a few words with Christien. Our translator then turned to me and asked, "When do you propose to dine?"

I paused an instant to feign some thought.

"Soon…actually, now would be fine."

The three exchanged awkward glances. Apparently around 6:00 p.m. was not their habit. I glanced at an antique clock mounted on the wall that was clicking away the seconds, searching for a compromise. I couldn't remember the last time I had eaten.

"Well, sometime soon would be great. Say, six-thirty?"

Noting Nini's and Carmi's reactions while Christien translated, I quickly added, "Or seven."

Around six forty-five we departed the flat. Nini drove us to a nearby restaurant, and we took a table in a pleasant alcove with rustic wood-paneled walls. A stuffed wild boar glared at us from a corner, its two large tusks jutting up in a menacing smile, providing a startling reminder of the wild world into which I was heading and why I was here. During the meal I constantly feared violating some unknown social protocol, being worn down by the sleepless thirty-hour marathon of packing and travel, and after inhaling the repast as discreetly as possible while responding between bites to questions and puzzled stares about why I was in Romania, I was grateful we returned directly to the flat. With no energy remaining to sustain even marginally competent socializing, I quickly escaped to the small, comfortable bedroom they generously offered, and wired but exhausted, slept surprisingly well.

The next day I learned my hosts would drive me directly to the cabin. They wouldn't hear of me taking the train. They liked going to the mountains anyway. Another fortuitous development, although I began to worry this was all too easy. I was seriously jet-lagged, yes, but where were the difficulties and dangers I felt were the necessary components of true adventure?

I got a taste on the drive to Zarnesti. As we left the brown and somber late-winter plains of Wallachia and began ascending into the Transylvanian Alps (as the southern arm of the Carpathian Mountain chain is sometimes called) on the winding, narrow mountain road, now lined with snow-clad spruce and fir, a seemingly inexhaustible stream of cars began to rush wildly by, passing us one after the other on sharp curves with no visibility of the road ahead. And what was ahead was a seemingly inexhaustible stream of approaching cars passing slower vehicles in exactly the same manner, forcing Nini into frequent evasive maneuvers. Thinking a train may have been the safer alternative after all, I was grateful that Nini, at least, chose not to participate in the frantic dash that seemed to rule the road this day.

We finally descended into the relative safety of the Transylvanian plateau and rolled along a quiet road through flat, open country. We passed a jumbled row of small, decrepit shacks, which I was to learn was a Gypsy village, and then came to a lonely intersection where loomed a large sign plastered with threatening symbols and exclamation points and prominent admonitions in three languages (Romanian, German, and English): "Warning: Entering Dracula territory!!!"

Nini clutched the wheel with resolve and continued on, driving us to and through a village called Rasnov, and a few kilometers beyond that we came to the outskirts of what seemed to be a more imposing settlement, as the narrow road soon became lined with a solid wall of modest but neat stucco houses. Beyond an intersection, at a break in the wall, stood a long line of pink, dilapidated, rust-streaked factory buildings. The dismal facility featured large gray façades of sooty windows that were checkered with the black holes of missing panes, and seemed abandoned.[11] More houses followed, regrouping around the road until another wall was formed. At what I took to be the center of the village, Nini pulled over and parked between two enormous craters, and we finally piled out into the dreary, dank cold of Zarnesti.

Since we were four hours from Bucharest, I was surprised when three or four men immediately recognized Nini and came rushing over to chat. I suppose I was introduced, but while friendly greetings were exchanged I could only stand silently and gape around at the village — at the chickens roaming the sidewalks; at the horses pulling rough-hewn wooden carts along half-frozen, mud streets; at the decrepit high-rise buildings that stood beyond the houses; at the somber sky filled with billowing gray clouds; and at my breath hanging in the frigid air — and wonder what I had gotten myself into. I seemed to have landed not only in another place, but another time. As the conversation continued around me in a tongue I didn't know, a large bundle of sticks on a steep roof above grabbed my narrowed attention.

[What the hell is that? Why would someone put a huge bundle of sticks way up on that steep roof?]

(I was to learn later that no person did; I had spied my first stork's nest.)

The Wolf Cabin lies along a rough dirt road six or seven kilometers from the center of Zarnesti. It is indeed primitive. I'm tired, jet-lagged, and hungry as it sinks in just how primitive. A large plastic container with a spigot and a catch basin underneath provides the "running" water for cooking, washing dishes, drinking, brushing teeth, etc. The water must be carried in buckets from a small stream in front of the cabin. There are small fish in the stream, so if we want a water supply tank and not an aquarium we must take care when dipping in the buckets. For cooking, a propane stove supplements the hulking ceramic woodstove that dominates the main living area of the cabin. Lighting is provided by a single compact-fluorescent light bulb powered from a battery that is charged by two solar panels on the roof. I'm told that we might get three or four hours of illumination in the evenings on a bright sunny day, otherwise candles do the job. The sleeping quarters are upstairs where a row of mattresses lines each wall. The loft is cold, dark, and cheerless, being lit only by the meager light trickling through one small window. We access the stairs through the "outroom" in the back, which is kept unheated and is used for storing food and supplies. As I settle into the one chair (besides the dining table benches) to take this all in, I notice that a large jumble of dirty dishes overflows a basin sitting on the floor.

A tall, slender young man has been showing me around and suddenly I realize there are others living here after all. After he completes some more urgent chore, the man leads me out back to another small log building and explains that this is where we can "shower" (sauna) once every three days if we have the time to chop and burn enough wood to heat it up. We then walk about thirty meters farther up the slope to the outhouse, from which is a majestic view of the Piatra Craiului (King's Stone) mountain massif across the valley.

Most enthusiastic about my arrival are the two canine residents of the cabin. Guardian is a rambunctious white-and-black speckled male shepherd dog, weighing perhaps fifty-five pounds, who wags his whole body whenever I glance his way. "Careful," I'm warned, "he sometimes nips at the backs of the legs of strange male humans." Curly is a smaller and more serene brown-black-and-white female, who looks at me with a smile and an intelligent, curious gaze.

Besides the dogs, I learn I'll be sharing these new digs with four human residents, at least for now. Titus, the man who stopped (most of) his busy chores to show me around, is a young student from Germany. He has been living here since November — a feat that impresses me. The quiet, petite, woman who has been inconspicuously performing various cabin chores during my orientation is Silverine, an eco-volunteer from France. She has been here a week and will stay one more. Another student, Vanessa, and another eco-volunteer, Joris, are currently out in the field.

As the afternoon wears on I try to get settled. I see the atmosphere in the cabin is rushed yet efficient and I try to fit in, but naturally, not knowing the ropes, I feel a bit in the way, although I do take on the pile of dishes.

Wolf monitoring and tracking is currently going on full-time, in three eight-hour shifts: 2:00 a.m.–10:00 a.m., 10:00 a.m.–6:00 p.m., and 6:00 p.m.–2:00 a.m. All other activities revolve around this schedule and supporting the rustic yet hectic life in the cabin: cooking, eating, cleaning, boiling drinking water, maintaining equipment, drying clothes and boots, keeping the water tank filled and the wood stove going, and the wolves and the dogs fed. I'm sitting here again in the chair next to the woodstove feeling very uncomfortable and wondering if this is crazy and how long will I last. A large paper sign posted on the wall reads as follows:

Things that need to be done everyday: 1) Fill up the water container; 2) Feed the wolves if they have no horsemeat!! 3) Cook dog food every!!!! evening and feed them every morning (cooking instructions above the stove); 4) wash dishes as soon as possible; 5) clean up the small table in the corner, personal stuff can stay in the outroom!!! 6) When the bucket with organic waste is full -> PLEASE empty on the hill; 7) when the bucket with normal waste is full -> take the bag out and bring it to Zarnesti before it overgrows and everything is on the floor!! 8) If you have time in between please broom the floor. Thank you!! PS: Everybody here in the cabin is out in the field and busy every day. But if everybody helps together, things go a lot faster And your support ☺ makes everybody's life here easier!!

I guess there is no escape from rules.

Thursday, March 6

The view from the cabin is spectacular, especially after a light snow overnight. Patches of blue sky mingle with white clouds and fog hanging over the mountains. The wolves are howling. Two captive wolves, Poiana (meaning "meadow" in Romanian, or more precisely, "a small meadow in the forest") and her larger brother Crai (King), inhabit a two-acre fenced enclosure sloping sharply up the hill behind the cabin. One wolf begins a low whine, which rises slowly into a long mournful wail. A second voice joins in, seeming to chase the first, which, as though not to be caught, abruptly shifts to a hysterical, high-pitched whoop. The first voice falls silent, while the second continues as a prolonged lonely plea. Then begins a series of short yelps that meld into a pulsing, high-pitch cry. The voices continue, rising and falling, sometimes in concert, sometimes not, interweaving in a forlorn acoustic dance that seems formed from some indeterminable number of wolves instead of two. While I gaze at the snow-covered landscape and breathe deeply the frosty mountain air, this eerie sonic tapestry confirms the reality of my dreams in an ecstatic thrill.

Vanessa and Joris have left for another day in the field. The 24/7 monitoring will continue for a month or until the radio collar goes dead. The routine will be much different after that. Silverine and Joris both leave next week and no more eco-volunteers will follow. They are the final volunteers in the ten-year history of the CLCP. Vanessa also leaves in April, and Titus is thinking about it. I know the project hosts eco-tourist treks and horseback rides, but what else? Will I soon be alone? What will I be doing? I'm still waiting to meet Christoph, and until I do my role here is not quite clear.

I have a minor sore throat and wonder if it's the start of something serious, as conditions here are not especially sanitary. Using the stream for water particularly concerns me, as we are downstream of a few houses and pastures. We boil the water for drinking, but not to wash and rinse dishes, hands, toothbrushes, etc. I've been volunteering to wash the dishes so I have at least some influence on sanitation. Today I also made a new handle for our axe and hand-planed the tool shed door so it would close more easily. I hope I'm being useful.

All my hopes for a modicum of sanitation are foiled when I see Titus and Silverine lugging pieces of a dead horse from the metal box near the outhouse to the wolves' feeding area near the cabin. The dripping red chunks of meat and bone are large, heavy, and rotten. It is odorous and disgusting work and very difficult for Silverine. I offer to help, but I'm exempted because I had already washed the dishes. While obviously not a fair exchange, it is clear that this is part of the eco-volunteer experience that Silverine is determined to see her way through, and I don't protest. This is just as well, because upon catching a particularly strong whiff of the foul odor, along with the sight of squirming maggots, it is only with great difficulty that I manage not to hurl.

After Titus and Silverine toss them over the high chain-link fence, the wolves tear into the gory prizes, their teeth cutting quickly through the decayed but sinewy flesh, tendons, and fat as though they were bread.

Friday, March 7
Yesterday afternoon Titus started baking bread in the wood stove, making the cabin much too warm, so I decided to take a walk in the quiet beauty of gently falling snow. While everyone here is pleasant, and we get along well enough, and we bump into each other far less than might be expected as we bustle about our daily chores, living in a confined space with five adult humans is not the experience I had anticipated, and certainly is not what I was used to. I craved some solitude, and some exercise as well, and this was my first real chance at both since I arrived.

As I left the cabin yard and walked out to the road, I found myself not quite alone after all. Guardian and Curly invited themselves along. But not being judges, canine companions present no hindrance to solitude for me, and as we disappeared into the snowy mists our loneness seemed only magnified by the howling of the wolves.

A few hundred meters from the cabin we came to a side road that, behind the curtain of falling snow, appeared to lead into soft and silent gray-brown hills. It was no difficult choice to take this enticing prospect of mystery and peace, and as we drifted along, Guardian and Curly were perk and alert, seeming proud and enthusiastic to escort their neophyte companion on a walk through their mystical haunts. The soft white flakes tickled my nose and eyebrows, and all was silent.

We soon came upon a lonely farmhouse where a sign said "no"-something in Romanian. Something wasn't allowed, I wasn't sure what, but I guessed we were likely trespassing. While I was contemplating how to explain that I just wanted to walk with my canine companions, suddenly it no longer mattered. Five huge dogs came charging around the farmhouse, barking and yelping and tearing up a storm. Topping a hundred pounds of terror each, they appeared on a mission to tear out my lungs. Guardian cringed near me while Curly calmly stood her ground. Just short of the final leap, the beasts pulled up short and formed a raging wall of barks and growls, snaps and snarls. Their message was clear, so I slowly stepped back, turned, and began to walk on as casually as possible.

The raging wall slid along beside us, leaving my left side feeling very exposed and vulnerable. I'm sure I cringed with each new surge, but I tried to ignore the deafening clamor and gazed calmly ahead. Curly pranced along in front, glancing back at me a couple of times to see if I noticed her noble example, while Guardian slunk along beside me. We finally reached a fence at the edge of the property where most of the dogs, very disappointedly it seemed to me, gave it up, although a couple of particularly dedicated characters continued escorting us along, quietly now, until they decided their duty had been accomplished.

I wiped the sweat from my brow, released my breath, and let go the tension gripping my neck and shoulders. We continued our stroll in a sudden peace that now seemed tenuous and surreal, but just as I finished congratulating myself on our survival I realized we still had a problem. How would we return? I chose a secondary track that led into a small valley to the left, into the same range of hills that are behind the cabin, hoping there would be a way through. We followed it a ways, but by now the snow and wind was picking up, it was getting dark, and I wasn't sure the dogs could make it through the deep snow that covered the steep hillsides. There was no choice; we had to go back. When I stopped and turned, Guardian paused in his tracks, turned only his head, and looked at me over his shoulders with eyes that asked, "*Are you crazy?*"

But perhaps satisfied they had already made their point, or perhaps being occupied with other shepherd dog duties, when we passed the farmhouse again only two of the brutes came out to greet us, and they were now subdued, entirely different creatures. They took a couple of sniffs, investigated Curly a bit, and let us pass.

Upon returning to the cabin I now knew the purpose of several hefty sticks I had noticed leaning against the outside wall. I resolved to never walk again in the Romanian countryside without one.

It was Thursday evening and I still hadn't met Christoph and was beginning to wonder if he remembered I had arrived, when he called on one of the project cell phones. (The recorded answering announcement for the CLCP field workers' mobile phone: "Sorry we are not *relevant* now. Please leave a message...")

"Sorry I haven't had time to meet you yet; come on over to my house."

"Where is it?"

"In Zarnesti. Ask Vanessa for directions and take the Suzuki."

Outside was very dark with snow falling heavily.

"It's not difficult..." Vanessa began, and for some reason I felt rushed, so I didn't bother to write down the directions that she quickly rattled off, while I contemplated the feasibility of making the journey in those conditions and wondered whether I could even legally drive in Romania.

Catching about half the directions, but thinking it couldn't really be that hard to find a house in a small village, I dashed out of the cabin into the swirling darkness and climbed into the frigid vehicle. The dome light didn't work so I struggled to find the ignition, but once I did the engine started robustly, and as I exited the driveway I was pretty confident of the first turn, a left, which, sure enough, after a six-kilometer ride, brought me to the village. All I could remember of the directions after that was a vague sequence of lefts and rights before or after train tracks and post offices and things like that. Soon I was lost amidst a confusing jumble of short, snow-covered streets, not seeing any train tracks or post offices, and realizing the village was a lot bigger and more complicated than I first thought (it turns out that Zarnesti is more properly a town, not a village, with a population of almost 27,000).

When I rolled down the window to expand my view beyond the tiny ice-free spot on the windshield, a scene of winter wonder greeted my eyes. People of the town were out and about, walking in small groups or strolling arm-in-arm along the white streets and sidewalks. Children were chasing each other, throwing and dodging snowballs, while a large, black horse, adorned with red tassels and silver bells, pulled its cart through the snow with a tossing of its head and the sounds of jingles and muffled clip-clops. Several other horses stood at their carts like statues, waiting patiently for their charges while the snow accumulated on their blanketed backs. The falling snow speckled the night air, the entire scene illumed by an orange-yellow glow from street lamps and from the light spilling from shop windows. It looked like a nineteenth century setting in an American Christmas card.

The scene was beautiful, even sublime, but I didn't have any better idea of where I was. So, with a feeling of remorse for disturbing the serene winter wonderland, I drove on, making a few quick turns, trying to feel my way around, looking for what I could take to be the "center," or a main street through it, or to it, or some railroad tracks, or a post office. Suddenly I remembered I had a cell phone, which I had fortunately grabbed on my way out of the cabin.

"Where are you?"

"I don't know."

"Do you see any railroad tracks?"

"No."

"A post office?"

"No."

This line of questioning continued while I meandered along, randomly making turns, the cold and snow blowing through the open window into my face. I searched for some landmark, or a hint of some landmark, that Christoph could recognize from my descriptions, and through this process, as well as some blind luck, I eventually found myself at the Prombergers' rented house on the far side of the rather large and complex "village."

Christoph and his wife Barbara had just finished dinner, and I don't know if they noticed me glancing at the leftovers with ravenous eyes — after a couple of days at the cabin on meager fare I was famished — but they immediately offered them up, and I wasn't shy about wolfing them down as I tried to converse gracefully between bites. On an almost full stomach I felt much better, and after a glass of wine even better, and we passed a pleasant evening discussing how was my travel and the project and small things I don't remember. To my great satisfaction we also made plans to go out into the field to track wolves the following day.

Christoph, in his mid-thirties, is tall and lanky with dark curly hair and confident blue eyes. Barbara, around thirty, with straw colored hair, has the fit and wholesome look of someone who spends a lot of time outdoors, and she mostly listened while she held and cared for their baby girl, Enya. The couple speaks English well, and since the house is surprisingly modern with wood-trimmed white walls and sparkling hardwood floors, as the evening wore on I almost forgot my unusual circumstances. I almost felt like I was visiting close friends back home. I tried to ignore the lurking problem of how I'd return to the cabin in the raging storm, and had a faint hope my hosts would offer to put me up for the night.

No such offer came, so when yawns started to replace words, back out into the wild night I headed, with better directions and more hope. I was pretty confident I could retrace my path back to the center, but from there I wasn't sure. The route to the cabin road is not obvious and I knew I must find a narrow lane inconspicuously tucked amongst a row of tightly packed houses. But I felt my way and eventually succeeded in leaving the lights of the town behind me and headed into the blackness.

Only the small sweep of my headlights broke the utter darkness. I wasn't certain I'd be able to see the driveway to the cabin even if I was on the right road, and I wondered where I'd be heading if I missed it — somewhere into the Romanian wilds? Tensely concentrating, trying to detect any turnoffs, hypnotized by staring into the swirling matrix, I was lost to time...

When I came to I had no idea of where I was and how long I'd been driving, but I felt sure I had missed the cabin — if I was on the right road.

I was struggling to stay awake and thinking I had better return to the town, if I could, when suddenly I sensed a disturbance, an ethereal movement in the chaotic flux. I knew Guardian's coloration would not be distinctive in those conditions, and I wasn't really sure I'd seen anything other than a temporary fluctuation in the random swarm of flakes — or in my own mind — but I had a feeling, or maybe it was just a hope, that I'd caught a glimpse of our loyal black-and-white cabin dog. Then, before I could stop, the image dissolved into the void like a ghost. But the fleeting mirage was my one hope, so I continued slowly, mostly awake now, searching for a place to turn, a broadening of the narrow road or a break in the snow bank. Finally I found a spot where I was able to eke out a four- or five-point turn. I drove back, intently gazing through the flying snow into the blackness beyond, until I saw it again. This time the apparition gradually resolved into something constant, something substantial, something real standing in the road, black and white, tail wagging. It was Guardian, and I was home.

With almost 23 million people living in an area not quite the size of Wyoming, Romania is about six times as densely populated as the state of Colorado.[12] For such a populous country, Romania has a remarkable amount of undeveloped, forested wilderness, especially along the rippled landscape of the Carpathian Mountains, which stretch from west to east across south-central Romania and then bend to the north, like a giant arm cradling the Transylvania plateau. The Romanian economy doesn't yet support automobile-dominated mobility, so suburban sprawl is practically non-existent. Most people still dwell in cities, towns, and villages, and most still walk to buy the goods they need for their daily lives in small shops, called *magazines*, which are seldom further than the next block.[13] While not offering the overwhelming range of products available in modern American supermarkets, the neighborhood *magazines* carry the basic necessities. Even the smallest shops, some barely the size of a large closet in America, are always well stocked with delicious fresh-baked bread and pastries, and most carry at least some fresh produce (in winter the selection is limited, but potatoes, carrots, tomatoes, and onions are common). And if one shop lacks freshly butchered meat, the next is likely to have it.[14]

It is commonly assumed that wolves require vast areas of remote, undisturbed wilderness in order to thrive, if not survive. While Romania's land use patterns allow for an impressive wilderness,[15] by North American standards the forests of Romania are neither huge nor inaccessible. They cover about the same area as the forests of the state of Maine, about 27,000 square miles, mostly over the comma-shaped expanse of the Carpathians. The Romanian forests are permeated by an ample system of access roads for logging and hunting, and they are rife with livestock trails and pastures. Yet here there are wolves. Lots of them. About 3,200 wolves live in Romania,[16] the most significant population of wolves in Europe west of Russia (approximately 30 percent). And the country is home to robust populations of Europe's two other large carnivores as well: about 5,400 European brown bears[17] (approximately 50 percent of the bear population of Europe, excluding Russia), and 1,500 Eurasian lynx[18] (about 25 percent).

The wolves of Romania live and hunt and raise their young almost entirely unnoticed by the general public (excluding shepherds), in some places right to the edge of large and dense human settlements. In the late 1990s, the CLCP radio-collared a wolf whose range included the forests immediately surrounding Brasov, a city of about 350,000 residents, and discovered that her pack was traveling at night into the city to raid a trash dump for food. A BBC film crew filmed these streetwise wolves crossing busy roads on their way to the dump from the forest-covered slopes adjacent to the city.[19] Investigations revealed that local people were never aware of the presence of the wild canine predators. If they did happen to see them, they probably assumed the wolves were dogs.

Lots of people, lots of wilderness, lots of wildlife. While many Romanians aspire to live the American lifestyle, as I watch the townsfolk — very few of them obese — bustling about the streets of Zarnesti, walking to the *magazines*, the schools, the churches, to the post office or bus stop or to visit their neighbors, I wonder which is the wiser and more sustainable way of life.

Today, finally, my first day of wolf tracking. Or backtracking, to be more accurate. I was teamed with Christoph, and our goal was to follow the fresh tracks backwards through the snow to see if we could find wolf scat or, if really lucky, a kill, or any other signs of interesting behavior. The pack the project is currently monitoring, the "Glajerie pack," inhabits a territory of approximately 157 square kilometers in and around the Bucegi Mountain range south of Zarnesti. It consists of only two adult wolves, a radio-collared female, designated "Turnu," and her male companion (the project only gives names to the wolves it has collared).

Christoph rarely works in the field these days. Instead, especially while focused on his latest project of creating a large carnivore information center, he most often navigates the political wilderness of Romanian and European bureaucracy, seeking elusive approvals, land deals, partnerships, and funds. I think he joined us today at least partially for my benefit. Although my primary role would be as a technical consultant, he knew I wanted to work in the field, and he seemed to take a special interest in providing me this experience. As an "older" person with a professional background, perhaps I am one of the more unusual project participants, and maybe he was curious. Since it was not given without merit, the students and volunteers greatly valued Christoph's respect, and I think they felt I was lucky to track with him. I know I did.

In 1990, when the time came to conduct his master's thesis, Christoph knew he wanted to study wolves. None were to be found in Germany in those days, and very few in Western Europe, so he got on a plane and flew to North America, making his way to the town of Whitehorse in the Yukon Territory, Canada. He walked into a government field office that was responsible for wildlife management and research and said he wanted to work and wanted to study wolves. They took him on — something that would be unheard of today, when wolves are so popular and competition to study them so fierce — and there he stayed for about a year. He conducted research on the relationship between wolves and ravens, which led to a master's degree in forestry. With his Yukon experience behind him and diploma in hand, Christoph returned to

Europe with a mission: to help conserve the most significant refuge for wolves remaining on the continent west of Russia. He headed to Transylvania.

Plowing through deep snow, following the wolf trail up and down very steep slopes, some nearly vertical, Christoph showed no hint of being out of shape from too little time in the field and too much in smoky offices, and I could feel his eyes on me until he was satisfied I could keep up. The wolves certainly didn't bother taking the easiest route across the rough terrain. Ignoring the gentler contours of land and spurning the concept of switchbacks, the wolves had climbed and clawed straight up, and plowed and slid straight down the steep slopes, as though determined not to be followed by nosey wolf researchers. We weren't using snowshoes, which would be impractical on the steep slopes and in the thick brush, so I was left to experiment whether it was easier to match the deep holes of Christoph's long stride or to break my own path.

While the tracks of dogs often wander randomly, showing little evidence of purpose other than to have a good time, those of wolves typically demonstrate a focus, a mission to get to a particular place. The stride of a wolf is surprisingly long,[20] especially while running, and when traveling in deep snow trailing wolves often save energy by stepping in the tracks of the leader, who in turn often saves energy by using a "direct register" gait (placing the rear feet in the holes made by the front feet).[21] Thus the trail of even a large pack of wolves can appear as a rather scant line of holes in an otherwise unruffled blanket of snow. There's an aesthetic quality to such a record of wild intelligence, efficiency, and mystery so recently cast in the sparkling snow of a still forest, and as Christoph and I followed the trail, we both avoided trouncing on the tracks. What thoughts, what anticipations, what motivations propelled these wild creatures so purposely along, loping and hopping and plowing through the snow, breathing vigorously with tongues hanging out, just a few short hours ago? Unlike us human intruders, they have no choice about where to live, they can't pick up and leave when things get tough, nor retire to a cozy cabin on a freezing night. This mountain forest is their home and in it they must eke out an existence: must hunt, must defend, must sleep, must reproduce, must use their wits to survive.

We had been trudging through deep snow for two or three hours when the tracks suddenly stopped, as though the wolves had simply appeared from out of nowhere. We circled around searching for a place from where they may have leaped, but found no sign.

"Sometimes they will turn and follow their own tracks back," Christoph explained, but I saw no evidence of a turn. Could they have hopped up and spun 180 degrees and landed in their own prints? And even if they did, from where had they come to make the trail we were following? We scratched our heads, but apparently such puzzles are common when following the ways of wolves. Retracing our steps, eventually we picked up another set of tracks that joined this trail, which, being some distance away, we hadn't previously noticed (wolves can leap a great length).

Following this new trail, again backwards, down a gentle, thickly wooded slope (there are *some* gentle slopes here) we came to a small, level area where we were greeted by a distinctive sight: a circle of padded-down snow flecked with pink-red spots along with a few smears. To Christoph the evidence was unmistakable: we had stumbled upon the site of the wolves' sexual activity of the previous night. Unlike dogs, which can breed year round, female wolves are reproductively receptive only once a year, for a couple of weeks or so, and in the Carpathians the time is now. Wolves here mate from mid-February to early March. With some luck for Turnu and her mate, the Glajerie pack may have five or six new members in about sixty-three days.[22]

By mid-afternoon we had followed the tracks into a dense thicket that was impenetrable even on hands and knees. We circled the thicket trying to pick up the trail, but failed to find any tracks exiting the dense brush. It was getting late, so we gave it up and began the long trek back.

I returned to the cabin in the late afternoon dusk, tired and hungry. Displaying the teamwork that made this whole operation possible, Titus and Silverine had the dishes cleaned and the sauna ready. I knew a long day in the field didn't excuse duty, and mine was to cook the evening meal. Then, finally, after the cheerful, candle-lit dinner, I got to enjoy a highlight of cabin life: my first, much needed, sauna.

The sauna is in a small building behind the cabin, structurally typical of European saunas, although with no electric lights or piped-in water, perhaps more rustic than many. An outer room with wood slats covering the gently sloping concrete floor is where we hang our clothes and rinse off. The smaller inner room, dominated by a huge iron water pot that sits on an iron woodstove, is where we sit on a two-tier slatted wood bench and sweat. Since at least four hours are required to get the pot boiling and the room hot, and since everyone is very busy throughout these late winter days, it's always dark by the time the sauna is ready, so the one small window is useless and we use candles to stave off the dark.

Europeans tend to like their saunas hot. Very hot. So hot one's nostrils burn (at least mine do). I can't say ours ever reached such a state of sweltering perfection, but it was hot enough for my tastes and enabled me on this occasion to effectively sweat away several days of accumulated grime and stress. After I had sat for a while and had become very relaxed, the prospect of rinsing off by pouring a bucket of frigid stream water over my head began to loom. While perhaps not a strategy condoned by sauna purists, who are prone to top off the experience with a leap in the snow, I added to the bucket of cold water a dose from the boiling pot, just to take off the edge. Still plenty invigorating, as the water's icy tentacles gripped my head, clamped my shoulders, and crawled down my back, I wondered if any of the small fish that populate the creek were involuntary participants in my dousing.

My cleaning ritual complete, as I tiptoed through the dark on the icy path from the creek, carrying two slopping buckets of water to replenish the boiling pot, I'm sure I never felt so rejuvenated and sparkling clean. The sauna is our one luxury.

Later, under a crescent moon floating in the twilit sky above the silhouetted hills, I learned the German pronunciation for Orion: "O-REE-on."

The wildlife of Romania is a valuable resource which can benefit the country's economy, and which can serve as a pool to revitalize the exiguous wildlife populations of other European nations. The mission of the Carpathian Large Carnivore Project is to promote the conservation of Romania's unique natural heritage by developing and implementing strategies to reduce the costs and increase the benefits associated with the presence of wolves and the other large carnivores. The project is utilizing a four-pronged approach of research, public awareness, conflict resolution, and sustainable rural development (especially eco-tourism) to achieve its goals.[23]

Upon my arrival, I was lucky to step into the midst of one of the project's more intense research activities: a "predation study." These studies consist of thirty-day intervals of intensive monitoring and tracking in order to determine everything a wolf pack eats during the period. The current study is the fourth in a series conducted over the last twelve months on the Glajerie pack. The data from the studies helps characterize the ecological role of wolves, the territorial and resource requirements to sustain viable wolf populations, and the nature and degree of conflict between wolves and humans (i.e., livestock and dog depredation). It is hoped this information will lead to the development of effective management and conflict resolution strategies. Barbara has been supervising this series of predation studies on Turnu and her mate and will use the data for her doctoral thesis.

Thus the associated hectic activity currently dominating life in the field and at the cabin.

Saturday, March 8

This morning at the weekly status meeting, after two hours of rather tedious, detailed reports about the wolves' location and activities 24/7 during the previous week, we finally arrived at a discussion of the last shift, the one that had just ended. Titus presented his observations of the locations, movement, and activity of the wolves throughout the night, and then casually announced, "and at 7:10 a.m., just before leaving early to come to this meeting, I found a kill, a wild boar, at GPS coordinates [such and such]" Leaning over the large map spread open on the table over which we were all huddled, the gangly young student pointed out the location.

Excited chatter and laughter erupted, pens dropped, hands flew up. Finding a kill is like finding gold for these dedicated researchers; it is why we are all here. Titus stood back and shuffled his feet, a bit bewildered, apparently trying to reconcile his desire to initiate his career as a detached and consummate researcher with our boisterous — but exasperated — response. "He might have said something at the beginning," was the general sentiment.

49

We rushed to the project vehicles and made the hour long, bone-jarring drive into the territory of the wolves. Stopping a short distance up a snow-covered track just off the heavily traveled highway to Bucharest — the mountain road of my harrowing experience on my first day in Transylvania — we spilled out into a stiff, cold wind and breathlessly followed Titus up an open, white slope.

Over a small rise was the dramatic site of the kill: bloodied snow stamped down by hoofs and paws in a circle several meters wide, with stiff dark hair, two forelegs, and a few flat sheets of hide scattered about. The (mostly) fleshless spine lay on the snow, resembling the back of a miniature stegosaurus, while a short distance away the large head sat upright, partially stripped of hair and skin but still looking formidable with its large, sharp tusks. Full-grown male wild boars in Romania can weigh up to 600 pounds, and if healthy they are very capable of defending themselves. As we examined the site, Christoph suggested that our two wolves could not likely have killed this large male unless it had been sick, or perhaps wounded by a human hunter. He then pointed to a thicket a couple hundred meters away. "There is where you and I tracked the wolves the other day."

As dramatic as the kill site was, I was especially intrigued when I glanced up and saw skiers swishing down the slopes of a small ski area on the other side of the paved road, perhaps 500 meters away. Were any of those recreational thrill-seekers aware of the violent drama that had transpired so recently and so near?

We assisted Barbara as she weighed and measured pieces of skeleton and collected samples of boar hide. She stuffed the gory head into a sack, thinking it might make a good display for the information center.

Later in the afternoon, it happened that my feet were the only means I had for returning to the cabin from the project office in Zarnesti, where I had been dropped off so I could check email. Initially disheartened at the inconvenience, I resigned myself to necessity and began the seven-kilometer walk, strolling along the muddy streets towards the familiar dirt road that exits the town and leads along the flat valley floor to the west. I was accompanied by the clip-clop beat of an apparently stray horse that seemed intent on following me through the town, as though eager to offer its services as a guide or a mount. With my Indiana Jones hat, sunglasses, and large companion, I was feeling a bit self-conscious, and was indeed greeted with many second looks and an occasional stare, but I carried myself as naturally as I could manage and tried to give the impression that I really had nothing to do with the horse.

Unlike towns in America, which usually fade out gradually, Zarnesti ends abruptly. The solid wall of houses and high stone walls and wooden gates that line the street suddenly stop, like at the edge of a fortification, which I suppose the town once was. Although the current municipality wasn't officially established until 1951, Zarnesti was probably settled during the twelfth century by Saxon immigrants from Germany on the site of an even more ancient Roman settlement called Zarnizis.[24] The continuous barriers of houses, walls, and wooden gates — many of the latter ornately carved — hide the yards from the view of the streets and narrow sidewalks, and are characteristic of the medieval Saxon villages and towns of Romania. The design was intended to defend the settlement's dwellings from attack.

The road to our cabin spills into the countryside and first passes for about a kilometer through a series of large, flat potato fields, which are rimmed to the south by sweeping, terraced slopes that climb the foothills of the towering Piatra Craiului massif. As I walked along the fields I was intrigued by the terraces, given the preponderance of level, arable land surrounding the town. Had they been intentionally designed by human minds and built by human hands, or had plateaus formed over untold centuries from the hooves of livestock and the feet of their human herders who led them up the slopes to graze?

A stiff, cold wind gathered force over the fields and seemed determined to hinder my progress. As I leaned into the gale and covered my face against the bite, occasionally turning and walking backwards to give my face a chance to thaw, I couldn't help reflect on the state of walking in America. Back home, except in the core of cities, does anyone walk for personal transportation anymore?[25] Does anyone walk even one kilometer to go to the post office or the grocery store? If there is a grocery store that isn't several miles away planted amongst commercial sprawl along some unwalkable highway. How many people ever leave the boundary of their property except with their rear ends on the seat of a car? And isn't this absence of walking a perversion of our natural, physical *being* in the world? Surely throughout most of human existence, walking every day has been the norm. Instead of being considered a waste of time, why isn't walking perceived for what it really can be: as pleasant a way to pass the time as any other? Indeed, for me, more pleasant than most. Although it's true I no longer have deadlines to meet and red lights to beat, what, really, are any of us ever rushing towards?

With these musings, and having little choice anyway, my initial annoyance at this inconvenience melted away. I settled into the experience and gradually began to feel privileged to be simply ambling along, enveloped by the new sights of terraced slopes and fresh snow-capped peaks, the new sounds of hoofs clopping and bells ringing as horse-drawn carts passed me by, and the new scents of fertile earth and of things burning (there always seem to be things burning in and around Zarnesti). When I noticed a family — a father, a mother, and three little children — trudging back to the village from the forest carrying bundles of sticks nearly as big as they were on their backs, my seven-kilometer walk suddenly seemed a leisurely stroll.

And had I driven our project's Suzuki, I would not have stumbled upon my first opportunity for a "real" conversation with local folks. When several young men on a horse cart passed me by, no doubt noticing my Western demeanor, if not attire, they asked in Romanian where I was going, and then pointed at their wrists, asking for the time. As soon as I struggled to reply in Romanian, however, my chance was gone. They seized the opportunity for themselves, and excitedly asked me in English why I was here and where I was going. My words *cabanna lupului* apparently told them most of what they wanted to know. They acknowledged they knew the place, with looks that implied they now knew what I was doing here, but not why, and then they waved friendly goodbyes.

I continued walking along, my feet repetitively crunching the frozen dirt of the road.

[I haven't been here a week. It seems much longer.]

The rhythm of my stride often catalyzes thoughts, and whether I want to solve a problem, or want a problem to solve, for me a walk is always the surest means.

[Is time different here…or am I different here? Don't we carry time in our heads?]

As I left the wide, open fields behind, the wind eased. The sun warmed the left side of my frozen face.

[What is special about the present moment? Isn't it only our consciousness that distinguishes the present from all other moments in the past and the future?]

The road approached the river that flows down the length of this valley, and I could hear the water trickling over the stones. The river runs low this time of year, and its music has a gentle, hypnotic quality…

[The present is simply that point in time at which our consciousness is observing, and it is a characteristic of consciousness that it moves through a succession of moments such that the "laws of physics" apply.] [26]

A group of ravens were feeding on something along the roadside ahead.

[Time only has meaning in consciousness, and consciousness only has meaning in time, and if our memories were perfect, if we could observe with equal clarity all past moments, surely we'd be lost in time.]

I made a note to remember this last point if I was ever back in America unable to find my keys. Meanwhile, as my thoughts faded I gladly experienced time at a slower pace — and finally, not at all — although I began to wonder why my feet were more tired from walking along a flat dirt road than hiking up and down steep slopes of snow and mud, tracking wolves.

When I arrived at our cabin in the gathering gloom of dusk, the windows were aglow with the yellow light of candles. I opened the door and was greeted by the homey warmth of baking and the aroma of fresh-made cinnamon rolls. Vanessa and Silverine were busy creating a perfect ending to a long day.

The wolf cabin has become home, and my new friends, family.

During the rare clear evenings, a million scintillating stars dominate one's consciousness in the darkness of this valley, where the only artificial lights are a couple of insignificant, dim, specks from homesteads further up the road, eerily glowing through vapors that rise like ghosts from the moist earth and drift from the creek.

Sunday, March 9

When the others first heard that today I would be tracking with Peter Sürth, the lead wolf tracker for the CLCP, they pronounced that I would soon be "in for it." Allegedly, Peter sets a fast pace. They were right. Even a quick lunch being too long a pause, Peter's standard fare for a day of tracking (eight or nine hours of arduous trudging through deep snow up and down countless steep slopes) is a banana and a coke.

In his late thirties with thinning reddish-blond hair, a moustache, and eyes that feature a mild version of the permanent squint typical of those who spend most of their time outdoors, Peter is of average height, and although sturdy, is not especially brawny. His strength and endurance seem to derive from his intensity and focus. He was born and grew up in Switzerland, began training as a veterinary technical assistant in Munich, Germany, and went on to study biology and wildlife management in Düsseldorf and at Van Hall Institute in Leeuwarden, The Netherlands. There he received a degree in Animal Management after completing his thesis on "Wolf Tourism in Transylvania."

Peter first joined the CLCP as a volunteer in 1996, serving as a tracker and research assistant, and playing a key role in raising the newly acquired wolf pups, Poiana and Crai. Since 1997 he has worked under contract for the project as a "wolf technician" and tour guide. He has designed and implemented eco-tourism events, assisted on film projects, and helped to trap and collar wolves, bears, and lynx. And of course he tracks.

The wolves of the Carpathians rarely hunt during the day, when encounters with humans are always a threat, so during predation studies the project field workers — staff, students, eco-volunteers, and professional consultants (Peter being the only consultant currently) — use radio telemetry to monitor the wolves' location and activity throughout the night, trying to ascertain whether, and where, the pack under study may have made a kill. Predation results, if they are found, are usually found during the day, when the wolves are usually sleeping or resting.

A wolf monitor using radio telemetry learns to appreciate the subtle nuances of an ethereal beep. A directional antenna intercepts signals transmitted by the radio collar and relays them through a portable receiver into a set of headphones. The orientation of the antenna in which the beeps are loudest roughly indicates the direction to the collar, the volume of the loudest beeps roughly indicates the distance, and the frequency of the beeps indicates whether the wolf is active (is moving her neck), resting (has not moved her neck for at least several minutes), or possibly dead (has not moved her neck for a long time). Such is the theory. Using radio telemetry to monitor wolves in the wild is as much an art as a science, especially in the rough, mountainous terrain of Transylvania, where the topology often distorts the signals. The task is also frequently complicated by snowstorms, frozen hands, stuck vehicles, suspicious forestry officials, or rapidly moving wolves.

How goes the night for a CLCP wolf monitor? If the location of the wolves is entirely unknown when you begin your shift, you drive along the roads and rough forest tracks abutting the wolves' large territory, using the directionless antenna on the roof of the vehicle, trying to peel the slightest hint of a subtle beep from the constant din of static. If you begin to hear something resembling a beep, or begin to think you hear something resembling a beep, you start exploring for a direction that makes it stronger. And if what you seemed to hear fades back into the static, as it often does, you return to where you heard it before. If you no longer hear it there, as you often won't — maybe the wolves have moved, or maybe the weather has caused a shift in the signals, or maybe what you heard before was only your imagination — you begin the search anew.

But, unless it *was* your imagination, you might now at least be in the vicinity of the wolves, so your next search probably goes faster. If you're finally successful — if you finally hear a definite beep that doesn't fade away as soon as you move your head or take a breath — then you hop out of your warm vehicle into the freezing night and hold the directional antenna aloft hopefully, rotating it back and forth through the blackness, searching for the direction, or *a* direction, which makes the beep the loudest. The variation in volume is slight and shifting as the signals bounce around the landscape, but with some luck you narrow the direction down, perhaps to within an arc of about sixty degrees. You guess at the midpoint and take a compass reading. Then, if you don't already know where you are, you use your GPS device to find out, you mark your position on your dimly lit map, and you draw a line from you to the wolves.

Allegedly the wolf wearing the radio collar is somewhere near that line, plus or minus a lot of degrees. But to know approximately where, you must do this all again, from another position some distance from the line you've just drawn. Using the signal volume to estimate the distance to the wolves, you try to find a new position that is roughly perpendicular to the line from the point where you believe they might be. And you must be quick about it, because the wolves may be moving. If you manage to get a second line, since this is all so imprecise, you should do it all again and try for a third. Finally, where the two or three lines intersect on your map is roughly, maybe *very* roughly, where the wolves are, or were.

If you now have some confidence about the wolves' location, and if the volume of the beeps seems steady, and especially if the frequency of the beeps tells you the wolf isn't moving its neck, you sit, you wait, and you listen again to that interminable beep, which will begin to haunt your dreams. Of course you shouldn't be having dreams, but it's 4:00 a.m. and that beep has become a sort of cosmic heartbeat embedded in the random hiss of the universe. When your head falls to the side you suddenly remember that science is depending on you, so you get out of the car for some fresh cold air and a few jumping jacks. Returning to the beep, you try to remain alert for any subtle shift in volume that might warn the wolves are moving. If they are, you try to move with them, exploring for the direction that will keep the volume strong. More groping in the dark, more readings in the cold, more lines on the map — thus it goes throughout the night. It's tedious, lonely work and without the glamour you may have expected. It's certainly nice if you have an eco-volunteer along to keep you company.

In the morning at the change of shifts, the day team meets with the night team to discuss ideas about where there might be fresh tracks, or even better, fresh kills. The activity of the wolves may provide clues. For example, if the wolves had suddenly ceased traveling and then remained active at the same location for most of the night, perhaps they had made a kill and then stopped to feed. If the day team manages to find fresh tracks, it follows them, usually backwards so as not to disturb the resting wolves.

Of course it's not usually possible to retrace the wolves' entire night journey, so the intuition of experienced trackers, along with much hard work and a good deal of luck, is required to find all the kills. Peter is about as experienced as they come, having tracked wolves and the other large carnivores for the CLCP for the past seven years. The more time I spent with him the more I came to appreciate his sharp observational skills, his ability to read stories from subtle signs left in the forest, and his keen intuition about wolf behavior. He and I were to have unusual success at finding kills in the days ahead.

Today, we backtracked the wolves to a site that was baited with a dead horse, put out by hunters for bears some days before. The carcass had been well fed on, but during the night the wolves probably still managed to tear few shreds from the scant frozen meat and gristle yet clinging to the bones. As I looked at the large skeleton dangling from a roughly constructed wooden frame, I recalled a story Barbara had told me about finding a horse along a trail, still struggling after some men who wanted to use it for bear bait had tried to kill it with axe-blows to the head. They had abandoned the cruel task not quite finished, but probably supposing the horse was incapacitated enough for the purpose. Barbara returned and finished it with a bullet to the head.

We left the bait site to search for more interesting activity elsewhere in the dark spruce (*Picea abies*) and fir (*Abies alba*) forest, eventually following a trough that had been carved in the deep snow by logs that were dragged out of the woods by horses in the employ of loggers. As we walked along, our feet crunching the newly scraped snow in the narrow depression (which we thought the wolves might use), Peter related a few of his more unusual wolf stories. He once followed a set of tracks to a small but steep snowy slope that the wolves climbed and then apparently slid down — several times. Evidently an exception to the rule that the tracks of wolves demonstrate only utilitarian purpose, Peter had stumbled upon the impressions of wolves that seemed intent on having some fun. He also recalled an incident involving the filming of a den site where a female wolf had just given birth to a litter of pups. He helped the BBC film team set up and carefully hide their quiet, remotely controlled cameras, but in spite of their best efforts, the wolves could not be tricked. Neither the adult members of the pack nor the pups ever showed their faces while the camera was recording, although the pack was obviously active when it wasn't.

The day warmed with the afternoon sun, and I was drenched in sweat as I followed Peter up a particularly long and steep open slope, my heart pumping vigorously. We had driven to a new area closer to where the wolves were currently resting, but we still hadn't found any wolf tracks. We stopped to catch our breath and plan our next move. Peter suggested I head back down the slope to search in a ravine at the bottom. I assumed he would continue climbing up the slope to the top of the hill, which was capped with the gray-brown trunks of beech (*Fagus sylvatica*) and mountain maple (*Acer pseudoplantanus*). I hated giving up the hard-won altitude, but eager to do what was best, back down the slope I bounded. The snow was especially deep in the thicket of small, bare trees that filled the ravine. I plowed through it for a while, finding tracks of hare, birds, and other small creatures, but nothing that looked like wolf. Peering back up the slope between the gray tree trucks, I could see Peter standing in the sun. He hadn't moved, and was waving for me to return. I thought he must have found something interesting. While I made the long, steady climb, Peter continued standing and watching patiently — too patiently, I thought, to have found anything of interest — and as I got closer I could see that he was smiling. Was he testing my conditioning, perhaps to plan for the days ahead? Kicking my feet into the snow to carve the final few steps, I struggled to restrain my rapid breath.

As it began to slant sharply from the southwest, the late afternoon sunlight lost its warmth. We had been at it nearly eight hours, and while we rested (or actually, while I rested), a chill crept into my wet body. Peter looked up the hill, turned and shielded his eyes from the sun while he scanned the shaded slopes on the other side of the ravine, and then came the words I was secretly hoping for.

"Let's go back."

I loved being out, and was ecstatic, really, that I was tracking wolves in this fantastic landscape of Romania. I had come a long way and this was a dream come true. But now, after my first full day of tracking, I admit we had been trudging through wet snow and climbing slopes and searching for tracks until I had had enough, and I was very tired.

"Ok."

The dirt road that wound down the open valley from the mountains was not so much potholed as riddled with miniature hills, like the moguls of a black-diamond ski slope. A torrent of water from the late winter snowmelt rushed around the mounds and over the stones and through the mud, following the same route as us. As I was jolted about in my seat, I observed, "This is more like a river than a road."

"Could be worse," was Peter's reply.

This evening is filled with warm domesticity, cooking and cleaning at the cabin with Vanessa, Joris, Silverine, and Titus, on one of the few occasions we are all at the cabin together. We make a strange but tasty concoction from our meager provisions, which we observe is "multicultural" since representatives from Germany, Belgium, France, and America all toss something in. The temperature outside is about 1°C, but we have no need for a fire because the cabin is well insulated and warmed by our bodies and the propane cooking stove. I wonder how my boots, soaked by the wet snow, are going to be dry for tomorrow without the radiant heat from a fire in the woodstove. I crave a sauna, which isn't scheduled until tomorrow, but crawling into my sleeping bag in the cold loft, I fall asleep with the satisfaction of true fatigue.

Monday, March 10

Light snow is falling. I heard something outside the cabin last night, along the back wall and the roof (where it is adjacent to the steep bank) — a scratching and rustling sound. The dogs had a fit.

The night team detected no activity to suggest the wolves made a kill last night, and Peter is guiding a tour group from Great Britain, so we won't be tracking today.

While I'm washing my clothes in a bucket, Peter enters the cabin with the tourist group as though it's a primary feature of the tour. I suppose it is, but it's also our home, so it feels a bit intrusive when a large group of strangers come piling in, tracking in mud and leaving the door open.

We try to entertain tourists with stories, such as we have, but people come to Cabanna Lupului primarily to see Poiana and Crai. It's extremely rare to see wild wolves here in the dense forests of Transylvania (project personnel working in the field rarely do) so our famous friends in the enclosure fill the experiential void.

When any of us cabin residents return to the premises unaccompanied by strangers, Poiana and Crai usually come bounding down from their haunts on the steep, brush-covered slope to greet us. The wolves usually start their descent when we're still at least a hundred meters away, so they're obviously able to distinguish strangers from friends at this distance, even when we arrive by vehicle. They don't usually come down to greet strangers unless they are enticed with cheese, which they have trained us well to offer. If the wolves do come down, they will solicit scratches through the fence, pose for photos, and they might even be coaxed into a howl. After the excited visitors finish their close encounters with Poiana and Crai, they crowd back into the cabin for additional observations and maybe a few photos of us crazy "kids" who live in these primitive conditions in the wilds of Romania, and who track wolves. Probably seems romantic.

Silverine and Titus finish entertaining the tourists while I go outside to rinse and wring my clothes. The tourists have to duck when I bring in my shirts and pants and socks and begin hanging them on cords stretched over our heads. I thaw my frozen fingers in front of the woodstove as we say our goodbyes.

In the afternoon I walk up the valley in the heavy stillness of a dark, foggy, positively vampire-like afternoon. On the return, Curly and Guardian stop to visit some neighboring housedogs along the way. It dawns on me that Guardian may actually have some canine friends. I continue on alone, strolling dreamily through the mists. Suddenly, like a scene from *The Hound of the Baskervilles*,[27] the thick silence is rent by an eerie howl and a series of agonized barks echoing violently across the valley from somewhere up in the shrouded foothills. Whether evil is being done to or by the screaming creature or creatures, I can't be sure.

Always quick to smile, Joris exhibits a muted joviality unexpected from a policeman. In his mid-thirties, he was a soldier with the Belgian army when it entered the Congo in 1991 to evacuate Belgian nationals from civil chaos. He remained for a time with the peacekeeping force, and he still walks with a slight limp as a result of shrapnel he took in the rear from an exploding grenade. There seems no subject on which he doesn't have some knowledge, and we've been closing many of our evenings with probing conversations in candlelight about anything that comes into our heads — history, philosophy, religion, art. Our discussions are occasionally lubricated by a bottle of Ursus, the local Romanian beer.

With limited English language skills, Silverine, in her mid-twenties, is a quiet listener. A recent graduate, she wrote her thesis about wolf re-establishment in France. She is always eager to help and seldom expresses her own wishes, but one senses this is because she's happy and satisfied to be here, not because she's meek. Her gentle manner and soft eyes belie an inner strength and strong determination. Last year she went to Mali for ten weeks as part of a school project, living in a grass hut with no clean water or electricity. Our modest but solid cabin probably seems extravagant. After she listened to Joris describe the harassment he experienced at the train station in Bucharest — lots of folks pushing up to him and insisting he needed the help which only they could provide — Silverine softly allowed, "It is nothing compared to Africa."

This evening Joris is sitting in the cabin's lone chair and rubbing Guardian's neck when he asks, "Have you felt the muscles around his neck and shoulders? This is no city dog." Guardian looks at me in delight, mouth open and tongue hanging out.

Being surrounded by people with an affinity for animals, Curly and Guardian get lots of attention. They both inspire sympathy. A few days after her sister disappeared last fall, Curly showed up at the cabin with Guardian in tow, as though she had recruited the black-and-white canine to fill the void. While the ownership of shepherd dogs in the valley seems somewhat fluid, as dogs associated with one shepherd might sometime later be seen with a different shepherd, Titus recognized the new dog as being associated with a certain neighboring shepherd, to whom he promptly returned the wayward animal. Guardian reappeared at the cabin some days later, followed soon after by the shepherd, who informed the cabin residents that he must be compensated for the loss of his valuable, if not loyal, assistant. The cabin residents demurred, and he left without an answer.

Between their hectic activities over the ensuing days the residents deliberated on this new matter, but a new dog was not in the project budget (and anyway there are always plenty of strays around if another dog is wanted), so Titus put on a collar and leash for extra emphasis and returned Guardian to the shepherd once again. A few more days passed and the dog was back again, sans collar and leash. With little extra time on their hands for extended negotiations and continued returns of a dog, the project workers conveniently assumed a deal had been consummated: Guardian in exchange for a leash and a collar. This was probably not an unreasonable arrangement for the shepherd, considering Guardian's questionable loyalty and the fact that one of the dog's hind feet had never healed properly from what was surely a break. The dog's paw stuck permanently out to the side, presumably rendering him marginally effective as a working guardian of sheep.

Although obviously powerful, Guardian is nevertheless extremely timid. He cringes from any hint of a rapidly moving arm or hand. And while the dog is loyal and affectionate to those he knows will treat him well, he fears human strangers.

He seems to have few friends of his own kind, either having made an enemy of every working shepherd dog in the valley, or they having made him theirs.

In spite of his physical and social handicaps, Guardian never relinquishes his role as protector of the cabin, its premises, and its occupants. He simultaneously fears and vigorously challenges all canine intruders and passers-by, and since these seldom come alone, he constantly gets beat up. More than once I've watched the obstinate dog come hobbling into the yard with a little blood seeping from around his neck through his not-so-clean black-and-white coat. As he looks at me, I see that his pride remains unscathed, however, and he's still eager to wag his tail at the slightest kindly glance.

"I wonder how long he'll last," Joris continues, voicing my own doubts about Guardian's prospects in the tough world of this valley and the role he chooses for himself in it.

Curly, meanwhile, descends from a family of dogs with a long history at the cabin. She is plagued by a wound festering in her side near her hip, presumably the result of a botched spaying operation. She's been brought to a couple of vets who have determined that there is something foreign inside, but they've been unable to find and remove it. The pain seems to come and go, but lately she's been yelping every time she gets up. The food we've been preparing for the dogs is entirely grain-based, so I modified the recipe by adding some of the ample supply of manufactured dog food we have as an emergency source for the wolves (it is old and the wolves will never need all that we have, as there is always plenty of meat), hoping the extra protein will help Curly heal. We've also started spraying the wound daily with an antiseptic wash. Hopefully we'll soon be able to stop cringing every time the dog gets up.

The large carnivores of Romania are relatively tolerated despite the fact that Romania's fragile economy and many of its people are highly dependent on livestock.[28] Agriculture accounts for about 15 percent of the country's economic production and employs about 40 percent of the labor force in the Carpathian region.[29] Raising crops and livestock not only provides a primary source of livelihood for Romania's rural communities, it also sets the rhythm for an ancient way of life. Horse-drawn carts still roll slowly along country roads carrying towering loads of hay, or bundles of sticks for firewood, or groups of peasants to work the fields. Cows, horses, goats, and sheep are still herded through the main streets of villages and towns, frustrating the drivers of cars rushing to meet their appointments in the hectic pace of the "new economy," which is just beginning to challenge the ancient rhythms. But whether people march to the old beats or the new, it is the attitudes formed over centuries of coexistence and conflict with livestock that still dominate the feelings about wolves in Romania.

During winter, most sheep and other livestock are confined near the lowland villages and farms. In early spring, after the snow retreats, the animals are allowed to graze the rich pastures farther up the valleys and on the lower slopes, tended by shepherds who are generally hired for the work, but who may also have a few animals of their own. Then, in late May, the sheep are gathered into larger flocks — numbering up to a thousand animals — and led further up the slopes, to the high summer pastures in the mountains. There the shepherds live with the animals for the duration of the summer in "shepherd camps," small clusters of rough-hewn wooden shacks and lean-tos, where they generate income for their employers by making cheese from the animals' milk.

Of course the large carnivores share this mountainous terrain, and there are conflicts; wolves and bears take about 1.2 percent of the five million sheep that graze within their territory each year.[30] This loss is a significant economic blow to people so dependent on livestock for their livelihood, and shepherds or farmers will sometimes kill a wolf that is known to be preying on livestock or dogs — with or without legal sanction.[31] Nevertheless, the same unrelenting hatred that led to campaigns to completely eradicate wolves in America[32] seems not to be prevalent in Romania, perhaps due in part to a certain *laissez-faire* attitude and measure of fatalism that seems not uncommon in the culture: traditional rural Romanian society does not seem possessed by an overwhelming urge to control every aspect of nature.

Still, until the fall of the communist regime in 1989, effective conservation of the large carnivores was due primarily to state authority, as Nicolae Ceausescu, the ruthless dictator and avid bear-hunter, instituted rigorous measures aimed at protecting bears in order to enhance his personal bear-hunting success. Ceausescu severely restricted hunting (except for himself), banned the use of poison, and set aside large tracts of wilderness as habitat for his personal quarry. Not satisfied with merely protecting bears (except from himself), the dictator also encouraged game managers to *produce* bears — and not just any bears, but the biggest bears possible. So the managers instituted feeding programs, placing copious amounts of fruit, corncobs, specially formulated pellets, and even dead horses, at special feeding troughs within their management areas with the goal of increasing both the number and trophy quality (which mostly means size) of the autocrat's favorite quarry. The practice continues today, although to a lesser degree, in an effort to nurture the lucrative trophy hunting industry in Romania.

During his "hunts," Ceausescu was flown by helicopter to whichever of these feeding stations had recently been identified as having the best trophy bear-killing prospects — possibly more a result of competition among game managers to attain the honor and privileges that might ensue, than the reality on the ground. The dictator then sat in a specially constructed shelter and blasted away at whichever bears were feeding or had been driven to the station for his benefit, while a nervous assistant reloaded the awesome hunter's guns.[33] He occasionally invited a foreign dignitary along to join him in the slaughter.

Regardless of the Romanian leader's motives, the protections designed for bears benefited other wildlife as well, including wolves.[34] When Ceausescu's regime fell, however, the legal protections ceased, and it was clear that the large predators would soon face the same pressures that decimated their numbers in much of the rest of Europe. Fortunately for the predators, as the young democracy began to gain traction in the early part of the 1990s, and as it began to consider the appealing prospect of European Union membership, its legislators decided to bring the country into compliance with European biodiversity and conservation goals. In 1993 Romania joined the *Convention on the Conservation of European Wildlife and Natural Habitats* (also known as the Bern Convention of 1979) and restored legal protection to wolves and the other large carnivores.

Whatever their tolerance and whatever the law, shepherds work hard to protect their flocks, and large, aggressive shepherd dogs are their primary tools. Although the dogs may directly fend off attacks, barking is usually their most effective function, as wolves will not challenge humans who are alert to their presence. Nevertheless, the predators are sometimes successful, relying on stealth and speed — and often, negligent shepherd dogs — to make their kills.

The CLCP has been working to develop and test new methods for protecting livestock. Especially promising are portable electric fences that are used to surround the sheep pens at night. These fences, powered by 12-volt car batteries, have proven completely effective at preventing the loss of livestock to predators in the camps. Since the fences are beyond the means of most shepherds, the project has also been raising and providing funds to help finance their purchase. Other protection measures have been suggested by the analysis of livestock predation case studies. For example, the project recommends better training and nutrition for the guard dogs, so they will spend more time protecting the flocks instead of running off to hunt for prey to supplement their typical inexpensive corn-based diet, which lacks sufficient protein.

Wednesday, March 12

Not much adventure these last couple of days, unless holding back a cough so as not to wake one's cabin mates be considered heroic, and bearing a sore throat without complaint brave, and constantly blowing one's nose an epic struggle. So, not being able to track yesterday, I spent most of the day in the office editing the CLCP's annual report. Later I chopped a little wood, retrieved a few buckets of water, walked across the horizontal "ladder" running from the slope to the cabin roof to clear snow off the solar panels, helped cook the evening meal, and washed the dishes. There's always work to be done.

Whether the solar panels are clear of snow or not, these days are gray so we have only a few minutes of electric light in the evenings. But darkness shared is not gloomy, and the warm, flickering candlelight adds to the convivial atmosphere in the cabin. We cook, eat, cleanup, discuss the day's events or the morrow's challenges, and share our personal stories. Poiana and Crai occasionally serenade us with resounding howls.

While the CLCP is little known in the States, a collection of magazines in the cabin gives evidence that most European conservation and geographic publications have featured the wolves of Transylvania and the CLCP at one time or another. Among media coverage accessible to North American readers is an article about the CLCP written by David Quammen in the December 2000 issue of *Outside Magazine*. Quammen also wrote an article about the bears of Romania, which appeared in the July/August 2003 issue of *Atlantic Monthly*, and his book, *Monster of God*, includes a chapter on the same subject. At least two film documentaries have featured the CLCP: *Transylvania – Living with Predators* (BBC, winner of Best of Festival in 2001 at the Wildlife Europe Film Festival), and a production by Valentin Thurn called *Lord of the Wolves* made in 2000 (which is specifically about Christoph).

Allegedly, every couple of weeks someone in the group makes a trip to a large modern supermarket in Brasov, called the "Metro" (which is a chain), to get food and supplies. We are currently in dire need of food, so I hope this happens soon. There are also two open-air markets in Zarnesti where local people sell vegetables from their small farms and gardens. They're open year round, although for only one or two days a week in winter when the selection of vegetables is meager. In order to best support the local economy, and to save money — for the locally produced goods are cheaper — we purchase as much as we can at the local markets.

Thursday, March 13

My cold is no better, my body aches with inactivity. The rain of last evening night has changed over to heavy, wet snow this morning. The gloom, along with this cold, clouds my brain. I literally have a case of cabin fever. As I'm writing, another British tour group arrives in horse-drawn carts and invades the cabin. Apparently tourist activity picks up here in the spring.

Later, I watched from the outhouse as Simona showed up with a television crew. I suppose they came to film the wolves, and perhaps us as well. After they left, Simona told us that they would come again tomorrow to snare one or two of us for an interview. I hope to avoid this, or at least to be in a less compromising position when they arrive.

Simona, a feisty, twenty-something resident of Zarnesti, is the CLCP's public relations officer. She handles most of the project's interactions with local media and develops and facilitates community outreach programs. These include presentations in the local schools about ecology and the role of predators. She moderates discussions and encourages the children to share their views, so not only do the children learn from the project, but the project also learns from the children about issues that concern them and their communities.

The presence of large carnivores is a sensitive matter in the rural communities of Romania, and the CLCP tries not to dictate opinions. The aim is to present accurate and balanced information about the nature and behavior of predators, acknowledging the problems they can cause while trying to dispel myths and suggest or stimulate solutions. The task is not easy, and recently has been made more difficult by rumors that the CLCP physically transports bears into the region (a belief that may be exacerbated by the project's name). In fact, when addressing CLCP representatives, people are beginning to refer to predators as "your wolves" or "your bears."

Thus Simona's work continues. With funding from various EU sources, she helped children in one Zarnesti school start an environmental magazine. The young publishers are completely responsible for all aspects of producing and distributing the magazine, which has acquired quite a following in the community. Especially interested in reading the next issue are the local Important Persons the students have interviewed, such as the mayor of Zarnesti and visitors such as foreign journalists and EU representatives. Simona also organizes summer activities for the children, such as visits to the wolf cabin to perform maintenance tasks (for example, they built the steps leading up the slope from the driveway to the wolf enclosure), and clean-ups of the valley conducted with groups of children from Western Europe.

As if this isn't enough, Simona and her mother operate the project's souvenir shop, which is tucked away on a Zarnesti side street and offers products made by local craftspeople (including warm socks, sweaters, and hats made from the wool of local sheep).

Friday, March 14
Our electric light only lasted about an hour this evening, so I'm writing by candlelight. Soft snowfall all day. Today will be a rare day off for the predation study (for the entire team, that is — both day and night), as no predatory activity was suspected last night and people need some rest. Personally, I've had a lot of days off lately, but my cold has finally broken and I hope to go back out with Peter tomorrow.

Silverine departs in the morning and Joris the next day. As I watch the last CLCP eco-volunteers sitting on the benches of our long, rough-hewn but glossy-finished wood dining table, reading in the yellow glow of the candles, I already feel the approaching loneliness.

Sunday, March 16

More snow yesterday and again today. The dark bluish gloom reminds me of the Transylvania setting at the end of the movie, *Bram Stoker's Dracula*.[35] The filmmakers managed to catch the ambiance of the place.

I made an attempt to go out with Peter, but by the time we stopped at the project office in Zarnesti, I decided I still wasn't fit enough. Coughing, sore throat, foggy feeling. Christoph, Barbara, and Simona have left for a wolf conference in Sweden. They'll be gone for two weeks, and Vanessa will keep the one remaining project vehicle while she housesits at the Prombergers. In spite of my previous advocacy of walking, I'd like a faster way to get about, given the distance of the cabin and the amount of work to be done, and I regret not calling Simona before she left to arrange to get a bike. The CLCP helped a local entrepreneur begin an eco-tourism business that provides mountain bikes for hire, and we can borrow a bike or two as long as they aren't in use by customers — not an issue at this time of year.

Before Vanessa and I brought Joris to the Brasov train station for his departure, he and I walked the road far up the valley, to an idyllic sylvan setting where several quality vacation homes are under construction. The new dwellings are being built on a hillside and will have a nice view of the valley. Apparently the drive to build trophy houses in spectacular "natural" settings is a worldwide phenomenon. Money finds its way to every place beautiful.

Curly and Guardian rustled up dogs at every homestead we passed, and I suspect the average rural Romanian household has at least three of the dutiful canine guards.

The cabin seems empty now, with Joris and Silverine gone and Vanessa staying in town, and our mood is somber. I suppose the fact we have had only one day of sun in the past two weeks might be adding to the feeling of emptiness left by the departure of our friends. Titus is working the 2:00 a.m. shift and he and I are rarely awake at the cabin at the same time. What will I do this evening after he retires at 4:00 p.m.? Our battery is low and there will be no one filling the dark spaces of the cabin. A week ago, when I came in from the darkness at the end of a long, hard day in the field, I was hungry, cold, and tired, but the cabin was warm and fragrant and full of cheer as Silverine and Vanessa cooked cinnamon rolls. Where is that happy moment now? All endings seem to tear away a part of me. Once I had dogs — beings brimming with life/love/happiness/curiosity/worry/fear. Where does such vital existence go? After twenty years of relative stability in my life, I now see that the perception of stasis is always an illusion, and faith in it always misguided. Well, I didn't know *anyone* would be here when I came...

Outside are children on sleds being dragged along the road by a car, and earlier I saw families sledding on a hill. That at least some local people have the time and inclination for a little recreation is a pleasing contrast to the austere activity that dominates rural life here. I often see folks walking back to the town bent over with bundles of sticks on their backs, gathered in the forest to provide heat for their homes. Women wash their clothes by hand in small streams or in the river, and beat the dust from the rugs of their homes, and perhaps from their lives, with sticks. There is always mud to fend off, and cows and chickens and pigs to tend to. Soon will be hoeing and planting, then weeding and watering, then harvesting and storing...

Poverty is defined differently here than in America. Here it means no refrigerators, TVs, CD players, electric ranges — or electricity, for that matter — and certainly no cars. Here, people wealthy enough to own a horse have the luxury of using a horse-cart to transport the sticks, and perhaps of being generous enough to do so for their friends and neighbors as well. Yet, regardless of their circumstances, nearly everyone greets me on the road with a pleasant smile and a friendly *buna ziua* (hello).

Earlier, on my return with Vanessa to the cabin, two old women and a young girl flagged us for a ride. Other than a word or two from the girl, they spoke no English, and as we rode along, one of the women constantly crossed herself and whispered chants. Whether for thanks or protection I did not know.

Turnu and a younger, female yearling named Leasa, were both caught in baited cages on the northern slopes of the Bucegi Mountain range and fitted with radio-collars by CLCP technicians in

February 2001. They were pack mates, and therefore probably sisters.[36] Their original pack, known then as the *Glajerie* pack, as Turnu's is now (referring to the local name for a valley within their territory), was believed to consist of at least six wolves at the time. Through subsequent monitoring and tracking it appeared that Turnu was dispersing from the pack, as over the next few months she traveled throughout the pack's territory, but mostly alone. Only occasionally was she found to be located near Leasa and the other wolves.

When young wolves disperse from a pack to find a mate, a territory,[37] and form a pack of their own,[38] as nearly all young wolves must eventually do,[39] they may wander near, like Turnu did in that late winter of 2001, or they may travel far; lone dispersing wolves have been known to travel up to 886 kilometers (532 miles). Wolves that disperse far, which tend to be younger wolves, usually do not wander aimlessly but proceed in a general direction, modulated by perceived opportunities for finding a mate, finding food, and avoiding danger. Most wolves disperse by age four, and most disperse alone, although sometimes they'll leave in groups of two or more, perhaps separating later. Dispersing wolves most often depart their natal packs in the spring, when social tensions are high due to the arrival of pups, or in the fall, when nutritional tensions are high due to the needs of the newest members of the packs, which have grown significantly but which cannot yet fend for themselves. Turnu, as a near disperser roaming alone within her pack's territory, would not have been announcing her presence much by scent marking or howling, as more distant dispersers usually do when traveling through lands without packs, looking for mates.[40]

Turnu rejoined the Glajerie pack in May, around the time the pack's breeding female gave birth to a litter of pups. During the next several weeks the formerly footloose wolf did not often venture farther than a kilometer from the pack's den site (at least during the day), nor later from the pack's "rendezvous site," which was located some 500 meters from the den.

Turnu probably had returned to her pack to help raise its new members. Most (but not all) wolf packs have only one breeding female (and usually only one breeding male), and thus only one litter of pups per year.[41] After the mother has dug her den, often with the help of the pack, she enters the dark underground shelter in late

April or early May to give birth. While she is incapacitated immediately prior to parturition and during early nursing, the father brings her food, either by carrying it in his mouth or in his stomach.

Once the pups start crawling from the den to explore the world, usually after their eyes open around twelve to fourteen days from birth, the entire pack participates in the care and rearing of the wobbly youngsters. While one or more of the pups' parents, brothers or sisters, aunts or uncles, grandmothers or grandfathers, cousins, or an occasional unrelated "adoptee"[42] — the adult members of the pack (in rough order of prevalence) — are off hunting, one or more of the other adults remains with the pups to defend and keep them out of trouble.

After the pups finish nursing at about eight weeks of age, the pack usually relocates to the aforementioned "rendezvous site," as wolf biologists call the small semi-sheltered or at least reasonably comfortable and defendable area where the pups are kept and reared until they can begin to travel on their own at about twenty weeks of age. There the youngsters can huddle and eat and play and wrestle, still under the constant supervision of at least one adult. And whenever an elder wolf comes loping back to the site, head held high and hopefully stomach full, the pups rush to their towering pack-mate and scramble over each other trying to nudge their muzzles into its mouth to stimulate regurgitation.

In mid-July Turnu left the pack again, keeping to a sixty-square-kilometer corner on the northeastern side the of the pack's territory, approximately the same area she had kept to before. By December, the female wolf had met up with a lone male disperser of unknown origin, and thus was formed another wolf pack in the Bucegi Mountain region. This method of pack formation, in which a wolf splits off from a pack, meets a mate, and carves out a territory mostly or entirely within that of its original pack, is called "budding" and is usually only successful in areas of abundant food. A predation study conducted in their first month of union showed that Turnu and her mate tried but were unsuccessful at hunting roe and red deer, and relied mostly on horsemeat at bait sites, where they also killed and ate at least two dogs. The new couple fed on at least ten daily occasions (usually at night) during the twenty-eight day period of the study.

While there is almost always avoidance and often aggression

between neighboring wolf packs,[43] though perhaps less so when the packs are closely related or competition for food is low (and the latter makes the former more likely), Turnu apparently maintained good relations with her former relatives, as one evening that December CLCP fieldworkers observed a brief but friendly reunion between Turnu and her former pack. And neither were the two radio-collared (probable) sisters ready to abandon their familial bond. A month later Leasa joined Turnu and her mate, remaining with them for about three months. Yet, as happened with her sister the year before, natal family duties apparently called, and in April Leasa returned to her original pack for the pup-raising period. By now her pack mates, the original Glajerie pack, had moved into a new territory, and thus Turnu and her mate came to inherit both the territory and the name of her former pack.

Leasa's loyalties and pup-raising proclivities must have been divided, because not long after Leasa left her sister in late April, Turnu gave birth to her own litter of pups. The new parents spent that spring and summer in the vicinity of two rendezvous sites, the first relatively remote from human settlements, but near some shepherd camps, and the second closer to dwellings. According to CLCP predation studies, Turnu and her new mate preyed almost entirely on sheep during the summer, but by winter they were preying on bait, dogs, and deer.

By the first snowfall, however, the tracks of the new pack no longer included the prints of young wolves. None of Turnu's offspring had survived. Since the bodies were never found, the cause of their deaths could not be determined. Given the success of the pack's predation, however, it is unlikely the young wolves starved. Perhaps they contracted a disease from domestic dogs, or were poached, or the novice parents lacked some key competency in their first attempt at raising a family.

Turnu's progeny were not the only casualties that year. In mid-December 2002, a mortality signal led to the discovery of Leasa's body. She had been caught in a snare and apparently died after a long struggle. Throughout the summer Leasa had been roaming in an area of many farms, hiding during the day in patches of trees as small as two hectares, probably in the company of her original pack and probably feeding mostly on sheep and dogs. It's not clear whether she was still with her pack in the fall, but judging from her emaciated body at the time of her death, she had not been faring well, although perhaps well enough for her predatory habits — being as contrary to the interests of humans as they were — to lead to her demise.[44]

Monday, March 17

The first completely clear, sunny day since I arrived two weeks ago. Finally off with Peter again to track wolves.

We learned from Titus that Turnu and her mate were somewhere up "Bungee Canyon." Not yet adept at remembering Romanian place names until I hear them several times, thus I labeled a gorge where a bungee jumping outfit operates in the summer, and where some of the bungee rigging can still be seen dangling from the cliffs. A dazzling layer of fresh white powder coated the half-meter of old snow already blanketing the head of the valley. No other vehicles had yet blazed a path up the narrow track, so we got out of Peter's Trooper, put on the tire chains, and then thawed our frozen fingers while we managed to drive another kilometer further up the canyon. The road widened slightly at a quiet, lonely spot, which in the summer surely bustles with cars spilling out excited and nervous folks who are eager, or at least willing, to climb up the cliffs and hurl themselves off. From there we continued up the road on foot, plowing up to our knees through the unbroken and slightly crusted blanket of snow. We soon came upon what we were seeking: a line of wolf tracks breaking the smooth field of white. The tracks led in the same direction we were traveling, up the road, and the large paw prints were filled only with a light dusting of new powder — no more than a day old.

We continued trudging along for about three kilometers, passing colonnades of bare gray beech trees that guarded the steep slopes of the canyon, and brushing past dark stands of snow-laden fir and spruce trees that crowded the road. As I struggled behind under the lingering effects of my cold-induced weakness, I concluded that Peter does indeed set a faster pace than anyone else with whom I have hiked. His natural stride is a bit shorter than mine, but his indefatigable legs pump rapidly and non-stop, like pistons. It probably doesn't hurt that his constant companion, Djanga, a Doberman/German Shepherd mix, usually pulls strongly at her leash as they march along.

Peter pauses only rarely, and only to listen for the beep in the ensuing silence. While we paused on one such break, he related that yesterday he had found the remains of a fox, "or a small dog with nice fur. There wasn't much left to tell the difference." As I stood in the snow, catching my breath, Peter glanced at me for a moment, then directed his gaze up the road, along the trail of the wolves. "Am I going too fast?" he asked. His eyes squinted as he scanned the bright slopes above. "I forget that most people can't keep up."

"No...no, it's ok."

"If you're having trouble, just say something."

"No problem," I managed between hurried breaths.

Although my heart was throbbing in my head and my lungs seemed ever incapable of grabbing sufficient air, I was still with him, and I wondered if his query might be due mostly to habit. Diverting the subject, I suggested that this gently ascending road seemed ideal for cross-country skis.

"Don't like them."

"Why not?"

"I like to walk."

"Skis would be faster, more efficient."

"I was guiding some tourists who used them. They were slower than me."

"Maybe they were slow skiers."

We resumed plodding through the snow while we discussed the tradeoffs of using skis. Dense brush would often make packing them on our backs impractical, so they would have to be left behind when the going got too steep or densely wooded, forcing us to return the same way. Likewise with snowshoes.

Occasionally the wolf tracks veered from the road and led into the surrounding woods, but the radio signals indicated the predators were still further up the gorge, where monitoring by previous shifts suggested they had been hanging out for about a day. The wolves had been taking short intervals of rest, an hour or so at a time, between periods of activity — a pattern that suggested they might be feeding on a kill. They were currently inactive, probably sleeping somewhere on the wooded slopes above and to our left, and our plan was to approach their current location while staying on the road and not getting so close that we'd disturb them. Then we'd follow the tracks back down, staying always with them so we wouldn't miss anything that they may have killed on their nighttime jaunt along the bottom of the canyon.

The air was still and the silence broken only by the crunch of our steps, the rush of my breath, and the beat of my heart. I paused for a moment to fill my lungs, to completely grasp the present moment, to fully wrap my mind and heart and soul around the sight and sound and smell and feel of being in the snow, the cold, and the Transylvanian wilds on the trail of wolves. I watched the breath from my slow exhale hang in the crisp, halcyon air, as though it was a tangible but ephemeral record of my dreams of adventure and feelings of contentment.

We had proceeded for about a kilometer beyond where we had last seen the wolf tracks when we came upon a distinctive trough carved through the snow by the low-riding body of a wild boar. The animal's dewclaws had poked dual spikes in the snow behind each of the hoof prints that lined the sides of the trough — another sure sign of a wild boar. A little further on and the tracks of the wolves reappeared in a small clearing, where Turnu and her mate had obviously romped about. The wolves had enjoyed the spot, so it seemed as good a place as any for a bite to eat, at least to me. I was ravenous. But Peter didn't yet feel the need for his banana, so while I unwrapped a chocolate bar and started savoring the calorie-rich sweetness, he took only a swig of coke. He then began following a single set of tracks that formed a short loop leading away from the road and behind some bushes. As he stepped off the road, he immediately plunged down into about a meter of snow.

The temperature was about 2°C, but it felt warm in the sun and still air so I peeled off a layer. As Peter came wading back through the snow from behind the bushes he quietly announced that he had found fresh wolf scat containing the hair of wild boar. He then stopped to take another swig of coke while I worked on an apple. Keeping our voices low, we had begun discussing our next move when Peter stopped talking in mid-sentence and shifted his eyes to a point above my shoulder on the slope behind me, on the far side of the road. "I see blood." I stopped chewing and turned to look. On white patches of snow that I could barely see through the thick gray-brown brush lining the road and covering the bottom of the slope were a few splotches of bright red.

We scrambled up the bank and clawed our way through the bushes. Amidst a thick stand of spindly bare trunks was an area of snow about ten square meters stomped down and covered with blood and clumps of dark, bristly, hairs. Wild boar. No significant remains were left, but a trough in the snow leading through the trees and up the slope indicated where the carcass had been dragged. We followed the trail, well marked by blood and broken twigs and tufts of hair clinging to prickly sticks and branches near the ground. After a few meters we came upon the intestines, looking like sausages lying in the snow, and a large patch of hide clinging to a foreleg. From here the slope curved sharply steeper. The wolves weren't far, and we didn't want to disturb them.

"We'll return tomorrow to find the head."

"Ok…Why?"

"So we can determine the age, sex, and something about the weight."

As we drove back through Zarnesti on our return to the cabin, I recalled how strange and alien the town had seemed when I first arrived. Then, my faculties of perception had been overloaded with novelty. I couldn't take it all in, couldn't absorb and process so much new information coming so rapidly. Now, just two weeks later, what initially struck me as squalid in the dreary weather and my travel-shocked state had become familiar, comfortable, and even charming. Now Zarnesti seemed a familiar town that welcomed me home from the long days in the field.

Back at the cabin, in the fading light of late afternoon, Titus and I are chopping and splitting wood when we're interrupted by Curly's bellicose barking. Two young men approach. One speaks broken English. They are out of gas; can we help? They indicate through gestures that they will pay, but I waive off their offer. Titus has a spare container of gas in his car, from which I fill their plastic soda bottle. With more gestures and an embarrassed affectation the man explains that the gauge doesn't work. They ask how long we'll be here, and indicate they'll return in a couple days to "give us something." [They never did.]

Tuesday, March 18

This morning, when he came to pick me up at the cabin, Peter informed me that the task to find the wild boar head would be mine. I didn't quite make out what he was going to be doing.

"What do I do when I find it?"

"Weigh the head and cut off the lower jaw and bring it back."

"Oh...I don't have a knife."

"I'll give you a knife."

"I don't have a scale..."

"I'll give you a scale."

"What do I put the jaw in?"

"Here's a bag."

Peter and Titus both grinned, sensing that hacking apart a huge, freshly dead but still smiling boar head was not my cup of tea.

We arrived at the foot of Bungee Canyon around 9:30 a.m. Shortly after we began driving up the road along the two deep ruts we had made in the snow the day before, we were confronted by a parked car blocking the road. The vehicle was facing towards us, and I assumed it must have broken down on the way out and had been abandoned. There was no way around through the deep snow, nor could we easily turn around, so we were pondering what to do when I noticed a movement through the iced-over windows. Something whitish was being jostled about. I thought maybe it was a road map that someone was holding aloft and trying to read.

"Do you see what they are doing?" Peter asked in an annoyed tone.

I stared until the blurry scene began to resolve. A person's back was moving up and down. We sat and waited for several minutes, hoping the amorous pair would notice us and wrap it up. Peter fidgeted with impatience. Finally, the man climbed off and took his position behind the wheel. The woman sat up and frantically brushed her hair. They flashed awkward smiles through the frosty glass as their car started with a blue puff of smoke. While Peter carefully navigated our vehicle backwards down the long embarrassing kilometer, their car followed ours face-to-face and we exchanged more awkward smiles. When they were finally able to pass around us, the man waved proudly. The woman turned away.

"In the springtime, the sexual activity of both wolves and

humans starts to increase," Peter offered philosophically, as he stepped on the gas, spinning our tires a little. He was clearly being more poetic than accurate; he knew that I knew the sexual activity of wolves in the Carpathians was now past its peak.

Following our encounter with the amative humans I set off up the road on my quest, treading in the holes carved by our feet the day before, with visions of a large, grisly boar head sitting on the snow. I was determined to do my part for science, and do it well. *[Finding the head should be a piece of cake, even if dealing with it after won't be.]* The head we had seen at the previous kill site had sat on the snow nearby, so this one would surely be just a bit further up the slope where the drag trail led.

The slope beyond the kill site was very steep and thick with thorny new growth. The snow was thigh deep and becoming wet with the warming day. Wolf tracks crossed the slope every which way, and as the smooth trough made by the dragged carcass dissipated, I soon couldn't discern which route the wolves had taken from the site. I tried picking out a single set of tracks to follow, but as I waded through the snow, ducking and crawling under bushes, this trail too soon mingled into the general hodgepodge of wolf prints. So I tried another set, with the same result, and then another. Finally I just began traversing the steep, nettlesome slope in a narrow pattern of zigzagging switchbacks.

After covering what I thought was a more than reasonable distance up the slope with no head to be found, I was puzzled, so I plodded back down to the kill site in search of a clue. Perhaps I had missed something, a set of tracks with a spot of blood or a strand of hair or a small piece of brains or something. A large, recently severed head couldn't have simply vanished without a trace. But I found no new evidence, so I trudged up the slope again, trying to cover different zigs and different zags. Again, I found nothing. I was losing hope, but there was no way I was going to go back to Peter empty-handed, so I bounced down the slope and tried once again.

This time I decided to ascend even farther up the slope, to a series of small cliffs near the top of the ridge, where most of the snow had melted away near the south facing rocks, and where the chaos of tracks dwindled. As I approached the cliffs I doubted the wolves would climb so high, but the bare rock enticed me to climb to the top of the ridge to see what I could see. If not a head, I hoped at least for a nice view. After looking for handholds on the rock face I looked down to plant my foot for my first step up and noticed scrapings and claw marks in the brown dirt and thin snow at the bottom of the cliff. The wolves had climbed this high after all.

I scrambled up the final course of rock and hauled myself onto the point of a long, snow-covered ridge. Catching my breath, I took in the scene. The ridge fell sharply away on three sides, yielding a spectacular panoramic vista of craggy gorges, forested hills, and snow-capped peaks. The top of the ridge was about two meters wide and covered by a platform of packed snow. The wolves had obviously used the outcropping as a bed, and what a site they had chosen! Apart from the scenery, the wolves could easily see danger approaching from any direction while they rested.

The air was fresh and clear as crystal, but a blustery wind bore a succession of threatening clouds and snow squalls that obliterated the occasional intervals of warm sunshine. After drinking in the scenery and the subtle sounds of nature's "silence," or as much of it as I could, I recalled why I was there and left the lofty berth, following a lone set of wolf tracks that led along the spine of the ridge to where the spur gradually broadened into a forest of young trees. I doubted, however, that the wolves would bother carrying a boar head so far, so I soon gave it up and returned to the outcrop. Looking down the steep slope and contemplating the scene of my former labor, I concluded a dead boar head might after all be very hard to see amongst all the gray and brown brush.

[Maybe the wolves cached it. It must lie somewhere down that slope, tucked under a bush or buried in the snow, and I must have simply missed it.]

So I descended back down to the kill site one more time. I chose yet another set of wolf tracks and began rather half-heartedly scouring the slope, which was now pretty much totally cut-up with my own wandering imprints.

It was now mid-afternoon and I had had enough. I had been searching the slope for more than two hours and was soaked from melting snow and sweat and thoroughly poked and scratched by branches and thorns. I was due to meet Peter in an hour. If the head was on that slope, I couldn't find it. Maybe with the help of Djanga's keen nose, Peter could have better results than I. I gave up and headed back.

"Couldn't find the head," I mumbled after I had slogged back down the road and approached Peter sitting in the Trooper. I took in a breath to begin a long description of my heroic efforts, but Peter interrupted. "That's OK. We often can't find the head. Maybe foxes dragged it off."

Wolves are opportunists and will eat whatever four-legged creatures they can kill, including small animals such as hares (*Lepus europaeus*), and foxes (*Vulpes vulpes*), wildcats (*Felis sylvestris*), the rare chamois (*Rupicapra rupicapera*), and when the opportunity presents, livestock and dogs (the latter are often strays, but shepherd dogs and pets can also be victims). They will also scavenge, as demonstrated by the pack that was discovered raiding a garbage dump in Brasov, mentioned previously. But the primary diet of most wolves most of the time in Transylvania consists of the three wild ungulate species that inhabit the region: European Roe Deer (*Capreolus capreolus*), European Red Deer (*Cervus elaphus*), and Wild Boar (*Sus scrofa*). A study in the Carpathian Mountains of nearby Slovakia found that red and roe deer comprised 68 percent of wolves' diet, and wild boar 26 percent.[45]

Capreolus capreolus is a relatively small, spry deer species weighing no more than thirty kilograms. *Cervus elaphus*, cousin to the North American elk, is a large, majestic animal, the third largest deer species in the world,[46] and in the Carpathians, where they are biggest, the males can weigh almost 500 kg. Wild boars are also substantial animals, with the largest males in the Carpathians tipping the scales at nearly 300 kg. To give an idea of how many of these prey animals wolves might consume, the CLCP estimates that the average individual wolf requires about eight red deer and eight roe deer per year to meet its nutritional requirements.[47]

Of course the wild ungulates of Romania are also of interest to human hunters, who might naturally assume that wolves are effective and significant competitors for their quarry. Studies have shown, however, that ungulate populations are not necessarily limited by predation.[48] The relationship between predator and prey populations is complex,[49] and conditions in which predator populations limit prey populations may be no more prevalent than conditions in which the reverse is true, or neither is true, or first one and then the other is true in alternating cycles of interdependency.[50] In addition to predation, the availability of food and suitable habitat, the presence of diseases, the characteristics of weather and terrain, and compensatory birth rates all influence prey populations, and animals killed by wolves are not necessarily animals that would otherwise be available for, or desired by, human hunters — they may be diseased or otherwise unappealing, or too old or too sick to survive until the next two-legged predator comes along.

Hunting in Romania is operated as a revenue producing activity for the state and private businesses, infusing much needed money into the country's economy. Hunting associations charge membership fees for permission to hunt in "hunting areas" that they lease from the state, and foreign trophy hunters pay agencies to organize and outfit hunts. There are approximately 60,000 registered members of the hunting associations, but not all of them are active hunters every year. "Trophy" hunting — maximizing the size and "quality" of target animals — is a primary goal of much of the hunting in Romania,[51] and non-association hunters are charged trophy fees for animals they take, as well as for animals they shoot at but do not recover.[52] Trophy fees can be substantial, up to $20,000[53] for a "high quality" brown bear. Of course, foreign hunters also contribute to Romania's economy by spending money on lodging, food, and other services.

Each of the 2,226 hunting areas (or "game management units") in Romania has a gamekeeper whose job it is to constantly roam his domain monitoring environmental conditions and game populations. The areas average 100 square kilometers, and taken together they cover most of Romania, including not only the mountain forests of the Carpathians, but also the tamer and more open country of the Transylvanian plateau, the broad Wallachian plains, and the marshes of the Danube delta. While these latter areas may be less remote, dotted with human settlements and lacking in large carnivores, many are still graced with significant populations of game such as deer, boar, and waterfowl. The gamekeepers of Romania tend to know their landscapes and the animals they contain intimately, and if an area contains bears, it is the gamekeeper's job to ensure the bruins are healthy, which usually means well fed. In addition to maintaining feeding stations, the manager may plant (or have planted) oat fields and fruit trees in the forest. Many gamekeepers take a personal interest in the bears, and can describe the personalities, habits, and antics of individual bears by name.

Gamekeepers feed data and advice about the game populations of their areas to higher-ups in the Romanian Forestry Department (within the Ministry of Agriculture, Forests, and Rural Development), who determine optimum game populations based on the size, environmental characteristics, and population trends of the areas. Using the population estimates, the managers then set annual hunting quotas for each game animal for each area, and from the quotas they determine how many hunters will be allowed in the areas each season (hunting is restricted to a specific season for each game species). When the numbers of predators in an area allow — or when predation of wild ungulates or livestock is considered too high — bears, wolves, and lynx can also be designated as game, and about 250 bears, 350 wolves, and 30 lynx are legally shot in Romania each year[54] (most bears are killed by foreign hunters; the annual quota for wolves is usually around 900, half of which is reserved for foreign trophy hunters, who typically do not take many). Sometimes a specific problem predator is identified, which then may be hunted outside the normal season for that species.

Thus game managers deliberately allow the significant numbers of large predators that are common in many hunting areas, presumably consistent with national conservation goals. Most hunters accept this, both because they value the predators as game, and because they believe that predators improve the health and trophy quality of wild ungulates. Such a beneficial effect seemed to be confirmed by a study in the Carpathian Mountains of nearby Slovakia, which found that swine fever among the wild boar population tended to occur only in areas where there were no wolves.[55] It is believed that wolves frequently eliminate afflicted animals rendered vulnerable by the effects of disease before they have a chance to infect other animals. Although wolves and other predators can kill perfectly strong and healthy animals, the weak and sick and those with less evasive traits are more likely to succumb. The stronger and faster and more intelligent predators are more likely to succeed. Over time, predators and prey create each other.

Wednesday, March 19

This morning while driving through Zarnesti on our way to the backcountry for another day of tracking, Peter and I had to wait while a shepherd, with the help of his mule and his dogs, herded a large flock of goats along the main street of the bustling town. Men in suits and shiny loafers and women in skirts, nylons, and heels who were hurrying to catch the morning bus to Brasov were forced to leap aside as the animals hustled by in fitful surges. I often saw these smartly dressed townsfolk stepping gingerly through the mud along the streets of Zarnesti, scattering chickens or dodging an occasional escaped pig.

During the night the wolves had left Bungee Canyon and crossed over a couple of ridges to the south and west. We drove up a snow-packed forest road to a fork where Titus was waiting to fill us in on the night's activities. The wolves were currently inactive, but Titus had located a set of fresh wolf tracks crossing the secondary forest road that branched off here at the fork, about 400 meters from where we stood. We found the tracks and Peter left me to follow them while he would drive further up the primary road to an area closer to the wolves' current location. We were in the midst of a twenty-four-hour activity-monitoring period, during which we record the wolves' activity every fifteen minutes (for a master's thesis study being conducted by Vanessa), and Peter wanted to get a clearer signal.

Since the wolves were some distance away, I could follow their tracks in either direction, and I chose to follow them backwards up a southwest-facing slope on the left side of the road. The slope was very steep, and where exposed to the sun the snow was melting and patchy. The wolf tracks soon intermingled with the chaotic depressions left by the large feet of red deer, the smaller feet of roe deer, and the torn up earth of rooting wild boars. Most of the tracks had disintegrated into nondescript holes in the snow and mud, so picking out the wolf trail was a slow business. Occasionally I had to retrace my route after a clear print indicated I had been following the tracks of a red deer instead of a wolf. After a couple of hours I concluded it was unlikely I would find anything dead in this direction. While the wolves may have killed something small and ate it all, they would not likely leave a carcass so far away from their current location.

I gulped down a quick lunch of my usual fare — bread, cheese, chocolate, and an apple — and headed back to where the tracks crossed the road. I followed the trail in the direction of travel now, plunging down into a deep, narrow, snow-filled ravine, where the cold air of night still lingered. I crossed the small stream at the bottom of the ravine and climbed up the steep incline on the other side, scrambling on all fours and pulling myself up through the snow and the brush. I hauled myself up the slope, first into the sun and then to where the incline gradually eased onto a wooded plateau. I plowed through waist deep snow following the wolf tracks into a thicket of spruce and fir. As I brushed through the thick wall of trees, giving every branch its chance to dump a little more icy snow down my neck, I came into a small clearing where I was greeted by another red-brown-and-gray-on-white scene of bedlam. The snow was less trounced than at the wild boar sites, the tufts of fur were softer, and the remains were smaller, but here was the usual blood, the stomach, the spine, some scattered ribs, and two forelegs. The evidence was clear: here a roe deer had met its end. The site was no more than a hundred meters from the road.

After a quick look about, I turned around and raising my knees to my chest to use the deep holes of my former steps, I followed my path back to the ravine, slid down the slope, hurried through the cold air and across the stream, and scrambled up to the road. Using my walkie-talkie, which was marginally useful in this crumpled land of ridges and deep ravines, I eventually contacted Peter.

After he arrived we followed my well-worn path back to the site.

"We have to find the head."

Yes, of course. Why do the wolves never leave the head?

A single set of wolf tracks led away from the site. The trail soon split, so Peter followed one set of tracks while I followed the other. A few more meters, behind some spruce trees, and I came upon the head lying on the snow, very much cleaned to the bone. The stubs of antlers and the completely worn teeth identified the victim as venerable old male, one whose time had probably been about up whether killed by wolves or not.

On the way back to the cabin, Peter noted that I seemed to be in good condition. "Most people can't keep up with me," he noted matter-of-factly. He asked how I stay in shape, and explained that he knows something about conditioning. He once was a trainer of decathlon athletes in Germany. I described my regimen of weight-lifting, running, basketball, and yoga.

"I was playing basketball too. In Germany."

"Yeah, basketball is great exercise. If you can stay healthy. I've gotten injured a few times."

"Ya, a lot of people somehow get hurt when I play."

Taxonomically, domestic dogs are classified as a subspecies of wolf.[56] But wolves are not dogs. You can tell when you look into their otherworldly, orange-yellow eyes; adoration is not looking back. A wild, aloof intelligence is looking back, and an intense curiosity. And if you've been accepted as a friend, a pack mate, then a kind of content serenity is looking back, as though the wolf knows its place, and yours, and there is no doubt or insecurity about either.

In *Mind of the Raven*, by Bernd Heinrich, which I'm reading this evening by candlelight, Heinrich refers to the possibility of "awareness" and "consciousness" in ravens and other animals, and how their presence might be established scientifically. While admitting a lack of consensus among behavioral and neural scientists, not to mention philosophers, Heinrich suggests that consciousness "implies awareness through mental *visualization* (my emphasis)" and that "consciousness is a *monitoring* (Heinrich's emphasis) of motor patterns…which are neurally engraved preferred pathways in the central nervous system."[57] He goes on to posit that the monitoring, which often includes mental constructions based on memory, can be conscious rather than unconscious so that whoever or whatever possesses this trait of consciousness can make *choices* (my emphasis) between alternative models, and that this capability evolved as a result of the survival advantages it provides. The world is too complex and unpredictable to manage well without it. Heinrich also implies that emotions are only emotions if they are *felt* (my emphasis), and they are felt only if, like consciousness, the capacity to feel them has evolved in a species as a result of the survival advantage they provide.

But what is it that *visualizes, monitors, chooses, and feels*? Heinrich acknowledges that the neural basis for this *something* is unknown, but a theory popular among neurobiologists is that it is an "elaboration on memory" manifested by complex electrical patterns generated by certain neural circuit(s). Thus, according to this hypothesis, one or more neural circuits is somehow able to stimulate and direct other neural circuits to create models of the world using memories — representations of physical objects, ourselves, or other living beings perceived through our senses (whether accurate or inaccurate) — and from these models and upon the receipt of additional stimuli from our sensory apparatus this executive neural complex is also able to create "feelings." From these models and feelings the monitoring neural complex somehow makes choices that trigger other neural impulses to direct the operations of muscles and glands, thus creating behavior (or perhaps more "feelings") — behavior that is hopefully (from the point of view of the actor) consistent with the choices.

All well and good, but what *perceives* the alternatives and what has the *free will* to choose between them? This question can continue to be asked no matter how precisely scientists are able to decipher the operation of the complex neural circuits in our brains. A computer operating an appropriate program can create and monitor chess strategies and "choose" among them. But if we are fundamentally different from a computer, some *thing* has to be free to choose, and "free" has to mean something not bound by deterministic physical law, something not derived from complex but predictable physical processes.[58] Otherwise the "freedom" is nothing more than an illusion and we are left with a term "consciousness" that describes a complex neural process but which says nothing fundamental about the subjective experience of being conscious, or about what distinguishes consciousness from the absence of consciousness, or about what distinguishes a lot of consciousness from a little consciousness, other than perhaps a measure of complexity. So when it comes to behavior, human or non-human, if we do not appeal to something transcending the physical, a Witness — that which perceives and wills — why use the term "conscious" at all? Why say a human is conscious and an ape is not? One can believe in the existence of consciousness, or not. It is only a matter of faith. Or is it? Quite possibly it is also a matter of empirical science, since in quantum mechanical theory and experiment "observers" are required to determine in time the exact physical nature of the small particles of matter and energy that make up the universe. And what are observers if not beings that are conscious?[59]

We know what it means to be conscious ourselves, but only as a subjective term impossible to define except by circular references to other descriptive behavioral and perceptual terms. We cannot prove that another human being has these subjective experiences — that there is some indefinable "someone" who possesses awareness — any more than we can prove it for a non-human being. Yet, while proof may be lacking, it's a logical and convenient assumption that other beings morphologically and behaviorally like ourselves share a similar subjective experience of what it means to exist. This helps us to generalize, analyze, and predict behavior.

Many behavioral scientists have traditionally assumed that "consciousness" is mutually exclusive with concepts like "instinct" and "conditioned response" — in animals if not in humans — and by implication (or by definition), non-human beings *operate* according to the latter, and therefore cannot *be* the former. (Humans on the other hand, are entirely rational beings, never operating from "animal" urges, right?) Yet scientists keep pushing the boundary of what is assumed to be some great chasm of kind between human and non-human cognition. Once it was tool use, until the use of objects to manipulate the environment was observed in several primate and bird species, dolphins, elephants, and sea otters (at least). Then it was "language," which became a blurred distinction when significant referential vocabularies (such as threat-specific alarms) were found in the vocalizations of several species of mammals and birds, and rudimentary syntactic abilities were discovered in great apes and dolphins.[60] Prairie dogs can use up to twenty different sounds to tell their associates about such interesting things as "a tall human in a yellow shirt, a short human in green shirt, a coyote, a deer, a red-tailed hawk, and many other creatures."[61]

If the language distinction is unreliable, or at least fuzzy, perhaps we can assume only humans possess capabilities like being able to know the intentions of other beings, or being able to deduce insights about the world through strictly mental models rather than by trial-and-error learning. Yet investigations of certain species have defeated this presumed distinction as well. Heinrich's book, for example, clearly shows that ravens posses both of these attributes.[62] And isn't it curious that dogs and certain other companion animals seem to be able to understand our intentions, moods, and vocalizations at least as well as we understand theirs, and maybe better than we understand them ourselves?

What about the ability to recognize oneself? (Or more precisely, the ability to recognize that one is seeing a real-time image of oneself, either in a mirror or as a video projection.) Unique to humans? Another former belief that has bitten the dust, as it has been observed in the great apes, dolphins, elephants, and European magpies (and the tests that have been devised and performed to date to test this capacity cannot really rule it out in relatively visually impaired species such as canines).

A scientist who recently reported the manufacture and use of tools by crows (the construction of "hooks" from twigs or grass to retrieve small insects and larvae) prudently advised that we must be careful about describing such behavior as "smart," because it may just mean that crows are very good at using tools.[63] To what extent will scientists apply this reasoning to other forms of manipulation by non-human animals, or to planning, anticipation, deception, cooperation, adaptability, and other attributes we normally ascribe to "intelligence," provided they occur in humans?[64]

Scientists must be careful, but why have so many animal behaviorists treated consciousness as though it is a poisonous concept to be refuted at all costs? Or at best, as a concept to be assumed absent unless proven otherwise. As a measure of complexity and adaptability, as a tool for prediction, or even as exclusively a subjective term, is it any less reasonable to assume consciousness is present, especially when behavior appears anthropomorphic?[65]

I see it there, in the eyes of Poiana and Crai. If consciousness is not there, it is not anywhere.

Thursday, March 20

Another dark and dreary day, with snow off and on, and some rain.

During the night the wolves had left the forested hills and crossed a river that flows down the eastern edge of a broad, open valley. They roamed among a few widely scattered settlements strung along a dirt road running up the middle of the dale. In the morning we drove along the road, listening to the beep via the directionless antenna on the roof (piped into a portable speaker), dodging or slowly bouncing through deep, iced-over, water-filled holes. We stopped to take a directional reading and to see if there were any tracks in the shallow, wet snow. Peter's intuition proved correct — a set of fresh wolf tracks crossed the road no more than ten meters from where we stopped.

Since the wolves were currently somewhere in the hills farther up the valley, we began following the tracks in the direction of travel, away from the road and towards the river, past a lonely farm house and into an open field behind. The hills from which the wolves had descended the night before rose sharply just beyond the banks of the river, the bare hardwood trees crowning the snowy hills like a stiff, gray-red mane. Before reaching the gushing river, the wolf tracks diverted sharply to the left, to the north, leading in the downstream direction through an open field behind a couple more farmhouses and an old military storage building. We soon noticed dog tracks wandering about, and since the snow was slushy and the prints not sharp, we began to wonder whether we were really following the tracks of wolves.

The tracks continued running straight down the valley, and we were regaining confidence that we were following the impressions left by purposeful wolves and not frolicking dogs when we came upon a large depression that was obviously formed by hoofs, not paws. A red deer print here, a wolf print there, both leading in the same direction…which tracks were laid first? We sensed we were now on to something interesting, if not dramatic, so we proceeded briskly, our attention entirely focused on the lines of holes in the snow, until the trail led into a large yard surrounded on three sides by a two-meter-high chain-link fence. The yard belonged to a small, decrepit hydroelectric plant that spanned the river.

Noticing a brownish spot on the snow across a small tributary stream, Peter handed me Djanga's leash and waded across, where he found a few drops of blood. Meanwhile, fiercely barking dogs brought a man out from one of the buildings. As the man approached he was screeching a rapid-fire monologue and I assumed he was informing me of the obvious — that we were trespassing — before I cut him off with my most diligently practiced Romanian phrase, *"Eu vorbesc foarte putsin Romaneshta"* ("I speak very little Romanian"). I signaled for him to wait while I pointed at Peter and restrained Djanga from delivering a message of her own. After Peter had finished wading back across the stream, the excited man had much to say with both his mouth and his hands.

"Four" wolves killed a "giant" red deer on his property last night. The deer's carcass was in his shed and he was in the process of butchering it. He led us around to where the kill occurred in the corner of the yard, where the ground was thoroughly trampled with hair and blood and snow and mud. The man pointed around as he shouted his story, and he showed us where the deer had inflicted a serious dent into the sturdy metal fence. He then took Peter inside the shed to show him the carcass while I remained outside with Djanga. They returned a few minutes later, and whether the expressive man ever finished telling his tale of a fierce night-time battle with wild beasts, we left to others to know. We had heard more than enough to satisfy our own curiosity, and took our leave.

We decided to follow the tracks back to see if we could reconstruct the detailed anatomy of this hunt.

The wolves encountered the deer about two kilometers back, near the road. As the majestic stag walked slowly through the dale, senses alert, kicking holes into the crusty snow to expose a few blades of grass or a few broken stalks of last year's corn, it suddenly stopped, lifted its head, thrust its wet nostrils into the cold night air, and twitched its ears. Something was wrong. Some disturbance — a slight scent drifting on a shifting breeze, or a delicate snap of ice shattering the deathly stillness, or a fleeting shadow wavering over the starlit snow — instantly crystallized the deer's being into complete and focused presence. Like an unobserved quantum of energy ready to act as particle or wave,[66] the deer stood with muscles twitching, perfectly poised between action and non-action, completely receptive, existing and perceiving existence with its entire nature, perhaps exchanging a final, instantaneous stare with its stalkers…and then it was off.

The deer bounded down the valley, fleeing for its life, barely noticing the tributary streams and the five rail fences it leaped with ease.[67] One deadly pursuer followed directly at its heels, just as focused, just as determined to survive, relentlessly shadowing every zig and every zag, jumping every stream and every fence. A second shadow darted along beside, but then veered to the right, towards the river, running past the ends of the fences, preventing the deer from reaching the water and possible escape.

Wolves will often quickly give up chasing as healthy and dangerous an animal as a large and speedy red deer. But not this time; at least not yet. These two predators had eaten just yesterday; they could not be considered especially desperate, so perhaps they were just evaluating, knowing they had plenty of energy for an extended pursuit of possibilities. Or perhaps they had already detected something vulnerable in this lone red deer. Or maybe they were just especially experienced, brazen, and confident wolves, suspecting at some intuitive level that as a pair they were at their peak hunting effectiveness.[68]

After about 1,500 meters, with its heart pounding and its lungs screaming for air, the deer recognized a chance. Its direct pursuer, the wolf that had once nipped its leg, had lost a few centimeters at the jump of a fence, and then a few more at the jump of the next. And now the wolf recognized it hadn't the power for another leap, so it diverted to the right to avoid yet another approaching fence. The wolves then swapped roles, the less fatigued herder dashing to the left to become the direct pursuer. But time had been lost and their quarry gained ground. Now the deer could hear the distance growing, could sense the retreat of death. But just as hope gave the fleeing animal a final surge of energy, just as it felt the impending triumph of its unyielding will to live, the end came in a violent crash. An invisible barrier intruded mercilessly into the deer's existence, instantaneously stopping all the momentum of its motion, its hope, and its life.

Perhaps the deer was knocked to the ground, perhaps not, but it was bounding no more and could not clear the tall, chain-link fence. Hope, ever tossed about by the vagaries of the indifferent Fates, having fallen from the deer was retrieved by the wolves. The predators tore at the deer's legs as the desperate victim tried to escape. The wolves sensed that their prey was now stunned and hurt, but the stag still managed to kick them off, and left tufts of hair on the fence as it rubbed along the confounding barrier trying to find a break. Where the deer's progress was stopped by yet another invisible obstacle, it swiveled to face its frenzied attackers. Stomping its feet and dropping its head to use its antlers as a shield, the deer drove the wolves back to the other corner of the yard. But there, trapped again and hurt, the large and once powerful red deer could find no escape, and whenever it turned to face one of the wolves, the other attacked ferociously from behind…

The wolves didn't get to realize much of the benefit of their wit and labor. Dogs joined the fray, likely kicking up a fierce storm, barking and charging at the intruders, both the wolves and the fallen deer. The electrical plant attendant heard the ruckus and rushed to the melee, and recognized that a large package of fresh venison had been delivered. Facing too many threats, the wolves were forced to give up. The predators retreated into the black and silent night.[69]

"So why did he say there were four wolves? Is there another pack around here?" I asked.

"People exaggerate about wolves. And when he came out, there also were dogs and he was confused. It was dark."

Apparently our wolves had become very efficient hunters. Our team had already found more wolf kills this week than during any other previous week of a predation study in the ten-year history of the CLCP, and more than over many of the month-long studies (or so I heard). And the week wasn't over. But Peter suspects that it wasn't usually the wolves that had been inefficient during those past studies. The researchers probably hadn't found all the kills. We had had good luck and seemed to be on a roll.

In the afternoon we drove through the village of Bran and up into the high hills beyond, where the radio signals indicated the wolves were spending the day. The quality of the houses and shops of the quaint village and surrounding countryside give evidence of the surprising impact a nineteenth century novel can have on the economy of a developing region. Bran is the site of "Dracula's Castle,"[70] an imposing structure built in the fourteenth century to guard against invading Ottoman Turks, and purported for the sake of tourism to be the abode of Vlad III Dracula (1431–1476), the Prince of Wallachia during three tumultuous episodes in the fifteenth century.

Dracula, of course, was the inspiration for Bram Stoker's novel, or at least the inspiration for the name of Stoker's main antagonist, as there is little evidence the writer knew much else about the historical Vlad. "Dracula" means "son of Dracul," referring to his father's surname Dracul, which can be translated as either "the Devil" or "dragon." For the purposes of legend the former is most often assumed, although the name actually derives from the fact that Vlad's father was a member of the Order of the Dragon, an order of knights created by the Holy Roman Emperor (and King of Hungary) Sigismund in 1408. The Order was chartered to defend the Cross, which meant primarily to resist the Ottoman Empire.

Vlad III is also infamously known as Vlad Tepes (pronounced "Tepesh") — Vlad the Impaler — for the incredibly cruel way he treated thousands of his enemies and people he judged as criminals: slow death by impalement on stakes. Impalement was not his only specialty, however, and, as evidence of the fascination that such brutal treatment of living beings seems to hold, there is plenty of literature documenting the gruesome details about how his many and varied forms of torture were designed to maximize pain, and how extensively they were applied: allegedly to tens of thousands of people — at a time. Because the stories were originally based on oral reports or descriptions in pamphlets published for political purposes by various factions who were not Vlad's friends (mostly by German Saxons and Catholic monks, who were often targets of his persecution), one can question the details and extent of his atrocities. Indeed, a careful analysis of some of the reports suggests that exaggerations are likely. But given the consistent nature of the stories across multiple languages and polities, and given the degree of precision about places and times, the fact that the Prince was exceedingly ruthless and cruel seems beyond doubt. Criminals subject to his ire included merchants judged to be dishonest and anyone who violated his strict moral code, especially unchaste maidens and widows, and unfaithful wives. Enemies included nobles (known as "boyars") and merchants who threatened his political power, and external invaders, especially the Ottoman Turks.

Dracula's role of Prince of Wallachia was not without strategic import in defending Europe from Ottoman expansion. He was the only European leader who responded immediately with more than words to a plea from Pope Pius II in 1459 to defend the Christian world, and in successfully defending Wallachia from the Turks during a dramatic campaign in 1461 and 1462, he demonstrated that he was a courageous and clever military strategist, effectively utilizing "scorched-earth" and guerilla tactics in resisting superior forces. But it may have been Vlad's brutality that finally tilted the balance towards the defenders, as his impaling of thousands of captured enemy soldiers reportedly so demoralized the leader of the invaders (the Sultan Mehmed II) that the latter finally gave it up. Dracula was defeated by the Sultan a few months later, however, and forced to flee to Transylvania; nevertheless, some chroniclers suggest that Western Europe gained the crucial time it needed for its defense while the Turks were delayed in dealing with the brutal Wallachian.

Vlad himself was imprisoned and mistreated by the Ottomans early in his life, which might explain some of his vitriol. His father had handed him and his brother over to the Turks as hostages to ensure their compliance with Ottoman rules of vassalship. And Dracula's enemies, internal and external, *were* dangerous. In the complex world of medieval politics, there was constant conflict between various factions of boyars and princes in the Romanian provinces, and assassinations of leaders were common. In fact, Dracula's father and elder brother (Mircea II) were assassinated by boyars and merchants of Wallachia, allegedly on the orders of the Transylvanian ruler, John Hunyadi. His brother was treated with special brutality, having been blinded with a red-hot iron before being buried alive, and revenge was likely a motivating factor for some of Dracula's actions. His fans have tried to further rationalize the Prince's goals, if not his methods, by claiming he was restoring much needed law and order[71] to a land ravaged by the anarchy and crime associated with constant political upheaval and war. This he may have accomplished — there are stories that a merchant could leave a cart full of goods in the streets of Brasov overnight without losing a trinket — but it hardly justifies, for example, skinning alive an (allegedly) unfaithful wife.

In spite of his thirst for spilling blood in creative ways, there is no evidence that during his time people considered Dracula to be a vampire. Like most Princes of the period, he was a patron and a builder of monasteries. After being defeated by the Turks and imprisoned by the Hungarian King, Dracula converted from Romanian Orthodoxy to Catholicism,[72] possibly in a bid to regain Hungarian royal favor.[73] His cousin Stephen the Great of Moldavia, with whom he was sometimes allied and sometimes not, is considered one of the great national heroes of Romania and was canonized by the Romanian Orthodox Church in 2006. Dracula's linkage to vampires, so ingrained in our minds today, had to await Stoker.[74]

Built in the 12th Century in a Teutonic style, like most medieval castles Bran Castle (its official designation) has its share of turrets with winding staircases, dark, narrow passages and stairways, and low doorways you must stoop to get through, but with its whitewashed walls and ample windows, the castle's many rooms are surprisingly light and airy. It has fabulous views. It's the sort of dwelling a prince or princess could be quite comfortable inhabiting and entertaining (if not torturing) numerous guests in. The Romanian royal family dwelt in the castle from 1920 until it was seized from Princess Ileana by the communist regime in 1948. The building was renovated in the 1980s, and after the fall of Ceausescu in 1989 it began its evolution into the tourist attraction it is today, associated with the legend of Dracula (as significantly modified by the Stoker novel, of course). The castle is now operated by the government as a museum, and receives between 250,000 and 450,000 visitors a year (I have found references to both figures).[75]

In fact, or more precisely, in legend, for there is no documented evidence, Vlad III resided at the castle for only one night.[76] I suspect, therefore, that the castle's touristy role has as much to do with its impressive medieval appearance as it does with the legend.[77] Perched high on a hill, the citadel looms ominously over the neat little village, where today restaurants and tourist shops selling Dracula paraphernalia line the main drag. Capitalizing on the presence of the castle, a vibrant agri-tourism industry has also developed in the hills around Bran, wherein tourists pay to temporarily reside on working farms.

The road we negotiated above Bran through snow and mud to get another bearing on the wolves was rough, narrow, steep, and very

Crai ("King"), a seven-year-old male (in 2003), one of the CLCP's two captive wolves, kept for educational, public relations, and research purposes. While friendly and relaxed around CLCP staff, the wolves were very wary and usually disappeared into the brush of the one-acre enclosure when strangers approached.
© SteffenLeiprecht/Froggypress.de (Inset © Thilo Brunner)

Cabanna Lupului, The Wolf Cabin, near Zarnesti, Romania.
© Alan E. Sparks

Piatra Craiului looking across the Barsa Valley from Cabanna Lupului. © Alan E. Sparks

Poiana and Crai howling.
© Jürgen Sauer

Poiana howling.
© B&C Promberger

Piatra Craiului. Photo taken near the cabin.
© Alan E. Sparks

Curly on patrol near the wolf cabin.
© Alan E. Sparks

Bucegi Mountains, on the eastern edge of the Glajerie pack's territory.
© Alan E. Sparks

Christoph Promberger listens for a telemetry signal. *© B&C Promberger*

Project status meeting with (L-R) Peter, Vanessa, Barbara, Silverine, Titus, and Joris. *© Alan E. Sparks*

Barbara Promberger at a wolf kill site (wild boar). Note the ski slope in the background.
© B&C Promberger

The cabin dogs, Guardian and Curly.
© Alan E. Sparks

Sheep in winter. *© Christa Schudeja*

Local transportation near
Cabanna Lupului.
© Alan E. Sparks

Local method of doing laundry.
© Jürgen Sauer 2005

Peter Sürth with Poiana. © Alan E. Sparks

Author and Peter examining wolf scat.
© Jügen Sauer

Poiana. © B&C Promberger

Vanessa using radio telemetry to locate the wolf Turnu in the Bucegi Mountains. © Alan E. Sparks

Farmlands near Bran. © Alan E. Sparks

Roe deer *(Capreolus capreolus)*. © Thilo Brunner

Red deer *(Cervus elaphus)*. © Peter Sürth

Wild boar *(Sus scrofa)*.
© Vladimir Chernyanskiy
(istockphoto.com)

ABOVE AND BELOW: Bran Castle, also known as "Dracula's Castle."
© Oana Vinatoru (above) (istockphoto.com); © Jürgen Sauer (below)

Following a horse cart near Bran. *© Alan E. Sparks*

Eurasian Lynx *(Lynx lynx).* *© B&C Promberger*

Bear tracks.
© Kathrin Merkel

European Brown Bear
(Ursus arctos arctos).
© Peter Sürth

The Zamorra Mountains looking across the Azuga Valley. This region is just to the east of Bucegi.
© B&C Promberger

Evidence of wolf sexual activity. © Alan E. Sparks

Indirect register. Wolf or dog prints?
© Jürgen Sauer

Piatra Craiului taken from the road to the cabin.
© Alan E. Sparks

Poiana. © *Steffen Leiprecht/Froggypress.de*

Crai. © Steffen Leiprecht/Froggypress.de

Poiana crossing a stream when she was about five months old, and a few months later on a snowy hill (inset). © B&C Promberger

Crai and author. *© SteffenLeiprecht/Froggypress.de*

Poiana. *© Steffen Leiprecht/Froggypress.de*

Poiana and author.
© SteffenLeiprecht/Froggypress.de

Poiana eating. *© Jürgen Sauer*

Cooking bones. *© Alan E. Sparks*

Wolf kill (red deer). *© Jürgen Sauer*

Meat for the wolves or the flies? *© Kolja Zimmerm*

Wolf kill (roe deer). *© Peter Sürth*

Barbara holds aloft a directional antenna to search for a signal. Christoph's dog, Yukai, is on the left; Barbara's dog, Chiron, is on the right. © B&C Promberger

Howling for wolves. © Jürgen Sauer

Pestera, Romania. *© Alan E. Sparks*

Coltii Chiliei (Rock Monastic Shelter), near Zarnesti. *© Alan E. Sparks*

Brancoveanu Monastery, Sambata de Sus, Fagaras Mountains. *© Jürgen Sauer 2006*

incongruous with the size and quality of several handsome farmhouses and towering inns lining it. The inns are only three stories high, I suppose, but they are narrow and appear especially imposing when looking up the slopes at them from down within the high-banked, deeply rutted track. As we rolled and bounced slowly along I imagined the difficulties that must have been faced in transporting the building materials up such a rough and steep path, and concluded that in America no one would bother, at least not without first improving the road.

Along a short row of much humbler dwellings just before the top of the ridge, the mud-and-snow banks rose to the level of our eyes, and our vehicle barely squeezed through the narrow chasm. We were trailing a horse-drawn cart that slowly wobbled along carrying its cargo of a man and two children huddled against the cold wind, bundled in brown and blue and pink coats and donning dark woolen hats. Were the children returning home from school? If so, what a contrasting lot from that of school children in America who ride in their parents' warm and smooth SUVs along sterile suburban boulevards!

The road opened up at the top of the ridge where the wind had blown the snow into hard-packed drifts. We couldn't go any further, and after taking a telemetry reading we got stuck while trying to turn around. We used chains to free ourselves and called it a day.

Friday, March 21

A long frustrating day in the snow and a very cold wind. Again the wolves were up in the highlands above Bran, and again we got stuck, this time while trailing a horse-drawn sledge. We got out and performed the usual activities people do to try to free a vehicle stuck in snow, in the usual order, beginning with shoveling and progressing to the placement of odds and ends under the tires for traction, and then to pushing. As I planted my feet in the snow and began to push in time with Peter's accelerations, I nearly got spiked through when a pipe he had placed under one of the rear wheels bolted out between my legs. Having by providence alone avoided that disaster, I nearly froze my fingers off when we proceeded to the next option of putting on the chains. But at least I was more helpful this time. I think. Yesterday, although it was my second experience with the chaotic masses of jingling metal, I had been a bit befuddled and pretty much just watched after it became obvious that Peter could put on four sets of chains quicker than I could put on one.

We finally got free and continued on our way to the top of the ridge. From there the road continues along the blunt spine of the open ridge before dipping down into a forest, but the drifted, hard-packed snow was navigable only by horse-drawn sledges (or, I suppose, in another time or place, by snowmobiles). Peter plunged the Trooper into the snow off to the side of the road as best he could so as not to block the local horse-powered traffic, and we stepped out into a stiff, frigid wind that howled in our ears and blasted our faces with swarms of stinging ice particles.

The fresh snow that had fallen over night was wind-whipped and hard-packed. As our feet plunged through the crust and deep into the snow on every other step, I tried recalling all the reasons we weren't using snowshoes. Our only practical method of loco-motion was to step in the narrow, deep ruts carved by the runners of a sledge, which probably had carried a load of firewood from the forest. We were forced to walk like tightrope walkers, placing one foot directly in front of the other — a direct register gait, human-style. I alternately sweated from exertion and froze from the wind, and after a kilometer or so the strange gait caused a blister on my right foot.

Between the snow squalls carried by ominous dark clouds we caught beautiful views of the white, rolling, farm-studded hills of Bran and the gray-brown lowlands beyond, but the only wolf tracks we could find were a few widely separated, short sets of holes that had not been blown away by the wind, and a short set of eerie, white, four-toed pillars that clutched the frozen, windswept ground. After our recent successes we were disappointed to find so little, but perhaps it had been an uneventful night for the wolves as well.

In the evening, after I finished my chores of walking Guardian, chopping wood, and cooking the dog food, I sat down with Titus to a most welcome hot dish he had prepared, of corn, red peppers, onions, and beans on corn tortillas. My face felt flushed and wind-burned and out of place in the warm cabin. Once again I retired to the cold loft feeling exhausted, nourished, and content — and won-dering if I had ever really lived another life.

Saturday, March 22

Cold day. –13.3 °C at the cabin when I awoke.

Today I heard tell another dream of wolves. While we were driving into the mountains, Peter discussed what would be next for him. Since the CLCP is ending the research program at the end of this month, his role here as lead wolf tracker will be over. It comes as no shock that opportunities for wolf trackers are rather limited.

"So what are you going to do?" I asked.

"I'm thinking about hiking along the Carpathians."

I paused, wondering what was new about that.

"The whole way," Peter continued. "From Romania to Germany. Next year if I can get sponsors."

I had no map in front of me, but I knew enough geography to know this would be no trivial undertaking. Was he serious or just dreaming? After having chased wolves with him for several days now in this rugged Transylvania terrain, I figured if anyone could do it, it would be him. Maybe he was serious.

He went on to describe how he and his team could collect the scat of wolves, bears and lynx in order to begin building a genetic inventory that could be used to characterize the distribution and movements of the large carnivore populations of Eastern and Central Europe. And by cataloguing evidence of large carnivore activity along the way, his project could help identify threats to the free movement of predators and the location of important corridors that should be protected from the development that is beginning to seep into the region. The exploit could also raise public awareness, especially for Western Europeans, both about the potential of the Carpathians for eco-tourism and their role as a reservoir of wildlife. It would be funded by people who would pay a fee on a weekly basis to join the expedition.

"I'll call it The Way of the Wolf."

[A name and all…he really is serious.]

"Wow. That's an incredible idea. Maybe you could even establish a route that could eventually be built into a trail, like the Appalachian Trail in America."

"Ya, I was thinking of that."

"What a crazy idea!"

Peter smiled, and after a pause in which it became clear he was not going to dispute this conclusion, I added, "Do you think I could come? For a while anyway?"

"Ya, I think so."

We drove along a snow-packed forest road leading up a narrow, densely wooded dell where Titus had monitored the wolves throughout most of the night. The radio signals indicated they were still not far off, somewhere up the steep slope that framed the east side of the valley. The night had draped the forest with a fresh layer of sparkling snow, and after Titus departed we drove further along the road scanning for tracks. Breaking the smooth soft whiteness of the forest floor were countless small depressions formed by clumps of snow that had fallen from the tree branches above, and countless trails left by sundry small creatures that had climbed out of holes or down from trees and scampered about on their business throughout the night, their small, nimble feet dabbing double rows of dots in the snow and their drooping tails engraving lines in between. Larger triangular patterns marked the seemingly random routes of hares, their two small forefeet and two larger hind feet having struck the distinctive impressions as they hopped about the woods. And the familiar tracks of roe and red deer were not absent. Apparently it had been a festive night in the thick stand of fir and spruce that covered the flat valley floor and stood guard along the small brook that meandered its length.

Further up the valley, at about 1,600 meters altitude, we came upon several sets of fresh wolf tracks crisscrossing the road. We got out, and while I looked for the clearest set of tracks to follow, Peter continued up the road on foot to see what he could find. As I entered the dark forest chamber on the left side of the road, wolf tracks were everywhere. I tried following the set I had chosen, which soon became interwoven with the prints of a much smaller canine. Were the wolves hunting this fox? Poiana and Crai had killed a fox in their enclosure several days ago, so I knew it was feasible.

Over tiny trickling streamlets, under fallen logs, through bushes…and then, sure enough, a tuft of fur and a single drop of blood on the snow. The fur seemed too brown and downy to be that of a fox, but maybe European foxes are different than their American cousins. But only one drop of blood? Could a wolf gulp down a fox in a single bite? I called Peter on the walkie-talkie and then headed out to the road to meet him. He soon came striding rapidly down the road. We rushed through the tiny streamlets, over the fallen logs, and under the bushes to the site of the "kill" — the single drop of blood and the lone tuft of fur. Peter confirmed my doubts. The fur was from a roe deer, not a fox.

We split up and each tried to trace a single route of travel from among the confusing jumble of tracks. At first we could easily hear each other's voice echoing in the silent forest as we both exclaimed our discoveries — a few hairs here, a drop or two of blood there — but as we gradually separated, our voices faded from each other's hearing and we finally ceased our announcements. I hadn't seen any remains for ten minutes or so when I heard Peter yelling from the direction of the brook, which here trickled along the far side of the narrow dell, no more than seventy meters from the road. He had found the main kill site on the bank of the brook. Upon my hasty arrival I noted the usual padded-down snow, but nothing remained of the deer except gray-brown hair scattered about like threshed wheat, a little blood, and the spilled contents of the stomach. As I examined the scene of the deer's demise, I imagined Titus, sitting in the Suzuki in the dark and quiet and cold and listening to that simple beep while the dramatic struggle ran its course nearby.

Sets of wolf tracks led from the kill site in all directions. The wolves had torn pieces from the steaming carcass and carried them off to eat, then returned for more, and fed thus throughout the night, within a circumference of about fifty meters. Small canine prints at the kill site indicated who had followed who — the clever little fox was alive and well and had joined in the feast, or at least had cleaned up the leftovers.

Peter sent an SMS to Barbara, who was still in Sweden. Her response was immediate and brief: "Find the head." The mantra of wolf tracking this week.

A lone set of tracks crossed the brook and climbed a precipitate slope densely covered with young spruce trees. The radio signals suggested the wolves were currently resting somewhere up the slope, and not very far, perhaps 300 meters away. We didn't want to disturb them, but we had our orders, so we began scrambling up the nearly vertical incline on hands and knees, as stealthily as possible, grabbing small trunks and branches to hoist ourselves up. Along the wolves' trail a few tufts of deer fur clung to the brush. We pulled and crawled up to where the slope leveled off, to a place where we could stand in the deep snow. We paused and restrained our breaths. Peter listened to the beep. The wolves were still inactive, now perhaps 200 meters distance.

We took one slow, cautious step at a time, stooping and twisting to avoid scraping against branches, until we came upon a site where the wolves had stopped, settled down on their haunches, dropped the choice pieces of deer they had decided to bring along, including, presumably, the head, and crunched down a few more mouthfuls. After a silent and cursory examination of the wolf impressions and the few red smudges and tufts of fur they had left in the snow, we had started to move on when I spotted a small bone pressed into the snow a short distance away. At first I thought it was a rib. I signaled to Peter. He motioned for me to pick it up. It was a lower jawbone. Great! The wolves had done the grisly work for us. As I held it aloft, Peter pointed to the teeth, which were not worn at all, and barely whispered, "young." He pointed in the direction of the wolves. We still needed to find the skull so we could determine the animal's sex.

We stood still again while Peter again listened intently to the beep. He opened one hand and three fingers of the other and silently mouthed "eighty." The wolves were resting about eighty meters away. We strained our eyes, looking up the slope through the dense fabric of gray-brown trunks and green branches. Our hearts were in our throats. Although we didn't want to disturb them, if we had the opportunity we certainly wanted to catch a glimpse of the elusive wild beings whose every move we'd been trailing for days. But suddenly I had a problem. I had to cough. I had been holding it back for some time — the residual effects of the cold I had had — and now I felt I would choke if I didn't finally clear my trachea. Perhaps it was one of those moments when you simply must do what you shouldn't do, like trying to restrain laughter in a quiet classroom. I signaled to Peter that my situation was urgent. While I struggled, we exchanged some gestures about how best to muffle it. Finally I buried my mouth in my gloves and coughed the gentlest, quietest cough I could manage. We waited. We listened; me to the silence and Peter to the beep. The wolves didn't move. We each took another step. My coat made a slight scratch against a branch. The wolves were up and off.

I was sorry I had disturbed them. I knew the energy balance of animals living in the wilds during northern winters is precarious, and a single extra incidence of flight can tilt the balance from life to death. I consoled myself with the thought that these wolves seemed to be faring well, given what we had found this week. Since they were now gone, we went on to examine their bed sites, the first about forty meters distance, and another about ten meters farther up the slope. They had been sleeping apart from each other, probably to enhance their ability to detect and escape from danger.

So that was it, the end of the predation study. Titus and Vanessa are overjoyed it's over. I can't blame them. Eight hour shifts in the field, plus transportation and debriefing time, nearly every day for a month is a lot of work, and they finished up with the tedious and cold night shifts. While excited at finding so many kills, I think even Peter is ready for a break.

This is also the end of an era — the end of all large carnivore research by the CLCP. We will continue to monitor the location and activities of Turnu and her mate until the batteries in the radio collar expire (which should be soon), but much less intensively. The Romanian authorities are not renewing the approvals required for continued research, and anyway the CLCP was first conceived and presented to supporting organizations as a ten-year project. Christoph and Barbara are now eager to move on to the next phase of promoting conservation in Romania — the creation of the Large Carnivore Information Centre.

I return in late afternoon to a cold, empty cabin. The gray and white ramparts of Piatra Craiului are catching the sun's final slanting orange rays and scattering them into the cloudless blue sky. It is already −6.6°C, and will be a frigid night. I'm vexed that the sauna is also dark and cold; it was scheduled for today and I had hoped Titus would have it fired up. I set about getting the fires going, first in the cabin and then in the sauna.

As I walk naked and steaming through the brisk night air from the sauna to the stream to fill the buckets of water, I step gingerly on the ice, mud, and stones along the path. The stars burn innumerable cold white holes into the black firmament of space above and into my consciousness within. Unlike in the urban centers and suburbs and even much of what we call "the country" in America, here in this dark valley at night the stars cannot be ignored. A meteor dashes across the glittering void.

When I enter the cabin the dogs are snoring. Time for me also.

Sunday, March 23

Peter called this morning to ask if I wanted to help find the roe deer skull, but I declined. I had to wash my clothes, clean the cabin, chop wood, repair the axe handle again… With only Titus and I here, things have been falling behind. The day is beautiful and sunny, but very cold. I think I may have slightly frozen the tips of my thumb and fingers while rinsing my laundry and hanging it in the cold wind.

Curly and Guardian are lounging peacefully in the sun when five huge shepherd dogs approach. Titus thinks they are Guardian's former mates. Curly tries to be friendly while Guardian hangs back, confused, jealous, and afraid. The dogs get rough with Curly, so Titus and I run out and drive them off, me with a stick, Titus with pepper spray.

Then I bring in my laundry, frozen stiff like cardboard.

Wolves have long been associated in the collective human imagination with the region we now call Romania. On ancient battlefields, the enemies of the Dacians (pronounced "Dachians"), the Thracian tribe which inhabited these lands as early as the sixth century BC, could be excused if they believed they were facing the largest and strangest wolf packs the world had ever seen, as thousands of Dacian warriors bore into battles the "Dacian draco" to inspire courage on one side and fear on the other. This unusual standard consisted of an open-mouthed copper or bronze wolf head to which was attached a cloth windsock resembling the body of a dragon-like creature called a "balaur."[78] When held aloft on a rod by a warrior riding astride a galloping horse, the draco produced a whistling noise, which presumably enhanced the intended psychological effects. This wolf-headed standard must have been very appealing in its way, or at least very effective, as it had a long career. Originally developed by the Sarmatians and Alans, tribes of the Eurasian steppes, the draco was adopted (and modified) by the Dacians by the fourth century BC, and later by the Romans.

The Dacians may have identified themselves with wolves long before they first employed the intimidating wolf symbol on a field of battle, as the name they called themselves, *daoi*, probably derived from the Phrygian word for wolf, *daos*. By the second century BC the tribe had established its Kingdom of Dacia, covering present day Romania, Moldova, and parts of Ukraine, Bulgaria, and Hungary, by defeating and expanding into territory previously occupied by Celtic, Bastarnae, and Boii tribes.

The Dacians had developed an organized and culturally rich civilization of their own before coming into conflict with the imperial ambitions of the Roman Empire. The kingdom's urban centers were supplied with water by aqueducts and pipelines, and they were defended by an especially effective (according to the Romans) defensive structure called a *Murus Dacicu* (Dacian Wall). Judging from the ancient coins that have been unearthed in the region, the Dacians actively engaged in commerce with their neighbors for centuries, probably exporting grain, honey, and wine, as well as gold and silver extracted from mines in Transylvania.

Conflicts between the Dacians and Romans began in 112 BC and continued sporadically over the ensuing years with victories and defeats on both sides. In 106 AD, after two especially bloody campaigns, the Romans finally prevailed under their emperor Trajan, who especially coveted Dacian gold. Dacia became a Roman province, and the culture became Romanized over the ensuing decades.

Rome's political domination of the province began to wane as its empire faded, but the Romanized culture and language did not, surviving fairly intact through centuries of foreign meddling by a succession of powerful neighboring empires: Gothic (third to fourth centuries), Hunnish (fifth century), Avar (sixth century), Bulgarian (ninth to eleventh centuries), Hungarian (eleventh to eighteenth), Ottoman Turk (sixteenth to nineteenth), Austrian (seventeenth to eighteenth), and Russian (nineteenth to twentieth). Waves of invading tribes from the steppes to the north and east, including the Petchenegs, Cumans, Magyars, and Tartars, swept the region in the eleventh and twelfth centuries.[79] They were followed by less violent waves of immigrants from the west, especially Saxons and Teutons from Germany and Szeklers from Hungary, who were encouraged to settle in the Transylvanian plateau by Hungarian kings in the twelfth century in order to counteract the eastern invaders.[80]

The struggle for political independence in the region was continuous, but through battle, compromise, intrigue, assassinations, and alliances under sundry princes and *viovodes* (the local word for military commander or governor), various small local states and dukedoms maintained some degree of autonomy throughout the Middle Ages, albeit always precarious, shifting, and compromised — and often tributary. By the fourteenth century the larger principalities of Wallachia and Moldavia had evolved, while Transylvania fell under Hungarian control, although with its own political organization.[81] All three provinces came under the control of the Ottoman Turks by 1541, as suzerains paying tribute but retaining most internal administrative autonomy.

For the next 450 years the principalities were continually pushed and shoved and traded and shared and fought over by their powerful, rival neighbors: Turkey, Hungary, Austria, and Russia (Moldavia also had the distinction of being a battlefield for wars between Poland and Turkey). In 1600 the three provinces — though containing peoples of diverse European and Asian ethnicities and cultures, still sharing significant vestiges of a common culture and language that could be considered "Romanian" — got a taste of political unity when they were briefly led by a single ruler, the Wallachian Prince Michael the Brave. Michael was killed in a battle with Austria a year later, however, and the chance for a more enduring unity was lost. The neighboring powers were quick to reassert their dominance. Transylvania remained mostly under the control of Hungary (which itself was sometimes controlled by the Ottomans), while Wallachia and Moldavia remained mostly as tributary states to the Ottoman Empire. In the eighteenth century the latter two provinces lost much of their previous autonomy under more exploitative Ottoman-appointed rulers, and in the nineteenth century they fell under the control of Russia for periodic episodes in a complex and ever shifting relationship with Turkey (and sometimes Austria), involving reparations and agreements allowing sometimes shared and sometimes exclusive influence or occupation based on the results of wars between the two (and sometimes three) empires.

Through all the political turbulence, the Romanian language and culture somehow held on, and with the revolutionary movements sweeping Europe in the mid nineteenth century, a movement for national unity and independence gained momentum. In 1857 the elected legislatures of Wallachia and Moldavia, under the leadership of nationalists, particularly one Mihail Kogălniceanu, declared the provinces united into the constitutional monarchy of Romania. The reality, however, first of the union and then of independence, had to wait until the Ottomans were defeated in yet another war with Russia, which this time was joined by Romanian nationalists.

The nation was finally recognized by treaty in 1878, and the first king of Romania, Carol I, was crowned in 1881. Transylvania, meanwhile, along with the smaller northern and western provinces of Maramures, Crisana, and Banat remained under the control of the Austro-Hungarian Empire, and Bessarabia, an eastern section of Moldavia, remained under the control of Russia, until the upheavals of World War I provided the opportunity for complete unification and the formation of Romania with the borders we know today.

The history of Romania during the twentieth century is no less fascinating and complex, and the country was no less influenced by foreign powers, but by now the point should be clear: the amazing survival of the ancient Romanian language and culture through centuries of foreign invasion, interference, and domination.[82] And neither has the legacy of the draco-bearing Dacians been forgotten. Thus the name of the country's automobile manufacturing company, created by the state under the communist regime in 1966. I don't know about the latest models, but the CLCP's old beat-up Dacia pickup truck and most of the small, rusting Dacia cars I see on the roads of Romania certainly bear no frills as flamboyant as the Dacian draco. But, like the language and culture of the people who make them, the vehicles are surprisingly durable, surviving decades of bouncing along on the rough, potholed tracks that pass for rural roads in Romania.

Poiana and Crai were rescued by the CLCP as small sibling pups from a fur farm in Romania in May 1996. Over the years they have well served their educational, public relations, and research roles for the project. They happen to be very photogenic and might be the most photographed wolves in Europe. A story goes amongst project volunteers that the pair is shown in stock footage in a documentary about wolves in Canada, although I haven't verified this.

The pups were hand-raised by humans with some help from various dogs along the way (especially Peter's dog Djanga and Christoph's dog Yukai). During their early years the young wolves were taken on walks for a couple of hours nearly every day by project volunteers or staff, and they were even let off their leashes occasionally. The wolves always returned on their own, but the primary risk was that they might kill a sheep. They tried a few times, but being the untrained, inexperienced, and likely inept pair of predators that they were, the shepherds and their dogs easily drove them off. One might think these incidents would have strained relations between the shepherds and the project, but apparently most of the shepherds viewed the fights between their dogs and the wolves with some amusement. Perhaps in addition to the entertainment value, the shepherds appreciated the training their dogs were receiving from the would-be sheep-killers. Nevertheless, the shepherds did sometimes get angry, at least briefly, and there would have been trouble had Poiana and Crai actually succeeded in taking a sheep, so the practice of letting the wolves run free was stopped as the wolves got older.

When Poiana and Crai entered early adulthood, at about nine months of age, they were both neutered in order to prevent or at least limit their natural urge to establish hierarchical dominance over their fellow pack mates: the project personnel who were caring for them. The procedure worked for Crai, who is a relatively gentle being. Poiana, on the other hand, is not. It is believed that the vet didn't quite complete the job, that some portion of Poiana's hormone-producing female glands remains intact. Not only can she be aggressive, but she exhibits other hormonally influenced female behavior as well, such as digging dens in the spring. Thus, although Crai is larger and stronger, Poiana is the dominant wolf. The relative rank of the siblings becomes particularly obvious at feeding time, when Crai is forced to wait his turn while Poiana satiates her hunger. To give him a chance, we usually put two pieces of meat into the feeding pen at a time, occasionally enabling the more docile male wolf to skirt Poiana's diligence and surreptitiously slink away with a morsel of his own. But more often than not Poiana notices, drops her hunk of meat, and chases her brother away from his. If Crai is especially hungry and determined, he will in turn grab hers. And thus it goes throughout mealtime in the wolf pen at Cabanna Lupului.

In fact, Poiana and Crai often "fight." Their battles are always initiated by Poiana, and they are often *very* rough. The disputes often begin when the wolves are being petted by people through the holes in the fence. If Poiana feels at all deprived relative to Crai (and she's very sensitive about this), she'll raise up on her hind legs, turn her head slightly, bare her teeth with a vicious snarl, and fiercely pounce on her brother, snapping vigorously at his neck. Presumably she's holding back, given that Crai is her sibling and pack mate and she doesn't mean to kill. Nevertheless, to see and hear the fury in her snarls and the power in her snapping jaws is to understand the fear and dread that wolves have inspired in superstitious human souls throughout the ages.[83]

For the benefit of Crai and other targets of Poiana's ire, the dominant female wolf's canine teeth were filed down. This wasn't enough, however, to prevent one of Crai's ears from being shredded during one of Poiana's recent tantrums. Yet Crai *is* the bigger and stronger animal, and he will only put up with so much. When he has seriously had enough, he stops Poiana's nonsense by twisting from her grip, throwing her off, and pinning her down.

While friendly to most human members of her pack (those of us living at the cabin whom she views as no threat to her status) and while she hides from most strangers, Poiana can be very aggressive towards humans whom she does view as threats to her position. Especially towards female humans who were involved at an early stage of her upbringing and who therefore were once more dominant in the pack than her. Especially towards Barbara. Poiana goes berserk whenever the slightest scent of Barbara drifts into her awareness, for example, when Barbara is still hundreds of meters away while driving up the valley towards the cabin. The wolf is not entirely sexist, however. She also once tore into Christoph, ripping up his leg pretty badly. After several incidents wherein Poiana attempted to assert dominance over female project workers who were taking the wolves for walks, her walks were finally stopped. Peter continued walking Crai until, at about five years of age, he also started exhibiting aggression towards non-cabin dogs and "a few people he didn't like."

Regardless of their occasional aggressive tendencies, due to their upbringing Crai and Poiana both crave social interaction with humans. The wolves are especially quick to notice who is accepted by Guardian and Curly; and if people are in with the dogs, they're in with the wolves. They appreciate being petted through the holes in the chain-link fence by people they know and trust (or by people who are visiting people they know and trust), which they often solicit by rubbing along the fence next to where their admirers are standing. And the two often howl when any of their pack mates, human or dog, leave the cabin premises.

We feed the wolves by putting animal parts into the feeding area, which is a pen about eight meters square adjacent to the main enclosure and separated from it by a small sliding door that we can raise or lower via a steel cord. The door is usually kept open, but we lower it when we want to confine the wolves either to the pen, to clean or maintain the main enclosure, or to the enclosure, to clean the pen or put in food and water. When we enter the feeding pen it's not unusual for several six-inch long, bright green Emerald lizards to scatter, and we must remember to place large rocks in the water bowls so the lizards can climb up and avoid drowning (which doesn't always work).

Tuesday, March 25

Today I was initiated into "the burning of the bones" — thus our sanitized label for the task of cleaning the wolf enclosure and burning all the scat and bones and uneaten flesh that has become too old and rotten to satisfy the tastes of the wolves.

We enticed the wolves into the feeding pen by putting in some new meat, and lowered the door so we could access the main enclosure without any risk from our appreciative but unpredictable friends. As we scoured the steep, brushy slope, collecting old scat in beat-up steel pails and picking up and tossing stinking body parts down towards the entrance, it became clear that the wolves had been fed far too much over the last few weeks. The fox that the wolves had killed a couple of weeks ago lay under a few scratches of dirt, leaves, and twigs, almost fully intact (I wonder if fellow predators are as tasty to wolves as herbivores). Cached under some bushes was a sheep head together with its eviscerated torso, full stomach, and intestines. Rusty horse shoes lay scattered about in the dust, some still attached to hoofs, and some hoofs still attached to desiccated, black hairy forelegs.

We gathered the remains off to the side of our driveway near the large stack of firewood that we had carefully prepared. A few lit matches to the heart of the structure, and the conflagration was soon underway. As we began tossing on the body parts, being careful not to smother the flames, an uncertain, shifting breeze coaxed the thick, black smoke first in one direction then another, defeating my efforts to avoid it until the sickly stench of burning flesh thoroughly permeated my clothes, my hair, and my very pores. A change of clothes and a splash in the stream had little effect; the fetor hovered about me like an unfriendly ghost long after the pyre had withered to a tiny pile of glowing embers and dusty ashes.

Titus and Vanessa explained that in the warmer weather of spring the usual practice is to burn the bones every three weeks or so. In the summer it is a weekly affair. After this experience, I resolved to implement a more reasonable feeding regimen for the wolves. People had been tossing in meat whenever it seemed the wolves weren't eating, or sometimes just because there was excess supply to be gotten rid of. Perhaps if we follow the rather obvious strategy of waiting for the wolves to finish what we give them before giving them more, we can reduce the frequency of this repugnant task.

Thursday, March 27

Last week was winter; this week is spring. The white snow is giving way to brown mud and green sprouts around the cabin. Some flowers are even beginning to bloom. I went with Vanessa today to a spectacular site in the Bucegi range, where deep snow still hides the mountain meadows and where the peaks glared dazzling white in azure skies. This was to be Vanessa's last venture into the field, and I wasn't certain whether the telemetry and activity monitoring she was doing was necessary for the project, or if she just wanted one last experience to color her memory of Romania. As we drove back to the cabin she sighed once to herself and quietly asked, "Oh Romania, when will I see you again?" But mostly she was silent.

Whenever I enter Zarnesti on the road from the cabin, a spry and thin old man wearing glasses and a big smile stands outside his house on the sidewalk and waves at me frantically, not letting up until long after I've passed. He looks a bit loopy, but as happy as a being can be. I've come to look forward to his cheerful countenance and joyous celebration of my arrival to town.

Without doubt, my most adventurous activity in Romania is to travel by car on its roads. Travel guides contain ample warnings about driving in Romania at night when people and horse-carts amble along the unlit country roads without taillights and often without reflectors. This is true enough, but it's not the greatest danger (provided one is aware of it). The mad passes on mountain curves and the sudden swerves by approaching vehicles to avoid the ubiquitous potholes are the bigger risks, I think. In addition to the hazards they create for themselves, drivers must also be constantly wary of pedestrians. As though the presence of cars has not yet entered the national consciousness, folks strolling along the streets take no heed whatsoever of motor vehicles, and are apt to step into the road without the slightest pause or turn of the head to see what may be coming — which very well may one of the many vehicles under the marginal control of frenzied drivers.

In the early 1970s the poignant message appeared periodically on our color TV, my family's first. An American Indian elder canoes serenely along a beautiful, gently flowing river, his body erect and his face carrying an expression of resigned pride. The camera slowly pans back to reveal the water, which is filthy and covered with foam and floating debris, and then the shore, which is lined with paper and bottles and cans, and then factories, which are belching smoke from tall smokestacks. The scene concludes with a close-up of the man's face showing a single tear running down his cheek, and the words "Keep America Beautiful" appearing at the top of the screen. Perhaps my memory plays the role of artist, choosing and combining several such TV spots from that era to create a more succinct and poignant version, I do not know, but that is how I remember it, and the message apparently sunk in. I'll carry a crumpled candy wrapper in my pocket for days until I think to dispose of it properly or it is washed into oblivion.

Yesterday as Vanessa and I were passing through the small village of Cristian on our return from shopping at the Metro in Brasov, I noticed that the banks of a small river flowing behind the row of buildings that form the center of the village are heaped with trash. Piles of shredded tires and rust-stained sinks and bedsprings and plastic bottles and paper and all manner of garbage line both sides of the river for at least a kilometer beyond the village.

I recently filled four large garbage bags with trash from along the small stream that supplies the water for our cabin, including assorted plastic sheets, potato chip bags, candy bar wrappers, beer bottles, and pieces of rotted cloth and canvas that I found half buried in the mud. I want to believe that our water supply is not a trash dump; that much of the debris simply blows to the stream from passers-by throwing it out of their car windows as they speed along the road, which is only about thirty meters away. But some of the trash was obviously too heavy to have been carried by the wind. Why are people so inclined to dispose of waste along rivers and streams? Do they think the water will cleanse it from the world, or at least, from *their* world? I suppose a springtime deluge might carry off paper and plastic, but what about the sinks and automobile axles and ancient TV cabinets that one might find along rivers?

Now that spring has arrived, on weekends people drive their cars onto the pastures near our cabin and along the river. They open the doors, turn up the radios, and dance and party throughout the day and night. By morning they are usually gone, but their trash is not. Paper, beer bottles, uneaten bits of bread and sausage, and perhaps a few condoms or even some human waste litter the ground. Often the same cars return to the same spot the following weekend, where the same party resumes amidst the same litter. Weekend after weekend throughout the spring and summer, the trash accumulates (or blows into our stream). Do the picnickers even perceive the unsightly refuse? It doesn't seem to inhibit their enjoyment of "the mountains," to which they briefly escape from the hot and crowded cities.

What fosters in a society an environmental aesthetic and the environmental ethic that follows? Is it primarily education? Did those "Keep America Beautiful" commercials during the 60s and 70s really work? Did they catalyze aesthetic sensitivities, or at least create sufficient peer pressure to cause people to be too embarrassed to toss beer bottles and Styrofoam coffee cups out the windows? (To be fair to Romania, I can recall plenty of trash dumps hidden in the woods of Maine, formed at the bottoms of ravines where people think their disposal habits will not be seen and their trash never detected.)

Or is it a matter of affluence? Trash tends to plague the poorer regions of the world. Does wealth provide the leisure to care, or simply the means to keep things clean? I'm not certain, but the picnickers have enough leisure to party the weekend away, and a trash bag is cheaper than a bottle of beer.

Saturday, March 29

A man is walking by the cabin, trailing his cart, which is trailing his horse. He stops for a moment and waves a friendly *buna ziua*. What does he think of me as I sit here writing? I guess his horse knows the way as it ambles slowly along, unguided and uninspired.

Earlier, a road crew came by making repairs on the road, the holes of which have gone from bad to harrowing. Perhaps this dirt road gets more attention than many in the region, since it services a chalet, known as Plaiul Foii, at a trail-head entrance to Piatra Craiului National Park, about six kilometers up the valley from the cabin.

Piatra Craiului National Park was formally established in 1990 from reserves that had been designated by the communist regime over the previous decades, beginning in the 1930s. The park encompasses almost 15,000 hectares, and is dominated by the narrow, 25-kilometer long massif for which it is named — "the longest calcareous crest in Romania." The spectacular ridge reaches an elevation of 2,238 meters, and consists of three primary rises: Pietricica ("Tiny Stone") on the southern end, Piatra Mare ("Big Stone") in the center, and Piatra Mica ("Small Stone") on the northern end. The reserve is home to a rich diversity of flora and fauna, including several endemic invertebrates and two endemic plants (including the symbol of the ridge, the Piatra Craiului Carthusian pink *[Dianthus callizonus]*). The park is bounded on the north by the Barsa River, which rushes down the valley floor across from our cabin and gives the valley its name.[84]

Sunday, March 30

A raucous group of European ravens has been hanging about the enclosure, scavenging from a calf the wolves finally opened up. A local man had dropped off the carcass a few days ago, unmarketable because the animal died on its own. The CLCP pays local farmers and shepherds for dead animals to feed the wolves, but is careful to pay below what an animal is worth alive or for marketable purposes. We do not want people slaughtering animals for our wolves. But we do want to pay something for meat that otherwise would be worthless, thus contributing to the local economy and gaining some measure of local support.

This morning we went to get another dead cow. At first I thought this might be a gruesome endeavor, but when I learned the cow had already been skinned, I hopefully imagined it wouldn't be much different than picking up sides of beef from a butcher shop. Vanessa, Titus, and I drove to the farm near Brasov where a young man — or boy really — met us at the barn and led us inside. The cow was hanging from the rafters, the large purplish-red, pink, and white body of muscle, tendon, and bone looking rather clean and bloodless, much as I had envisioned. The boy cut the carcass as we directed, first quartering it as it hung and twisted in the cool air of the barn, expertly separating the muscle sheaths with a sharp knife and then hacking through the hip and shoulder joints with an axe. Once the large parts of cow were on the ground he chopped each leg into a couple of lengths and divided the torso into portions we thought would be manageable and would fit in the project freezer. Finally we loaded the chunks of meat, bone, and sinew into our pickup truck and headed back to Zarnesti.

The project freezer is located in Moserel's barn. Mosorel is the owner of one of the two guesthouses in Zarnesti that have been established with the help of the CLCP's rural development initiative. Moserel is also the CLCP's landlord, as the project's office occupies a room in his guesthouse, on the outer side with a separate entrance from the street. I hadn't yet met Moserel. All I knew of him regarded an incident with the shower in the project office. One cold night a week or so ago Titus and I were passing through Zarnesti on our return to the cabin after a long day, feeling a bit dejected that we wouldn't have time to fire up the sauna for our scheduled cleaning. Titus happened to mention that the project has an arrangement with Moserel whereby we can occasionally use the shower in the office.

"A shower?!? Say no more!"

Although the diminutive shower stall crammed into a corner of the tiny bathroom left much to be desired, as the hot water splattered onto my dirty hair and spilled down my chilled shoulders and back, I was sure I had never experienced a more satisfying dousing of water in my life. I really don't think I lingered all that long, but our indulgence ended up causing a complaint from Moserel. Apparently our impact on the hot water supply for the guesthouse did not go unnoticed.

After returning to Zarnesti with the cow parts we drove our pickup around and behind the guesthouse to Moserel's residence. Across a narrow dirt lane, a collection of shacks and sheds and the barn, which allegedly housed the project's freezer, stood around a dusty barnyard where scores of chickens were strutting and clucking and scratching out a living. As we entered the gate of his back yard, Moserel came out to greet us. But I didn't take much notice of Moserel. I only saw the enormous black beast that was shrieking and lunging and straining at the end of a heavy chain clamped to a sturdy post. The raging monster was oblivious to the fact that the collar and chain yanked him off his feet at every violent lunge for our throats. He just twisted in his collar and tried again, barking more furiously with each frustrated effort to tear us apart. No display of affection could win him over and I concluded that the dog, while certainly an effective alarm system and guard, was quite insane.

Moserel led us into the barn where he pointed at the freezer and explained that it hadn't been working since September. Great. With the warmer weather we now had way too much meat. Our only option was to take the remains to the cabin and put as many pieces as possible into the "can" — a rusty but sturdy metal box that sits partway up the hill near the outhouse. When we returned to the cabin and took the large rock off the can and opened the heavy lid, our senses were stunned. The can was crawling with absolute putrid filth: reeking horse parts (I assumed), a hot, gaseous stench, and lots of beetles and maggots. We held our breaths as we tipped over the can and tossed in buckets of water to try to wash it out. The results were marginal, and we concluded the can was currently no place for fresh meat, so we gave two pieces to the wolves, reasoning that what they currently had — several horse pieces, a sheep, and the calf left several days ago — was getting too old anyway.

Of course there was now, once again, too much rotten carrion about, so I suggested we burn at least the old horse pieces from the can and the stinking sheep carcass, which the wolves had barely touched. The wolves had not been eating much lately, and maybe they would start fresh with the new meat. Vanessa and Titus assented. "Yes, you have a good idea," Vanessa offered. "Yes," Titus agreed, "have fun." My suggestion, my job. They would help me gather the animal parts, but they definitely had other chores to keep them occupied. My second flesh burning in as many weeks.

I knew I had to create a large bonfire in order to burn the entire sheep (I did not want to hack with an axe or operate with a knife on a rotten carcass), so I constructed a stacked dome of wood about 1.5 meters high by 1.5 meters in diameter, strategically placing each piece of wood to enhance the flow of air while simultaneously bemoaning the growing dent in our wood supply. As I was kneeling by this wooden hill, blowing into its tiny glowing heart, with the sheep carcass and the head of a horse and various other animal parts lying about on the driveway, who should pull up in a car but Nini and Carmi, my rather well-dressed friends, fresh from Bucharest.

Ignoring their uncomfortable glances, I stood and greeted Nini and Carmi pleasantly. I could see Poiana and Crai having their disputes and tearing lustily into the new cow pieces nearby. I knew that my last sauna and shave was four days past and that my face, hair, and clothes were grimy and smeared. As I stood there awkwardly, grasping an axe in my left hand, I absent-mindedly wiped my right hand on my pant leg before extending it for a shake, and then self-consciously held it back. We exchanged a few tentative "hellos" and they asked me to visit them in Bucharest, managing to say, "Our house is your house" in English. But given the circumstances, there wasn't much else to say, so they didn't linger.

Just as the fire was blazing well enough to throw on the sheep, it started to rain.

After the conflagration died down a bit, I asked Titus and Vanessa to keep an eye on it while I went for a walk and some fresh air. When I returned, Vanessa was standing over a large cauldron in the midst of the smoke, looking like a sorceress as she stirred the boiling contents with a stick. She had taken time off from her other important chores to cook the meat off some of the animal bones and heads so she could bring them with her back to Germany — for what purpose I did not know.

The sky has cleared and the recently fallen rain is steaming from the earth and the trees. The large black circle with its center of smoldering embers absorbs the peaceful orange glow of sunset.

As I sit in the sauna, sweating the smoky stench of death from my body, I suddenly realize I've been here almost a month. Was it really me who once lived that former life in the States? Was it so long ago that at the end of the day I might have contemplated with satisfaction a software problem I had solved, instead of this carrion I have burned? What is it that connects me to that person who once commuted each day to the office, lifted weights in the gym, shopped at the supermarket, watched the evening news on TV? Some large portion of the atoms in my body has likely been replaced since I arrived in Romania. And given how many new things I have experienced, I assume many of my neural circuits have been reconfigured as well. Physically I'm a different being living in a different world. Is it only a continuity of consciousness through a succession of moments in time that connects me to my past? Yet my conscious awareness is interrupted almost every night by sleep. So what is it? If consciousness is time, memory is self. If someday I'm back in my former life, doing again the same things in the same places, then surely *this* will seem like a dream.

Tomorrow Titus will begin packing. He leaves early the following day. Soon I'll be here alone, although another student, Anja, is due to arrive in a few days.

Wednesday, April 2

On Monday we had planned a departure party for Titus and Vanessa, but first we had to go to town to buy provisions and attend a project status meeting. In the morning, Guardian's former pack of shepherd dogs, which I called the "vicious seven," stopped by for one of their usual visits while they were on patrol with a flock of sheep. Soon after the typical highly charged confrontation between Guardian and the pack was over, we heard the sound of sporadic gunfire echoing from down the valley, presumably from one of the military exercises that occasionally occur in the area. When we opened the cabin door Guardian rushed in, mouth grinning and body wagging; the dog's defensive responsibilities were obviously not to include dealing with firearms. He then plopped down and went to sleep while we finished our chores — unusual for him, especially in the morning.

With the longer days and warmer weather of spring, activity is picking up in the valley. A flat, stony pasture stretches across the valley floor between the steep slopes behind the cabin and the steeper slopes of Piatra Craiului on the far side, beyond the Basra River. Every morning the hollow clanging of cow bells and the plaintive baying of sheep drift into the cabin as livestock leisurely graze their way up the valley. Usually (but not always) a shepherd accompanies the flock, and often (but not always) he is the well-tanned, mustached man of about thirty-five who wears a black conical wool hat, tattered greenish-brown woolen pants, a rough, off-white linen shirt, and high rubber boots. He usually has a thick sheepskin thrown over his shoulders, which he can pull over his head if it rains, or use as a bed if he chooses to recline on the meadow, chewing a strand of straw or dozing for a spell while the dogs guard the grazing animals. The shepherd is also never without a sturdy wooden stave, which he might use to encourage a lagging sheep with a whack on the rump, or to threaten a disobedient dog, or to lean on if the progress of the flock is particularly slow and he decides to stand for a while.

But whether a shepherd attends the flocks or not, shepherd dogs always do, and they always pay us a visit at the cabin. And since there are always several, there is only so much Guardian can do to keep the intruders at bay. The dogs wander in, sniff around, sometimes even wag their tails, either fearing to attack the human occupiers of this turf, or recognizing such is not their role. After exhausting their curiosity around the cabin, and helping themselves to anything that might be edible, the dogs usually remember to visit Poiana and Crai as well — and the wolves always heartily tear into the challenge. Once the opposing parties spot each other, either by nose or ears or eyes, the dogs charge the fence, the wolves charge the fence, and the dirt and dust fly along with a terrible din of barks, yelps, growls, and snarls. Observing the violence of these encounters, I'm certain that sturdy chain-link fence has saved many a foolish dog's life (although Peter has told me that in confrontations with dogs outside the enclosure back in the days when she occasionally roamed free, Poiana — strangely, given her typical disposition — often yielded and rolled over in submission, apparently unaware of her superior power).

The spring weather is also bringing an increasing stream of human visitors to the cabin. More people are driving up the valley to the chalet, and a few stop to have a look at the wolves and at us. Sometimes an adventurous foreign tourist who has read about the cabin and the wolves in *Lonely Planet*[85] or *The Rough Guide to Romania*[86] comes wandering onto the premises, or arrives in a car for hire; sometimes folks from the cities, from Bucharest or Brasov, who have read about the project in the newspaper or seen it on TV, make a special trip to the cabin; and sometimes even a curious group of local farmers or townsfolk tentatively approaches for a chat, all the while sneaking nervous glances at the enclosure.

Guardian is particularly aggressive towards local visitors, but can be a threat to anyone, so for his protection and that of human guests — especially since he was behaving strangely — we considered leaving the dog in the cabin where he wanted to be as we prepared to depart this day. However, Guardian is no housedog, and we couldn't keep him in the cabin throughout the spring and summer whenever we were gone, so to avoid a precedent, out he went. As we left I closed the gate to our driveway for what meager protection it offered.

When we returned to the cabin around 4:30 p.m., Curly greeted us happily — but no Guardian. It wasn't unusual for him to be absent, although if he was off somewhere usually Curly was with him. We convinced ourselves that there really wasn't much cause for concern, and we had a party to prepare for, but we each, I think, silently recalled Guardian's desire to remain in the cabin, and we were a little quieter than usual as we set about making dough and preparing the toppings for a pizza we'd bake in our woodstove. It happened that only Simona and Vaso would be joining us, as Christoph and Barbara had to attend to their baby daughter Enya, who was sick. Vaso, a heavyset, affable man in his thirties who converses primarily by yelling, serves as the project's jack-of-all-trades and primary liaison with local institutions and authorities. It is to Vaso's flat in an apartment block in Brasov that we go when we need to replenish our money, or need something repaired that we can't fix ourselves. It is also where I will go to get a visa if I stay longer than ninety days.

Our gathering was pleasant enough, but not particularly festive. My final two companions were about to leave Romania, and they were no less happy about it than I. And in the back of our minds we were all wondering about our missing canine friend. A gloom had settled in, it began to rain, and the conversation lagged. Our guests left as the final glimmer of day melted into a still, heavy presence of fog, mist, and darkness.

As soon as they were gone Vanessa and I began our search. Without a word, Vanessa crossed the pasture to check along the river, so I walked along the road, up the valley towards the distant houses where Guardian sometimes went. As I treaded through the mist and the gloom I couldn't help envision a final stand made against seven ferocious opponents. I searched for a couple of hours and then met up with Vanessa, and we returned to the cabin in nearly complete blackness.

There wasn't much we could do. Before retiring for the night I went out and shined a flashlight into Guardian's empty doghouse a few times. I slept fitfully and apparently noisily, jumping from my bed when Vanessa gave me a kick to silence my snore. By early morning I had developed a sore throat and had lost most of my voice. I arose in the faint light of an obscure dawn and went out to meet a cold and blustery day. Vanessa soon joined me, and we thoroughly searched the steep, wooded slopes behind the cabin, returning only to have our final breakfast with Titus and to see him off. He had driven his own vehicle to Romania and was returning to Germany the same way. A deeply religious man, Titus said a prayer for us and for the safe return of Guardian, and then he departed.

Vanessa was leaving later in the day and as we resumed our search I appreciated her dedication to a dog she would not likely see again even if we found him. Because of the shooting we had heard yesterday morning, I assumed Guardian went up the valley, not down, so again I walked up the road, this time past the new houses being built and as far as Plaiul Foii. Again I found no sign.

On the way back I encountered the vicious seven along with their shepherd tending the flock of sheep. By now this shepherd always greeted me as a familiar neighbor, with a friendly smile and a shake of hands, although he could never understand a word of my Romanian. I often wondered what he thought of us, strangers from foreign lands who harbored his traditional enemy, the wolf. I tried to ask if he had seen *alba negro cuine* (white black dog), but once again he didn't understand, or pretended not to.

Guardian's broken foot, his timidity, his persistence in ditching his former master were all indications the dog's life had not been easy before his arrival at the cabin. He had always received affection with a sense of wonder, never quite expecting it and never completely trusting it. So wondrous was love to him that he wagged his whole body even when Curly was the one receiving attention.

[Well, he had a few months of a better life, and at least got to know there is some love in the world]

As I drifted back to the cabin, I wanted to think that mattered. And I wanted to keep some hope. Perhaps he had simply left in pursuit of a female in heat.

Guardian is gone, Titus is gone, and now Vanessa is gone. I dropped her off at the *gara* in Brasov today. So it's just Curly and I at the cabin now. Curly doesn't seem much affected, although she just convincingly told a lone shepherd dog about 50 percent larger than her to get lost (they had a dispute over one of the horse forelegs that we sometimes gave to the dogs). First time I ever saw her agitated.

Anja arrives tomorrow.

Thursday, April 3

I picked Anja up at the train station, recognizing her as the only young woman with a large, western-style backpack draped over her shoulders. A 28-year-old student from Germany, Anja will be working on her master's thesis in sustainable tourism. She had already done a stint with the CLCP last fall, and is volunteering again primarily to work on eco-tourism projects, mostly as a guide for horseback tours during this late spring and summer. Of average height with a round, smiling face and medium length dark blond hair, Anja's sturdy bearing suggested this wasn't the first time she's hoisted a heavy pack onto her back.

Vanessa had informed me that Anja had become quite attached to Guardian and was even considering taking him back to Germany when she returned in the fall. She was to be the final long-term occupant of the wolf cabin, and she knew that homes would have to be found for both of the cabin dogs. Christoph had told me of other dog adoptions by project volunteers. Most, if not all, were failures. Any local dog robust enough for life in this valley possesses at least some strain of shepherd dog, and the Romanian shepherd dog, while not an identifiable breed, and in fact varying greatly in size and appearance, has evolved over countless generations to be an aggressive defender of property, people, and livestock. Typical was the story of one young woman from Sweden who returned home from the project with a sweet and gentle puppy in tow. As the dog grew into adulthood, sweet and gentle it did not remain. When it began attacking the woman's male friends the dog was put down.

I broke the news about Guardian as gently as possible. We arrived at the cabin, Anja unpacked, and we had a bite to eat. Then we immediately continued the search, exploring again up the valley and along the river. We stopped at the house where Guardian sometimes lingered, presumably associating with the non-working dogs residing there. A man came out who spoke German. He knew of Guardian but hadn't seen him recently.

Further up the valley we came upon our shepherd friend, tending his sheep with the ever-present dogs, which were now lounging about lazily in the pasture. Evidently even shepherd dogs occasionally need a break from ferocious attitudes and diligent duties. Barely lifting their heads when we arrived, maybe they were also becoming used to these strange folk wandering about with no obvious purpose.

Anja had told me Guardian's original name, so now when I asked about our missing dog, the shepherd actually seemed to know what I was talking about. He excitedly pointed at one of his dogs, one which I had previously noticed bore a resemblance to Guardian, and exclaimed, "*frate, frate!*" (brother). He was obviously very pleased to finally understand something I said, but then just shrugged his shoulders.

Saturday, April 5
We hadn't been able to reach Christoph or Barbara since Anja's arrival, so yesterday in the late morning we paid them a visit. They were going horseback riding later in the day, would we like to go?

"Sure, but I don't have much experience. Well, almost none, really."

"That's ok. You can learn," Barbara reassured me, before adding solemnly, "But we'll be English riding."

Seeing as I hadn't been on a horse but three or four times in my life — and most of those in my childhood for casual walks of about a hundred yards each while my Aunt Dawn walked in front holding the reins — I was sure it didn't matter. From my viewpoint, the distinguishing feature of English riding was that there was no knob on the front of the saddle to hold onto. I did imagine this could be a disadvantage, but concluded it must not be all that critical. At least I hadn't heard that the English suffer more horseback-riding casualties than Americans, and imagined that if they had, they would have added the knob to the front of their saddles by now.

After all the activities required to prepare huge beasts with minds of their own to willingly, if not happily, accept their human burdens — known to the adept, I supposed, as "saddling up" — it was late afternoon by the time we got underway. We rode directly from the stalls up a gently sloping forest road not far from the Prombergers' house. My fellow riders, Christoph, Anja, and especially Barbara, who has won various horse-riding awards in her home country of Austria, are accomplished riders, and they all thought it ironic that an American would be cutting his teeth on horseback in Romania. I guess we all should be cowboys.

My first impression of my horse, Andrei, was that he is big.

Bigger than the other horses, and bigger than anything else I had ever ridden atop of in my life, that being (other than my aforementioned brief stints on a horse) the 1971 450cc Honda motorcycle of my college days. Someone had said something about Andrei being an "eccentric bastard," but there was some reason why every other available horse would have been even less appropriate for a novice such as me, so Andrei it was. As I "led" the giant from the stable he stopped to pee, taking no pains to avoid spattering me as far as I could tell.

It was obvious from the moment I mounted who was in charge. Andrei went pretty much where he wanted, when he wanted, and however fast he wanted. He seemed to delight in testing his novitiate at every opportunity, and there were lots of opportunities. Augmenting my mount's natural disposition was the fact that none of the horses had been out for a while and they were all anxious for a run. As my fellow riders effectively managed their rambunctious steeds, they were quite amused by my predicament, and were quite generous with advice, but I couldn't help thinking that no matter what I did, there was no reason a thousand pounds of horse need take orders from me. Meanwhile I was nearly falling off more often than I wasn't, and though I hadn't really thought about it since those days when I was first considering this venture, my new perspective high off the ground renewed my speculations about the quality of health care in Romania.

When I had the presence to notice, the scenery was spectacular. We were riding through a broad, roadless tract of countryside that reminded me of the rolling hills and lush forests of New England, dappled with Wisconsin pastures, and surrounded by the snow-capped mountains of Colorado, all on a vibrant spring day. Periods of warm sunshine alternated with brief, light showers that washed the world clean and released the new green life waiting to spring from the earth. I gradually learned how to stay mostly in my saddle, and after an hour or so we ascended from out of the forest onto an open knoll with a panoramic backdrop of gray, purple, blue, and white peaks. As I watched a small flock of sheep grazing the soft, green grass atop the knoll, I suddenly realized this was the very scene I had idealized in that long ago moment when I was back home in the States, searching for meaning on the Internet and dreaming of wolves.

As much as I enjoyed the idea of the scenery, after about two hours I was saddle sore and my nerves had been rattled long enough trying to control Andrei and not bounce out of my saddle during his many spontaneous, unrequested trots. I had been given the impression our ride would be short, and as there was no sign yet of turning back, I concluded that I had been seriously misled, or else "short" had a much different connotation for my experienced companions than it did for me. Just when I was about to ask about our plans, however, we paused, and while I mostly tried to keep Andrei in one place, the others chatted about presumably important matters, maybe even about whether we were turning back. In any event, we finally turned our steeds about. Actually, Andrei turned himself about, having no intention of being left alone in the backcountry with a greenhorn atop his back. But turn he did, and my spirits rose.

Not for long. Christoph soon realized his dog Yukai was no longer romping along beside us. Thinking his companion must have continued on unnoticed while we had stopped and talked, Christoph rode back to find Yukai while we waited. He found no sign of his dog.

It happened that the trail formed a long loop, so we could return the long way by continuing on past where we had last seen Yukai. Our "short" ride had now officially become a long one, but I was rejuvenated by the mission to find Christoph's dog. Yukai means "northern lights" in the tongue of the member of the Yukon Indian tribe who gave the Siberian husky pup to Christoph some thirteen years ago. I could only imagine what she must mean to Christoph as we rode in silence now, eyes focused for any hint of a track in the muddy trail or any movement of gray in the thick trees, and ears listening for any rustle or bark from the woods. In my concentration I almost forgot that I was riding high atop an unmanageable "eccentric bastard." I even started to feel a little like John Wayne in the saddle after Andrei decided to take the lead, as though he too was determined to find a missing friend.

Arriving at a place where the trail fell away in a precipitous, open slope, we were forced to dismount. The hard clay sod of the slope was thoroughly gashed by rows of foot-deep ruts that must have been turned by a tractor. I could hardly imagine more difficult footing for a horse, and I felt very inadequate standing next to

Andrei as I gathered his reins and prepared to guide him down the treacherous decline. Nevertheless, as we started down, the immense horse seemed to sense that his fate was in my hands and he obediently followed my lead.

Andrei's trust was soon betrayed. After not more than two short, tentative steps, both of his towering front legs became entangled in the reins. I must have left too much slack. Realizing that if he attempted one more step there'd likely be a ball of ponderous horse and insubstantial man rolling down the steep slope, I clenched the reins close to Andrei's neck. I spoke to the horse softly, trying to convince him not to move, while with one hand I guided a rein slowly from around his left leg. He seemed to understand and stood still. Once around, then around again, and his leg was free. I took a deep breath and clutched the reins tighter, hoping he wouldn't try to test his newly found sense of freedom before it was complete. His thigh muscles twitched, he snorted, but he held his position while I slowly disentangled his other leg. My giant companion was now free.

We started down again, one careful step at a time. I continued speaking softly while guiding Andrei's steps to where I thought he had the best prospects for sure footing; the horse followed, pausing to look at me and await my decision when he was unsure. Slowly, methodically, we finally we made it to the bottom of the slope where the others were waiting.

For the remainder of the ride, Andrei was a changed horse, pretty much doing as I asked — if he could figure it out. And I was a changed rider. I was more relaxed and no longer constantly striving to control the horse's every move. We had become a team, if not "one." But I still couldn't figure out how to keep myself attached to the saddle during my partner's occasional trots. These were now almost always by request, in order to stay with the group, but as I watched the other riders glued to their saddles while their horses trotted along, I simply couldn't get my body to resonate with the frequency of Andrei's bouncing back. I actually preferred galloping, which, while more intimidating due to the speed, was easier than trotting.

As we rode down the final hill towards the stable in the gathering darkness, Christoph was lost in his own thoughts. Barbara, meanwhile, explained that Yukai had disappeared before and knew well these hills and the way home, so we had some hope the dog would show up on its own.

This morning we awoke to a cold and dreary day of mixed rain and snow. I had developed a severe sore throat during the night and was feeling much like the weather: foggy and miserable. But we had a mission — to find Yukai — and today I had a brilliant new plan. I would try a more manageable steed. So while the others prepared their horses and donned their ponchos, I got a head start on a mountain bike. No more trying to control a half-ton of stubbornness. Although yesterday Andrei and I seemed to have developed a workable relationship, if not a mutual affection, still, I was more certain a bike would pretty much do what I wanted — go where I wanted, when I wanted — and anyway I'd be much closer to the ground if I fell off. So up the forest road I peddled, feeling weak, and feeling pain at every swallow, but otherwise in decent spirits and proud of my cleverness.

My hubris was short-lived. About a hundred meters into my odyssey I came upon three large shepherd dogs patrolling the road. Just as I caught sight of them, they stopped in their tracks, scanned the ground with their noses, and lifted their snouts to the air. We exchanged a brief stare, an implicit acknowledgement of each other's existence and relative roles in the world — and then they charged.

By now I thought I had acquired a certain expertise in handling shepherd dogs. I knew that confidence was the key, so I pedaled on as nonchalantly as possible, with no intent to increase my pace. However, from a dog's perspective, a human on a bike is an entirely different animal than one on two legs — a revelation that came a moment too late, as an intense burning pain seared my right calf and I was brought down in a tumble of bike, mud, and dog.

As I struggled up and tried to shake the beast off my leg, it was apparently stunned by my sudden change in stature and released its grip. The entire trio backed off, barking furiously to cover their retreat, but then they riled themselves for another advance in a tempest of raging paroxysms. My vulnerability already having been clearly established, and from a certain look in their bearing, as the dogs charged again I surmised they were no longer intimidated by my two-legged appearance. So, kicking wildly with one leg to fend them off, I straddled my bike with the other and put my foot to the pedal. But after one or two wobbly meters it was evident that fleeing on wheels was hopeless. My only option was to ditch the bike and face the onslaught. The dogs were still in a frenzy, but now I was just as charged with adrenaline and rage as they were. With arms akimbo and a roar from my gut, it was now *I* who rushed *them*. My foes were astonished, and in their instant of hesitation I grabbed a large stick from the ground and swinging it wildly chased them away.

I returned to my bike and sat on a rock to assess my wounds. A few small punctures were beginning to bleed, but most of the hemorrhaging appeared to be internal, from pinching and bruising. I applied some Neosporin® from the first-aid kit in my ever-present daypack, mounted the bike, and was on my way. I knew what it was like to lose a dog, and in spite of my sore throat, foggy brain, and burning leg, I was as determined as ever to help Christoph find Yukai.

At first I made good progress along the gravelly road where it traverses a well-drained forested hillside. But where it exits the woods and meets the bottom of an open valley the road became a quagmire of spongy sand and soft mud. The bike continually sank to its axles, forcing me to dismount and push or drag the obstinate machine along until I came to the next solid stretch of road. While I was thus bogged down at one particularly irksome spot at a fork in the road where the valley split, my horse-borne friends overtook me. Riding tall in their saddles and smiling at my predicament, they were kind enough not to state the obvious and simply agreed that I would proceed up one of the vales while they rode up the other. With a grin that seemed intended to wish me good luck without expecting me to have any, Barbara leaned from her horse and handed me a walkie-talkie.

I progressed in spurts while trying to remain alert for some sign of Yukai: a paw print in the mud, or a movement through the fog and drizzle on one of open slopes, or the sound of a bark. Long since weary of struggling in the mud, I decided I'd have a better prospect by ascending to higher ground. I climbed a steep muddy slope, constantly trying to find a less awkward technique for hauling along the heavy, mud-encrusted bike, which I didn't want to leave because I didn't know if I'd want to return the same way. I stopped occasionally to scan the valley floor and the other slopes, and to search the sky for a gathering of ravens. I spotted the white dots of a few sheep scattered here and there on the distant slopes, surrounded by the roving specks of guard dogs, but nothing that looked like a lost and lonely husky.

The slope was covered with tussocks and the going was difficult and slow. Finally I gave it up and descended back to the valley floor so I could try to continue further along the miserable ribbon of mud that in drier times might be considered a road. By early afternoon I was soaked in sweat and rain, covered foot-to-head in mud, and feeling sick, exhausted, and dejected. I called Barbara on the walkie-talkie. They also had found no sign of Yukai and were ready to return to the stables. I turned, took a deep breath, and began the long journey back. I felt relieved when I finally reached the solid forest road and could easily coast down its gentle decline, although I kept a wary eye out for its canine guardians. By the time I reached the stables, it had begun to pour and I was shaking with chill. The horse riders were there, looking like specters in their glistening wet ponchos as they silently put up the horses in the gathering gloom.

"Yukai is old," Christoph said, his words injecting puffs of steam into the cold, drenched air. "Sometimes dogs will go off to die alone…"

Later in the evening after it had cleared, Christoph rode back out again by himself.

Two lost dogs in one week.

Sunday, April 6

Our yard at the cabin covers perhaps an acre, not counting the wolf enclosure on the slope above. It is dubiously shielded from livestock and other invaders by a shaky rail fence that appears to have been pieced together from various odd tree parts as time and circumstances have allowed. The fence runs to the west from the driveway gate, composed first of four or five lengths of double rails nailed to tottering white birch logs stuck in the soft, wet ground along the stream, and then it continues through a thicket of small trees lining the stream, as a series of log rails simply jammed and

146

woven among the trees. The fence then turns northward where it soon fades away in a swampy area abutting the slope. On the other side of the driveway there is no fence at all, but there is a dense thicket of young trees along the stream that forms a fairly effective barricade as far as the short picket fence running along the eastern boundary of the yard, from the stream to the woodshed. Abutting the woodshed is the wolves' feeding pen, which completes the eastern perimeter of our lot.

Such is the shield that defends our property. Any four-legged creature even moderately determined can get in, either by going around the fence and through the swampy area to the west, or by squirming through the thicket on the eastern end, or, if small enough, by going under or through the rails, or, if big enough, by simply knocking the fence posts over. Thus it is not uncommon to arrive home to find a few stray sheep or cows or even a horse or two roaming about the yard, happily grazing the verdant new growth that is just now springing from the earth, and ignoring their ancient enemies who are watching intently from up the slope.

Regardless of the fence's limitations, as spring arrived I began to realize that our little plot was a sort of Eden — perhaps the only wild, ungrazed patch of vegetation remaining in the valley. And I suspected that as the new verdure of the pastures became more and more depleted, the temptation to raid our unique garden would become more and more irresistible. I also wasn't too keen about the prospect of livestock eliminating near the little stream that supplies our drinking water. So now that I wasn't so preoccupied with tracking wolves, the condition of our fence began to haunt me. If they weren't pushed over, or blown over, it wasn't difficult to imagine that the fence posts would soon fall over on their own. I resolved to repair the fence, and I began today. I dragged down to the yard a large white birch tree that had been felled in the forest on the slopes above the cabin. This I would work with a handsaw into sturdy and handsome new posts.

Tuesday, April 8

If you were to see Dr. Allistair Bath walking along the side of the road, you might think you had stumbled upon an aging but content proponent of world peace and free love on his way to a Rainbow gathering. A thin man with graying, shoulder-length hair and a scraggly beard through which peaks an ever-present smile, Allistair is an associate professor of geography at the Memorial University of Newfoundland in St. John's, Newfoundland, Canada. He specializes in studying the human dimensions of recreational resource and wildlife management and in resolving associated conflicts, particularly those involving the presence of large carnivores. Allistair served as a consultant for the Yellowstone wolf reintroduction program, and he and Christoph met at a wolf conference sponsored by the International Wolf Center in the United States some years ago. They became friends, and Allistair has since been an advisor and consultant for the CLCP. He is staying at the Prombergers' this week to facilitate a series of all-day meetings to formulate the mission and education strategy for the Large Carnivore Information Centre, and to help us brainstorm ideas for the exhibits, which Barbara has already begun to design. With its high-tech interactive displays and green features such as passive solar heating and a photovoltaic power supply on the roof, as well as its many hectares of land for live large carnivores, the Centre would be amazing anywhere, but seems almost unreal for Romania.

As we were gathering for the meeting, I grabbed a moment with Christoph.

"What do you think about my dog bite?"

"How is it?"

"Fine. But, well…what about rabies?"

"It's possible. But not likely. I wouldn't worry about it."

By now I had gained a great deal of respect for Christoph and what he has accomplished in Romania, but his conclusion seemed contraindicated. Rabies possible, but don't worry about it? You can count on two hands the number of people who have developed symptoms of rabies and survived. Perhaps his admonition against "worry" was rhetorical, meant in general: act, but no use worrying…

"Should I do anything about it? Maybe have the dog checked?"

"You can if you want."

His look implied I shouldn't want. I gave it just another moment's thought, quickly evaluating everything that might be required: locating and identifying the dog, locating the appropriate health professionals, confiscating and killing the probably innocent dog so its brain could be tested, going through the shots, probably going to someplace unpleasant in a city somewhere to get the shots. There are times in life when you just take your chances. I decided not to worry about it.

Later, during the meeting, Anja called from the cabin. When Christoph handed me the phone, it was natural to suspect a problem.

"What's up?"

"Come quick…Curly is stuck in a hole!"

I struggled momentarily to conceive of the possibilities that could cause the urgency in her voice. A dog stuck in a hole did not on the surface seem an insurmountable difficulty.

"What?"

"Curly. Somehow she got herself trapped in a hole. I can't get her out by myself!"

Not happy about leaving an enjoyable and productive meeting (a rare event during my engineering career), I dashed from the house and hopped into the Suzuki. Rocks flew as I bounded along the road to the cabin. When I got there, Curly was indeed stuck in a hole.

A narrow pathway runs along the lower fence of the wolf enclosure, cut into the slope just above the roof of the cabin. It is on this ledge that people stand for close encounters with Poiana and Crai. An area underneath the ledge near the corner of the cabin had been seriously eroded, and it was here that Curly had apparently been digging, perhaps for an old bone or choice scrap that had somehow escaped the enclosure. As she dug, a rock or large chunk of earth must have collapsed from underneath the old beam of timber that holds the ledge in place and rolled down the slope from there. Curly either fell or tried to crawl through the resulting hole and out from under the beam. She didn't make it. Her hips and rear legs were trapped under the beam while her upper body stuck through the hole and dangled down the slope. I had taken to calling Curly "Buddha dog" because nothing seems to perturb her. This was no exception. As I strode up the steps to evaluate her predicament, Curly's eyes followed me calmly with an expression of complete, though misplaced, confidence in my imminent wisdom.

The dog's upper body was twisted at a strange angle relative to her hips, and her wound complicated matters further. After a few delicate attempts, it became clear there was no way to simply lift her out. She was stuck and we were going to have to dig, and dig a lot, while being careful not to collapse the entire section of ledge. Rocks tumbled down the slope and the narrow ledge shifted slightly as we methodically dug, causing a few anxious moments, for us if not for Curly. The dog waited patiently while we worked, until she was finally able to half-scramble and half-tumble down the slope, shaking herself at the bottom and looking up at us as if to ask, "What's the problem?" I then filled in the hole with rocks I carried from the roadside that I hoped were large enough to stabilize the ledge and prevent further erosion.

Wednesday, April 9

Today I accompanied Simona on one of her visits to the elementary schools in two remote mountain villages. We left in the morning, driving from Zarnesti toward our first destination, a village called Pestera (pronounced "Peshtera"), along a very rough dirt track that initially skirts the northeastern foothills of Piatra Craiului, then traverses southward across a rolling open plain just beginning to turn green, and finally turns to the west, snaking for several kilometers up a succession of long, steep, open slopes.

The crisp mountain scenery sparkled with a thin layer of fresh snow that was melting rapidly in the strong sunshine. Simona seemed at ease navigating the project's Suzuki briskly up the rutted, twisting track, bouncing over the holes and careening around the largest of the craters, and, when the smoother course dictated, staying to the left even on curves. We never saw another motorized vehicle, so it was not really an issue, but a question had been lingering in my mind since my first ride on the mountain roads of Romania.

"I notice drivers here take a lot of risks."

"Yes," Simona replied with her usual joyful smile and a shift of gears.

"Why? Don't they recognize the consequences of things like head-on collisions?"

"It's fun," she offered while swerving around a hole with a little extra enthusiasm, I thought.

"What about pedestrians? I've seen many have to jump out of the way."

"We're Easterners, not Westerners. We don't worry about such things."

I was left to ponder whether it was a cultural trait based on longitude or a matter of experience. After all, for many Romanians, the ubiquity of the automobile is a relatively recent phenomenon.

Consisting of a few whitewashed buildings collected along a short, straight stretch of the muddy track, Pestera is a small hamlet perched on an open ridge with a spectacular broadside prospect of the Piatra Craiului ridge to the northwest. Farmhouses dot the surrounding hills and sit precariously along the spines of ridges, seeming to hang in the thin, invisible air that blows cold from the snowcapped peaks beyond.

Pulling up to the brilliant white schoolhouse, we were greeted enthusiastically by the principal, a slight, nervous man of about fifty, and were ushered immediately into the building, to the teacher's room, where another man and two women were apparently awaiting our arrival. They stood up from their seats and offered warm, ardent greetings, and seemed quite surprised and honored to have an American visitor at their school. Feeling that I was the one who was honored, I wondered if I was the first.

The six of us barely fit in the tiny room. Simona remained standing while I obliged the principal's insistent plea to take a seat with the others around a small table. After a few exchanges of pleasantries we got around to what seemed to be the important business. The principal broke open a bottle, just as Simona had warned ("You better be prepared for a drink"). He grabbed several smudgy shot glasses from an ancient cabinet, filled them with a colorless liquid, and sent them on their way around the table with a nod of respect and a smile for each one. It being ten o'clock in the morning and me not being a drinker, I wasn't enthusiastic about imbibing and made a mild refusal, but protocol superseded principle — after all, as far as I knew the toast was in my honor — so I relented and in unison with the others quickly downed the clear, burning fluid. I redeemed myself by staunchly refusing a second round.

＊

Sitting on rigid benches in the stark, cold classroom, bundled in their winter coats and hats, the small cluster of sixth graders listen attentively as Simona describes ways to publicize the presentation they will give to the village community next week. The meager heat from the single wood stove is lost in the immensity of the large, whitewashed classroom, which dwarfs the small cluster of children. Hanging crookedly on the wall is a tattered map of the world, depicting nations that have not existed for half a century. Through the tall windows, which rattle and sing as gusts of wind seek entry through the loose fittings and cracked panes, can be seen the spectacular panoramic view that graces this small Transylvanian village. As the students walk hand-in-hand to school, which is an hour and a half journey for some, their hearts may quicken from more than just the exertion of the trek and the beauty of the scenery, for they hear stories...

It is commonly believed in Romania that wolves are dangerous to humans. Although they are usually curious about Poiana and Crai and find them to be *foarte frumos* (very beautiful), local visitors to the wolf cabin are almost always reluctant to approach the enclosure, being satisfied instead to look up the slope from the relative safety of our flat driveway. This fear of wolves is rooted in stories about wolf attacks that are passed around repeatedly until they become unverifiable folklore. An investigation of forty-one such stories circulating within the country in the last half century confirmed that eight were based on factual events,[87] but in every case the wolf was either rabid or injured, or was trapped or cornered and defending itself from further attack by people or dogs. There were no unprovoked attacks and no serious injuries to humans (although one person had to stay in hospital for a month as a precaution against rabies).

As part of the CLCP community outreach program, Simona has commissioned these students to investigate stories of wolf attacks that are currently circulating in the village. No computer or Internet is available to aid them in their task; the students must query their relatives and friends to discover who told whom what, tracing the stories back, if possible, to the sources. They will report their findings in a presentation at their school next week, and the community is invited.

Leaving Pestera, we packed a teacher and several excited children into the Suzuki for an afternoon ride to their homes along the way back down the steep, winding track. Our next destination was another small school in another mountain village, Moieciu de Sus, which lies in the hills south of Bran. Simona would be meeting only with the principal this day.

A large, gruff man, whose smile felt insincere, if not malicious, met us at the door of the rustic school building. Here was the Maurice Minniefield[88] of Moieciu de Sus, both in manner and in bearing. More than merely the headmaster of an elementary school, reportedly he is also the "big man" of the village, controlling or at least dominating most of the local civic affairs. I wondered whether he was one of those former officials of Romania not content with the new democratic order, one of those unwilling to let escape the power and privilege enjoyed under the previous communist system.

Simona translated a few of his initial jokes and condescending remarks, but he was soon off on a long, vociferous harangue. Simona occasionally interjected a few choice comments of her own (or so it seemed), and as far as I could tell was holding her ground. I was clueless about the content of the discussion, but I hoped I had misjudged the man's smile and the "conversation" was only passionate, not antagonistic. On the drive back, however, Simona explained that the principal's attitude toward the project had inexplicably turned negative and he had been aggressive and rude to the point where she had become a little afraid. Apparently he had tried to provoke me as well, making snide remarks about America, which Simona left untranslated.

As she dodged potholes with renewed vigor, Simona described the serious problems that have plagued the Romanian educational system, most of which have been caused by lack of money. Many teachers have been paid barely enough to survive, at least until recently. It's not long past that some teachers, especially in isolated communities, supplemented their income by threatening not to pass students unless they received bribes from parents.

Upon our return to Zarnesti, Simona invited me to have lunch with her and her mother. I was treated to a delicious bean soup and fresh baked bread in their modest but comfortable flat in one of the town's large apartment block buildings, not far from the CLCP souvenir shop. Again I was struck by how much nicer the interiors of the flats are compared with the exteriors of the buildings, which are generally ugly and decaying. During the meal Simona described the incredible skill of Romanian pickpockets, which apparently are more common in the cities than I realized. A friend of her friend once challenged her boyfriend to detect his stealthy lifting of the latter's wallet while he was fully aware it would happen. The "thief" was successful every time. From travel warnings I had read I knew this could be a problem, but now I realized I should be a little extra diligent when in Brasov, at the train station or exploring the beautiful center of the city.

After I related the story of our horse riding adventure, Simona finished chewing her bite of one of the tasty pastries her mother had offered, and then noted, "I don't ride horses anymore."

"Why not?"

"Last year I had a very bad fall. I had to go to the hospital. Four of my ribs were cracked."

"Wow. Sorry to hear of that."

"Yes, the horse was very difficult to manage. And he was very big."

"What was his name?"

"Andrei."

Thursday, April 10

My leg wound is healing fine.

Because I often walk, I think people in town are becoming used to seeing this unusual American striding along. I now receive fewer dubious stares and more familiar nods. As for me, I've become used to seeing the townsfolk walking about carrying white plastic bags emblazoned with the American flag. On pleasant Saturday mornings when many people are shopping, it looks a bit like the Fourth of July in small town America.

There has been a shift in Poiana's personality lately. She has become exceedingly affectionate. Is this a precursor to denning behavior, which will be occurring soon in her wild, un-neutered cousins?

I've noticed frogs' eggs in some of the pools dotting the meadows of the valley, but strangely I haven't yet heard the songs of their progenitors. I look forward to the springtime symphony — as sure a sign of the earth's enduring vitality as there is.

I continue working on the fence when I find the time. Today I cut some beech saplings, three or four inches in diameter, from amongst thick clumps in the forest above the cabin to use as rails. Being a proponent of low-impact living — after all I am working on a conservation project — I was a little uneasy about cutting trees, but for a single sapling to emerge from the competition for light and space and form a healthy, towering tree, the clump must eventually be thinned, by nature if not by me. Or so I rationalized. I've been taking pride in reusing old nails, or none at all where I weave the rails into the thick stand of small tree trunks lining the creek. It isn't just a matter of principle; we have only a few rusting, random-sized nails to spare.

Sunday, April 13

A dark and gloomy day. This morning a tourist group used up most of our electricity while they were in the cabin so tonight I'm writing by candlelight.

We learned from Paul, the Romanian tour guide, that there is a cave containing a religious shrine of some sort on the slopes of Piatra Craiului directly across the valley from our cabin. Anja and I decided to check it out. We started out after lunch, walking down the road in fog and intermittent drizzle, accompanied by Curly on the soggy ground and the howls of Poiana and Crai in the heavy air. We crossed the small bridge that spans the river and began climbing a viscid, muddy track that winds its way up an open slope behind our shepherd friend's house. As we trudged up the slope, our feet slipped and sank and stuck to the mud and lifted up large heavy gobs of the stuff, making our legs feel like lead and leaving clumsy imprints that obliterated the tracks left by the deft hoofs of countless sheep.

On a slope beyond a small ravine to our right the roof of a rustic house floated mysteriously above the trees and the fog. A thin line of smoke wafting from the chimney provided the lone evidence that the mistral structure was likely occupied by people. Suddenly several dogs charged from house like soldiers from a castle, dashing across the slope to intercept us. Once they got close

155

these canine guards were not as aggressive as most; they investigated us briefly and allowed us to pass. Perhaps they were friends of Curly.

We continued climbing up to a dirt road that traverses the slopes, coming from the direction of Zarnesti, and followed it westward, to the right, where it disappeared into the woods. Entering the darkening forest, we became even more enshrouded in swirls of fog and mist. We followed the road to a large log house that was still under construction, presumably the residence of monks somehow affiliated with the cave. As we approached the building we glimpsed a bearded man ducking into the basement door, but his demeanor did not appear welcoming, so we followed the path past the building and up the forested slope beyond.

Water dripped relentlessly from the green needles and gray branches of the forest. We ascended a steep, slippery path running alongside a cliff, which soon formed into a stairway of sorts, with steps cut by logs and with a rickety railing on the right made from miscellaneous boards and tree parts. The trail passed under a natural rock arch reaching out from the cliff on the left, and then ended about ten meters beyond, at an old wooden door set in rock and painted with colorful runes and images. The door was not locked, so we opened it and entered the cold, dark interior of the cave. In the dim silver light we could see the glint from the numerous icons, pictures, and ornaments hanging on the walls, and as our eyes adjusted we began to make out the images of Christ and saints. Near the center of the chamber, next to an altar set on a cone of rock topped with candleholders, stood a small spruce tree also decorated with ornaments, photographs, and images. I sensed rather than saw a succession of inner chambers, although in the darkness I could be certain of nothing. We hadn't brought a flashlight and didn't want to risk stumbling over any sacred relics, so we didn't explore beyond the outer chamber.

We sat for a while on the floor to meditate and ponder the age and significance of this cold and damp sacred space. As Curly sat next to me, injecting ghostly puffs of breath into the dark stillness, I began to wonder whether there is any reason to suppose that all beings are conscious at the same moment in time. Could what is "now" to me be a distant memory, or an unknown future, to Curly? Is it necessary for the operation of the universe that all observers are observing simultaneously?[89] Einstein's Special and General Theories of Relativity portray the universe as a four-dimensional space-time continuum (three dimensions of space, one of time) in which there is no need to suppose there is anything special about the coordinate of time that is "now." And certainly if the universe were to operate deterministically, if the state of the universe at any moment were exactly determined by its state at the preceding moment according to immutable and ubiquitous "laws," then there would be no special role for consciousness and nothing unique about "now".[90] In such a world, would "now" for Curly need be "now" for me, even when she's sitting quietly beside me?[91]

The theory of quantum mechanics suggests, however, that the universe is not deterministic but probabilistic and unresolved until observed, and therefore there is something special about "now": everything before now has been determined, and everything after now has not (and is open to multiple possibilities).[92] But determined by what, if not by observers that are free to determine? And what is an observer that is free to determine — that has free will — if not something that is "conscious"? So must the universe be determined by all consciousnesses at once everywhere, or can it be determined by separate consciousnesses that may be aware here in this body at one moment and aware over there in a different body at a different moment?

If the latter, if all sentient beings are not consciousness at a universal "now," then wouldn't each consciousness observe and decide in its own individual universe, since what other consciousnesses have frozen into being at other times could not influence the determination of what is occurring "now"? Wouldn't each consciousness be lord of its universe, and wouldn't it be an illusion to suppose that anyone else in it has free will? All others would have either already made their choices, or would not have yet, and therefore would be "currently" inanimate: not affected by their own will, but only by the will of the one who is "now" conscious — the one currently free to observe and act. There would be as many universes as there are sentient beings.[93]

On the other hand, if we're all necessarily conscious at the same moment, then consciousness itself is a special plane of time passing like a wave through the entire spatial extent of the universe, freezing existence into being as it observes and decides. And since

Einstein's Special Theory of Relatively guarantees that quantum determinations made at one point (or body) in space cannot instantaneously effect determinations made at another point, every embodied consciousness would be free from every other, and therefore could *feel* separate, even though all would be manifestations of the one special "time-plane of consciousness."

After our bones and my mind had became sufficiently stiff, we left the cave and descended back through the enchanted forest, past the building, down the muddy track to the flat pasture near the river. There we encountered another poignant mystery, a fitting end to our pilgrimage: our shepherd friend was proudly holding aloft two newborn lambs, umbilical cords still dangling. "*Copi, copi!*" (babies, babies!). He placed them on the ground, where they shook like leafs and could barely stand. Keeping a wary eye on Curly, the mother stood guard over and began to nurse the wobbly infants.

I later learned from Simona that the cave is called Coltii Chiliei ("Rock Monastic Shelter") and local inhabitants have used it since at least as early as the twelfth century as a refuge and a church. Eight hundred years ago it was Tartar invaders from whom people hid in the forests and caves of Piatra Craiului, and later it was the Turks, and later still the foreign invaders of two World Wars. The refugees needed a place to worship during these tumultuous and dangerous events, and this cave was a natural choice. Well hidden in the forest and guarded by a natural rock arch, legend maintains that pious refuge seekers have never been discovered at Coltii Chiliei — a sure sign the cave is blessed by God. And when you pass under the arch, half of your sins are forgiven, but it only works once, and you cannot choose which sins.

As a sanctified Orthodox Church, dogs are not allowed in the cave, and women no further than the altar in the outer chamber. I can't say for sure whether Anja passed the altar, but, while the guilt is surely ours, Curly was zero for two. (The building nearby now serves as a more standard and larger church and monastery.)

Coltii Chiliei isn't the only cave in Romania — there are over 2,000 scattered throughout the Carpathian Mountain region of the country. And it isn't the only cave with religious significance. A few are enshrined with monasteries more refined and on a much grander scale than Coltii Chiliei (such as the Pestera monastery at the Ialomicioara cave in the nearby Bucegi Mountains, which I never got to visit).

And monasteries are not the only distinctive features of caves in Romania. In a cave called Pestera cu Oase (The Cave with Bones), located in the southwestern corner of the Carpathians near a small town called Anina, a skull of an ancient human was recently discovered that is estimated to be 40,500 years old — the oldest fossil from a modern human ever discovered in Europe. At least as intriguing as its age, the skull, along with bone fragments from two other individuals, shows a combination of characteristics from early modern humans and Neanderthals, evidence which suggests that early human arrivals into Europe interbred with existing Neanderthal populations before the latter disappeared.[94]

We completed this sublime day with a profane task: another cleanup of the wolf enclosure. Although we have improved the feeding regimen and the volume of rotted flesh has been reduced, the wolves have almost stopped eating recently, so there was still more than enough to be disposed of, especially given the slightly warmer weather. I had been dreading one particularly large sheet of hair-covered horsehide that had been festering on the ground since before the last cleanup (it was relatively fresh at the time). I held my breath, but I could feel the explosion of warm stench as I lifted it off the ground and watched the underside writhe with white maggots. We decided to drag this and the other parts some distance into the forest rather than waste time and wood to burn it. As I stood and hurled the repugnant hide as far into the brush as possible, I struggled mightily not to lose my last meal — to Anja's amusement.

In the evening Poiana emits a plaintive whine as she paces near the fence. Why aren't they eating?

Tuesday, April 15
Back up to Pestera to attend the presentation given by the sixth grade students. It seemed it was most of the village that eventually wandered into the classroom, as neighbors, friends, and relatives

gathered first in the hall outside, where they busily chatted and caught up on the latest news, before slowly filing in to take their seats. At the front of the room the teacher stood patiently watching the audience grow, while the children fidgeted in their chairs.

Once on their feet the young presenters were surprisingly confident and the presentation began well enough, but the audience became rather boisterous and skeptical when the students reported that they were not able to verify any of the village's wolf-attack stories. A thin, drunk man, and a woman who was neither thin nor drunk, did most of the shouting. Apparently a bear had recently killed the woman's donkey. I felt sorry for the woman, and for the donkey, and for the children stuck in the middle of the boiling controversy, although the latter seemed to be holding their own. After long vociferous discussions, which included Simona, many of the villagers admitted that their fear of wolves was probably not justified and that they have more problems with bears.

This evening when I stepped out into the cool night air to brush my teeth one of the wolves began to howl. Since I had never before had my nightly teeth cleaning thus celebrated, I was wondering what was up when I suddenly realized I was hearing not a howl but a scream of agony. One of the wolves was shrieking and yelping frantically like a dog hit by a car. I dashed up the steps to the fence, followed by Anja who had rushed out of the cabin with a flashlight. Poiana was half hanging from the fence by one of her front legs. Her paw was jammed through a hole of the fence, her foot was bent and twisted at an unnatural angle, and she was hopping on her rear legs in order to remain standing as she struggled to pull free. While Anja and I stood at the fence trying to take it all in, fortunately Poiana calmed down and stopped struggling. I then gingerly touched her paw to see if I could push it out, but it was jammed tight and her panicked screams resumed.

A wolf's paw is large and can spread wide, especially the front paw, which for the biggest wolves can splay up to 5¾ inches wide when it's placed on the ground. This is a wonderful design for keeping wolves afloat on deep snow, but it's like a hook in a fish's mouth when a paw is stuck through the hole of a chain-link fence. The metal of the fence is very thick and not easily bent or cut, and I knew of no tools we had that could do the job. The only way I could see to free Poiana's paw was to first straighten her foot and then squeeze her toes together — no easy task while a hurt and scared wolf hangs from its foot and struggles.

But there seemed no other choice, so Anja went to get gloves to give my fingers some chance of staying intact while I stayed and tried to calm the agitated wolf. By now Poiana was alternating whimpers with screams, and we had to hurry. I was concerned that if her leg was not already broken, it might be by any manipulations I might try, and I dreaded what was to come. I stood there feeling helpless and racking my brain for other options. Meanwhile Poiana had rotated into a twisted position with her belly partially exposed. It was a situation that Crai couldn't resist, and he began to nip at his sister's belly. Fearing this would agitate Poiana further and worsen her plight, I decided I couldn't wait. I lifted my foot, which I hoped was well enough protected by my leather hiking boot, and, clenching my teeth in fear of the impending fracture, was about to push it against Poiana's paw, when suddenly Crai tugged on Poiana's stomach so hard that she reacted with a surge of defensive fury and pulled herself out.

I don't know whether Crai's help was intentional, but he was the hero, intentional or not. Poiana limped from the fence and thanked her brother by attacking him furiously. I guess no slack is allowed in the rigid hierarchy of wolf social structure, and she must have felt compelled to immediately remind him that her position had not changed one bit as a result of her embarrassing blunder. Having sufficiently made her point, Poiana then solicited some sympathy from her human friends by rubbing along the fence. I was a little reluctant to pat her, thinking that she may have associated the problem and the pain with me, but she responded warmly.

Amazing is the extent to which we carry our worlds with us. Here I am, embedded in completely different surroundings and circumstances, amongst new people, involved in activities I hadn't previously dreamed of, with entirely novel concerns. But as I sit here in this cabin, which now seems so familiar after one month, I do not feel different at all. I still have that "thin" feeling — that lack of connection with the world — that has been with me since my dogs died, as though part of my spirit left the world with them. Place and circumstances do not heal this wound. Will time?

Wednesday, April 16

My task this morning was to locate Turnu for the benefit of a German tour group the project is hosting. Once I identified the general location of the wolves, Christoph would bring the group to the area and we would then demonstrate the techniques of radio telemetry and wolf tracking. Since this was to be the first time out on my own to locate the wolves, I wasn't completely sure where I was going or what I was doing, but I was determined to be the best expert I could be.

I drove south from Zarnesti to Tohanu Nou, a small cluster of buildings gathered around an intersection lying in a flat, open plain near the center of the northern edge of the Glajerie pack's range. The core of their territory lies to the south in the Bucegi Mountains, and this is the usual place to first try for a signal. I put the directionless antenna on the roof, connected the receiver and put on the headphones, and sure enough I heard a very faint beep. Easy enough; now I had to make it stronger.

From my previous travels with Peter I assumed the small dirt road across the intersection was only a short village track, so to get a better signal I could either follow the main road to the left along the broad valley towards the northeastern corner of the wolves' range, or go right towards Bran, the southwest end of their range. I chose left. The signal weakened by the time I reached the first village, and was absent entirely at the following village, Glajerie. I had chosen wrong, so I turned around and drove back toward Bran thinking how unfortunate it was that I'd have to drive up the difficult road in the hills above the village, and weighing the odds of getting stuck.

[That would impress the tourists. Perhaps they could tour Dracula's Castle while Christoph pulls me out of the mud.]

There was no longer a signal back at Tohanu Nou, so it was with some doubt that I continued on to Bran. As I had suspected, the steep rutted track above the village was primarily mud and I barely avoided becoming stuck several times before making it to the top of the ridge. There I could hear nothing but static in the headphones. Wrong again. My role as expert wolf finder was now definitely in jeopardy. But at least I could now pretty safely rule out the southwestern end of their range, and since I hadn't picked up a signal anywhere between Glajerie and Bran, the central area was suspect as well. Perhaps I'd been misled at the beginning. Perhaps the wolves were actually at the complete opposite end of their range: Bungee Jumping Canyon.

So back down through Bran and toward the northeast I went, retracing my earlier route. Arriving in Glajerie around 9:30, still with no signal, I wondered how effective Christoph would be at making excuses for his wolf expert. I called him and left a message to the effect that I was confident the wolves were not near Bran. Hopeful this tidbit would hold them for a while, I continued on, ignoring the Dracula warning sign and driving past the Gypsy village and on up to the base of Bungee Jumping Canyon. There I heard the beep, loud and clear. Christoph arrived about ten minutes later with the tourists. Receiving my message, he had already made his own guess. "Welcome," I confidently greeted the tourists as they piled out of the van, "The wolves are up this valley…"

The wolves were indeed up the valley, and the signal indicated they were resting. They were not so close that we were a threat, so we led the group into the forested hills adjacent to the canyon. As we walked along I offered each of the tourists a chance to listen to the beep, while Christoph explained the ways of wolves, and the ways of expert wolf trackers. Continuing up a park-like slope covered with tall, stately beech, we came upon an area where dirty white patches of shredded plastic partially obscured the soft brown layer of decaying leaves blanketing the forest floor — artificial snow presumably left from the filming of the American film, *Cold Mountain*,[95] which had been filmed in the Zarnesti area the year before.

In addition to enhancing the wild aesthetic of a landscape, predators can provide measurable ecological and economic benefits.

In certain forests of central Europe, where no significant populations of large predators exist, damage to trees from over-browsing and bark peeling by wild ungulates is a serious problem. Over-browsing inhibits the regeneration of forest,[96] which can lead to secondary problems such as soil erosion and the invasion of non-native plant species. A CLCP study found that browsing damage to trees in Bavaria (where there is human hunting but no large predators) was up to ten times greater than in comparable plots of forest in Romania. While many factors influence the amount of browsing damage caused by ungulates,[97] large predators may help prevent over-browsing in certain situations, especially when browsers temporarily exceed the carrying capacity of a landscape due to transient conditions caused by drought, fire, or heavy insect infestation. Natural predation tends to be a consistent, adaptable, and self-regulating force that helps to maintain (or restore) the composition and dynamics of ecosystems. The reintroduction of wolves in Yellowstone National Park, for example, has been linked to the return of a more historically typical vegetative mix in certain parts of the landscape.[98]

The recent popularity of eco-tourism creates significant economic opportunities for regions blessed with unique or especially beautiful natural features, and the wildlife of Romania — and especially the large carnivores — is no exception. This presents an opportunity of particular importance for Zarnesti. During the communist era of the last century, Romania's state planners decided that the town's economy would be based on two large factories: a munitions plant and a paper mill. (For security purposes, the munitions plant was officially designated as a "bicycle factory," and is still sarcastically referred to as such by local people today.) Thousands of workers and their families were forcibly relocated to the town from other parts of the country. In recent years, both of the factories have fallen on hard times, with the paper mill being all but shut down. The unemployment rate of Zarnesti has soared to nearly 50 percent. Consequently there is strong pressure to develop extractive industries in areas around Zarnesti that are currently wild, and that contain wolves. For example, a quarry was recently proposed at a location near the wolf cabin. If economically attractive alternatives can be found, there is a better chance the unique natural heritage of the region can be conserved.

The Carpathian Mountains of Romania offers the closest relatively large, wild, and historically natural ecosystem to thousands of harried tourists from Western Europe seeking to escape the crowded and confining conditions of their controlled, industrialized world. To tap this potential market, the CLCP is helping local entrepreneurs develop eco-tourism businesses by providing business advice, establishing relationships with West European travel agencies, and soliciting sustainable development funds from various public and private sources. To date, these activities have aided the establishment in Zarnesti of two guesthouses, a horseback riding center, a mountain bike rental business, and a tour guide training program. While a small beginning, a CLCP analysis concludes that the local revenue generated by tourists attracted by the region's natural features — and especially by the mysterious and elusive large carnivores — already exceeds the calculated costs of game and livestock predation and protection. Nevertheless, the people who realize these benefits are not necessarily the same people who bear the costs associated with the presence of large carnivores, so controversy remains regarding the merits of this equation.

Thursday, April 17

I seem to be often interrupted in my glamorous chore of washing clothes in a bucket outside the cabin. This morning it was a group of journalists and a photographer from the DDP News Agency of Germany. At least my hand was only wet and not dirty when I extended it for a shake. The journalists must be doing a fairly in-depth story as they interviewed Anja and me extensively, and the photographer took several shots of us interacting with Crai and Poiana. The newsmen weren't quite out of sight when I returned to hanging my dripping clothes on a rope we had strung from the cabin to a tree.

In the afternoon, as Anja and I approached our shepherd friend's rustic house while driving back to the cabin from town, the shepherd and a companion were standing alongside the road. Their purpose seemed uncertain, but as soon as they spotted our Suzuki careening along, dodging the usual holes and kicking up the usual dust, they began frantically waving. They flashed huge grins while seeming very determined to get us to stop. The companion — a tall, grimy man with a band of dark stubble on the lower half of his face — was presumably the driver of the large logging truck parked in the yard of the house.

As I pulled up, the truck driver half ran and half stumbled to my side of the vehicle and offered his hand through the open window. When I extended my hand in turn, instead of the shake I expected he took hold of my hand and tried to kiss it. My embarrassment overrode what might, I suppose, be considered proper regard for protocol and I yanked my hand from his grasp. He persisted in his attempts to ravage my hand while his shepherd friend leaned on his stave nearby and watched, grinning happily.

Between his grabs for my hand this amorous man had much to say in Romanian. We didn't know what for sure, but certain words and signs suggested he might be pleading for diesel. So I signed for them to wait for five minutes while we went to the cabin to fetch a can. Upon my return (Anja opted to attend to other duties), I held the can aloft through the open window hopefully. The truck driver immediately climbed into my passenger seat, accompanied by a reek that seemed to have a life of its own. He gestured and spoke excitedly, trying desperately to be understood. He took some money from his pocket and offered it up, but I refused to take it. After successfully avoiding further advances on my hand, I began driving, assuming we were heading into town to fill the can with diesel, and wondering whether the interior of the Suzuki would ever smell the same again.

Still doubting what this was all about, I suddenly thought of calling Simona for translation. My passenger was puzzled when I handed him the phone, but he nervously took it and after listening for a moment he began yelling his replies.

"So, what does he want?" I handled the phone gingerly and not too close to my ear, wondering how I might clean it later.

"He wants a ride to Zarnesti to get a drink."

"What?! Why is he so excited? I thought he was in trouble."

I was already on the way and couldn't in good conscience ditch him on the long road, so I decided to finish the ride, but I'd been duped and wasn't pleased. I silently fumed.

[I'm not a taxi service for alcoholics. Next time I'll at least take the money.]

When I dropped him off at the first bar I came to in town, he tried again to lavish my hand with kisses, but I pushed him away and told him to get lost in language I thought he might understand.

On my way back to the cabin I was resolving never to be so fooled again when I came upon the shepherd, still standing alongside the road in front of his house and again waving for me to stop. I did, if for no other reason than to express my displeasure. The shepherd had much to say. More than usual, I thought. I made out the word *casa* (house), but he finally realized I wasn't getting it, and more, that I wasn't particularly interested in getting it, and gave up.

This evening at dusk I'm privileged to see an incredibly beautiful, ethereal sight: looking up the slope of the enclosure, the two wolves are at the very top, silhouetted against the darkening, blue-orange sky, gently wrestling, leaping, nipping each other in the neck, engaging in a silent, playful dance.

Friday, April 18

A rainy day. While I was at the project office emailing foreign embassies in Bucharest to ask for meetings to discuss grants, I got a call from Simona. She was at the cabin, and someone wanted to leave a dead sheep. The carcass was skinned, gutted, and decapitated. I really didn't think we could handle more meat now, but I knew it was not good politics to refuse such a conscientiously prepared and delivered offer. I called Christoph to ask whether we should spend project money for meat we didn't really need.

"Offer them 300,000." (Meaning lei, the Romanian currency, about nine dollars.[99])

"What about Curly?" I asked.

"It's ok if she eats a little."

"We can't put it in the can because we just put some cow parts into it this morning. And the freezer still isn't working."

"Well, have them leave it there, we'll figure something out."

Of course "we" meant Anja and me. When we arrived at the cabin about an hour later, Curly was walking along the road with a large bone in her mouth. All that remained of the sheep was most of the skeleton with a few red shreds clinging to the bones. Curly? By herself? Couldn't be. Not that quickly. Must have also been shepherd dogs, maybe with some help from ravens.

At least we didn't have excess meat to deal with.

Saturday, April 19

This morning I noticed that Crai had a large, blood-engorged tick on his forehead. I didn't have much hope that the wolf would hold still long enough for us to remove the parasite with our little tick-remover (essentially a pair of tweezers), but Anja and I both gave it a try, and we both failed. Poiana, however, either seeing what we were up to, or simply noticing the tick herself, gently used her front teeth to bite it off (after a couple of attempts). Christoph later reported that as far as he knew such "grooming" behavior has never been documented in wolves.

Later I joined Anja at the stables. She was preparing to go up to a logging road that will be used as a horseback-riding trail in the summer. She intended to clear the trail of brush and overhanging branches, and I had agreed to help. While Anja saddled up Andrei, I started to walk. Arriving at the trailhead at nearly the same time, I discovered that Anja had brought only some light garden shears, and she discovered I had brought nothing. We each thought the other was bringing a saw. As Andrei passed me by with Anja riding high on his back, I was sure the horse gave me a sly look of recognition.

I walked along behind the towering legs of the horse, feeling unimportant. Not far up the road, Andrei came to a stop where two huge green spruce trees lay across the trail. Anja dismounted and began attacking one of the trees with her shears. As Andrei and I stood and watched, I couldn't help thinking that if the huge horse ever had any respect for the wisdom of humans, it was surely lost now. After she had managed to hack through a couple of small twigs, Anja stepped back, took in the thick, long trunk spanning the trail, obscured by a dense tangle of large branches covered with still living green needles, and then looked at her shears. We broke up laughing and gave up the idea of trimming the trail today.

In the afternoon I was chopping wood at the cabin when a luxury car with tinted windows and small flags on the front of the hood pulled up in a cloud of dust. I was a bit annoyed because our prior visitors — an affable American couple in their fifties who were working on a USAID water project in Romania — had just left; this was our third set of tourists today, and we were having trouble getting anything done. The day was cold so we needed firewood, and I was especially anxious to finish the fence. The yard was almost closed in and if any livestock came in now it would be difficult to get them out.

A large, bald man with sunglasses (unusual in Romania) and wearing what appeared to be something between a safari outfit and a military uniform got out of the car and lumbered towards me. When I tried greeting him in Romanian, he simply barked, "You speak English. Good!" Then he grabbed me by the arm. "Come!" As he pulled me towards the car, I wondered if I was under arrest for cutting saplings in the forest.

Meanwhile, a short, not quite bald man, also wearing sunglasses, was escaping from the car, along with two small boys. "This is the ambassador from Canada." My captor paused for a moment to give me time to process the gravity of this information. "Show him the wolves." After freeing my arm, a bit indignantly, I did as I was commanded and showed the ambassador around, giving him a brief version of my speech about the project and the wolves. He seemed in a hurry. I tried to interest his boys in the wolves, but they were more fascinated by the fish and frog eggs in our creek. From the annual report I knew the ambassador had arranged for a grant to the project last year, which he mentioned, and as they departed I thanked him for Canada's support.

Before the day was over, my fence work was interrupted by two more groups of visitors and a drunk.

It has cleared after a snowy, rainy, foggy, cold afternoon, and Poiana and Crai are howling, sitting together up the slope a ways, heads lifted, noses pointing towards the sapphire blue evening sky.

Wolves are capable of a wide variety of vocalizations that have been categorized by scientists, in rough order of effective signal distance (recognizing that some of these categories are not really discrete but blend in a continuum), as whimpers, whines, moans, yelps, growls, snarls, woofs, barks, and howls, with various combinations being common. The meaning of these sounds, in rough correlation with the forms, has been determined to include: greeting/sexual arousal, frustration/anxiety/sexual arousal, submission/appeasement, pain, dominance, threat/attack, warning/defense, more aggressive warning/defense/protest, and reunion/bonding/spacing/mating. Most all of these vocalizations can also occur during play without necessarily carrying the same meanings, or at least not with the same intensity or seriousness. Excluding howls (the characteristics of which are especially conducive for long distance transmission) and yelps (when used to express pain), these wolf vocalizations, like the vocalizations of most mammals and birds, appear to be consistent with a theory that suggests that more peaceful and harmonious intentions are conveyed by higher pitched, harmonic sounds (which might be expected from smaller animals), while more aggressive intensions are conveyed by lower pitched, noisy (non-harmonic) sounds (which might be expected from larger animals).

Howls are relatively low-pitched and harmonic, characteristics which maximize the distance they can travel over rough and often forested land (non-harmonic and higher pitched frequencies attenuate quicker). Since they are often used to provide location information for the purposes of reuniting, spacing, or finding a mate, howls are usually highly modulated (varying in pitch), as anyone who has heard their eerily beautiful melodies can attest. When intended for spacing (warning other packs to stay out of their territory), it is better if howls do not contain too much information about how many wolves are howling, and best to mislead on the high side. Measurements have established that chorus howls do indeed provide little information about pack size, and most human listeners overestimate the number of howling wolves they think they hear.

Wolves are known to change the characteristics of their howls to be consistent with their purpose. For example, a separated wolf trying to find its pack will typically start off with higher-pitched, less modulated howls, so that less information about its location is conveyed and more distant wolves not in its pack are less able to hear. A separated wolf is trying to find friendly wolves by getting a response; it is not trying to be found by unfriendly wolves.[100]

To those who hear the howls of wolves, the role of howling for social bonding transcends scientific analysis and proves that the creation and enjoyment of beauty is not the sole purview of humans. Scientists say that wolves howl to reunite, to delineate their space, to find a mate, and to bond, but I believe, as I walk the road up the valley with Curly at my side, that wolves also howl to lament being left behind, to say goodbye to friends, and in the still evenings, as we're settling into our warm cabin for the night, wolves howl to proclaim the joy of existence.

Sunday, April 20

Today Anja and I hiked in Piatra Craiului National Park, entering on a trail just above the Plaiul Foii lodge. The skies were clear and the scenery replete with craggy peaks, towering cliffs, dark green forests, and blazing white fields of snow, although several heaps of garbage were scattered along the otherwise pristine, cascading headwaters of the Barsa River. Hiking appears to be none too popular in these parts, at least not at this time of year, at least not on trails far from the road. We saw no human tracks in the deep snow that still blankets the trail in the darker woods of the north-facing slopes. Yet, while humans may still be reluctant to venture into these forests, being content to continue hibernating in their villages, towns, and cities, the bears sleep no longer, and have found this human-made path through the forest to their liking. Looking at their large prints in the snow, I wondered what they think of the meat we have stored in the can near our cabin. Their stomachs must be empty after several weeks of slumber.

Thursday, April 24

I was awoken this morning — late, after celebrating my birthday at the Prombergers' last night — by a noisy disturbance at the enclosure. People were yelling and something was crashing through the brush. I ran out of the cabin and saw three men silhouetted by the bright morning sunlight high up the slope along the eastern side of the fence. They were carrying what I thought might be guns. I also thought they may have cut the fence, as one of the wolves was bounding frantically down the slope on the opposite side and at first I thought it might be outside the enclosure.

Gradually the sleep faded from my eyes and the menacing figures resolved into three teenage boys who were carrying cameras, apparently intent on getting some close-up photos of the wolves. Several of their more timid companions waited nervously at the road in front of the driveway. Not the least intimidated by my appearance, or perhaps too wrapped up in the excitement to notice, one of the boys near the fence attempted to climb it. *"Nu!"* I yelled. Anja sprang from the cabin and gave chase.

I approached a boy who had descended the slope and was standing near the lower corner of the enclosure. I tried to ask him in Romanian what they were doing and where were they from. He seemed contrite enough, so I waved for him to come forward, into the yard, and I then tried to explain with gestures, to him and his friends in the road, that they could take photos, but they must only approach the enclosure from the front. In the meantime, Crai was going berserk. Having entered the feeding pen, he was dashing from one end to the other and leaping so high that his head was crashing into the wire ceiling.

After they saw their fellow adventurers conversing with me and getting superior opportunities for photos, the boys who were still up the slope somehow resolved their differences with Anja, came down, and got their pictures.

For my birthday celebration last night, the Prombergers prepared a tasty meal from a sheep they had personally picked out for slaughter by a local farmer. This was not a sort of ritual sacrifice in honor of my birth. They had already intended to buy a sheep (most of which they would freeze for later use), and had just learned of my birthday yesterday from a friend of mine in the States who had sent them an email.

The festivities were well underway when Christoph's cell phone rang. Overhearing the near side of the conversation, Anja and I exchanged resigned glances before Christoph asked us the question we were dreading. "Do we need a horse?" Glancing again at Anja for validation, I reluctantly replied, "Yes, we do, although there are still some cow pieces in the enclosure, and the can is almost full. But to be honest, I think it is a bit gone." This latter was surely an understatement, and realizing that warmer weather was upon us, I quickly added, "But only if the freezer is working."

"When can you pick it up?"

"Where is it?"

"Pestera."

"Ten o'clock. Ask them to cut it up."

A quick call to Vaso confirmed that the freezer was still not working. Anja and I did our best to enjoy the rest of the evening.

So this morning, after our brief interlude with the teenage photographers, and after assurances from Vaso that the freezer would be fixed today, it was on to Pestera. We could not expect anyone in the remote mountain hamlet to speak a word of English, but armed with the Romanian word for horse, and given we'd certainly stand out as strangers, from foreign lands no less, we assumed we'd have little trouble finding the dead horse and the man who would sell it to us.

Arriving in the remote mountain hamlet we were directed to a white farmhouse set back from the muddy street of the village, not far from the white schoolhouse I had visited before with Simona. A couple of very excited men in much used and dirty farm clothes waved us around to the back, to a dusty barnyard framed by the white house on one side and a collection of dilapidated wooden structures resembling barns on two other sides. One of the men swung open a large door to one of the sheds, and there lying on the dirt floor amongst splattered gore and in a pool of red blood was the object of our quest: four or five enormous pieces of horse. The hide, thankfully, had been removed, but the large body parts would be difficult to handle and were much too big for our freezer. The horse would have to be cut up further.

The men dragged the heavy red pieces into the yard, where a few people had started to gather, presumably having noticed our vehicle driving through the quiet village and deciding to see what was up. We signed to the farmer to cut the body parts into smaller pieces. Girded with encouragement and advice from the growing crowd, the farmer enthusiastically set to work chopping with an axe, occasionally checking with Anja and me for guidance about where to attack. Blood and gore flew from the pieces of horse like wood chips from logs. Among the spattered were a trio of recent arrivals, two dapper men in suits along with a fashionably-dressed lady who had apparently been on their way to some important destination when they discovered the more interesting activity occurring in the farmhouse yard. Conversation and laughter and good cheer continued all around as the butchering proceeded and the crowd grew. Some amicable folks were doing their best to urge Anja and me to laugh as well, although I wondered whether we were being laughed at or with for being so foolish as to pay good money for this worthless bloody carnage.

A particularly begrimed and shabbily dressed man with a single-toothed smile stood in front of the throng and pointed and gestured and danced about trying to elicit laughs. Pointing with one hand at a few innocent cows in a fenced pasture peacefully chewing their cud, with his other hand he grabbed my arm and gently directed it towards the cows, as though to offer them up. He then turned his head towards the crowd with an exaggerated laugh. Obviously the cows were not his, and obviously his attempt at humor was at my expense. The jester then implored me to follow him into the barn. Realizing I was likely playing the fool, I followed him into the pitch-black, stygian enclosure, where I could barely breathe the foul and stagnant air. As my eyes adjusted to the darkness I began to sense the presence of a large, living, being. A horse was crammed into a stall with just enough room to stand. My guide chatted gleefully from somewhere in the darkness and I surmised he was offering me this horse as well. After we returned to the livable world of air and light, he pointed at the butchered pieces of horse and then back at the barn and slapped his knees and laughed. I curtly responded, *"Nu, nu. Unul cal…she nu vaca"* ("No, no. One horse…and no cow.") I wanted to dissuade his farces before they led to something more ominous, although I wondered what might be the better fate for the poor beast in the barn.

While Anja and I continued to give directions about where to chop, and tried to answer questions we didn't understand, and smiled at jokes we didn't get, a few of the local characters occasionally mimicked our English words with great amusement. When an especially large splatter of gore hit several people, including me in my face and hair, sending the assembled dogs and cats scurrying after the morsels, we all brushed off a bit, but no one seemed particularly bothered and even the finely dressed folks continued chatting merrily. Meanwhile the village comedian had a new inspiration. He began gesticulating and laughing wildly and pointed back and forth between his mouth and the horse's head. Yes, of course: Would we spare the horse's teeth? He could use them.

As the last pieces were being loaded into our truck the farmer asked us to take the head, but I knew that Poiana and Crai don't usually touch the heads (unlike their wild cousins), so I tried to suggest he give it to his funny friend instead.

After all the horse pieces were loaded into the back of our truck, the farmer brushed his bloodied hands on his pants, we paid him, and the party reluctantly began to disperse. We drove back through the little village while the people strolled merrily back to their lives. They smiled and waved and seemed grateful to us for providing the day's entertainment.

Upon arriving at Moserel's barn, we discovered that some of the horse parts were still too large for the freezer, so I found an axe and chopped them smaller.

We returned to the cabin, and while we set about our chores I noticed that I didn't feel compelled to immediately dash into the sauna, pour freezing buckets of water over my head, and scrub myself raw, as I would have a few weeks ago.

Every way we will ever be and every thing we will ever have is transient. Life is change, and feeling my change, I felt very alive.

Friday, April 25

Curly has been having a tough time recently. She's been in a lot of pain, and last evening she lay on her wound on her bed site by the creek and would not move, not even for food. Thinking she might spend the night there, after the chill of darkness set in I covered her with a blanket. About fifteen minutes after we retired, we heard her barking. I let her into the cabin and she seemed okay. Later, when I told Simona about it, she told me she had seen in a TV documentary that stream bank soil has healing properties which animals will make use of.

The owner of the small patch of land between the slopes and the road that abuts our yard just beyond the woodshed is clearing and burning brush, along with a few tires. Fortunately the wind is carrying the black billows of smoke away from our cabin. I wonder if he intends to thin or eliminate the dense line of trees along the stream, which would breach our defenses on that side from grazing invaders.

We have visitors from Bucharest, a young couple who have come to see the wolves. They saw the project featured on TV. The man is dressed in something resembling a racecar driver's outfit. They speak broken English and are really pleasant and even offer a donation. The man proudly tells me about his "American bloodline" pit bull. The dog has ten victories in the pit, but is as gentle as a baby to humans and even to other dogs (presumably excepting when it's in the pit). "I love dogs," the man says, almost with tears in his eyes. He can no more imagine I might have a problem with staged dogfights to the death than I can imagine that it is perfectly okay with him, a self-professed dog lover.

Saturday, April 26

Peter and Anja will be working as tour guides for the project this summer, so they are doing a lot of exploratory hikes over the next few weeks to check out route possibilities. During these treks Peter will also teach Anja about the local flora and fauna — the names and interesting tidbits about behavior and ecology that she can share with her clients. I plan to tag along as much as possible. Today the three of us, along with a woman from Germany who runs a tour guide business in Zarnesti, hiked the northwest side of the Piatra Craiului ridge. I heard my first cuckoo (Common Cuckoo — *Cuculus canorus*), a sound I had heretofore associated not with the forests of Eastern Europe, but with the relentless passage of time. Can clocks measure time as accurately as they mimic this bird?

For my benefit, as well as the fact that many of the tourists would be British, the two professional tour guides and their apprentice stuck mostly to English as they named every creeping and leaping and flying creature we came across. Sometimes they didn't know the English names, however, especially of the birds, and I regretted missing out (I had little hope of remembering the German pronunciations, whether or not they would serve me well in Romania or America). Although I strive to see things for what they are rather than what they should be, classification helps us understand and appreciate and the world.

We continued hiking along through fog, rain, and sun, ascending switchbacks on steep forested slopes and crossing steaming meadows, and catching occasional glimpses of the snow-capped Fagaras Mountains drifting in the clouds to the north. Snow still lay deep in the cool, dark woods on the north facing slopes, where the crusty snow of the trail was broken occasionally by the tracks of wolves. In a *poiana* (a small forest meadow) on the top of a rounded ridge we came upon a small tree that had recently been seriously abused by a bear. Bears will sometimes use trees to mark their presence in the world, standing up to gouge the bark with their claws and break off branches.

Eventually we split up and bushwhacked to look for hiking

A horse enjoys a spring day. Piatra Craiului is in the background.
© Oana Vinatoru (istockphoto.com)

Barbara guides a horseback tour near Zarnesti. © B&C Promberger

Brancoveanu Monastery, Sambata de Sus.
© Jürgen Sauer 2006

Young shepherd near the wolf cabin. © *Jürgen Sauer*

A shepherd and his dogs tend a flock
of sheep near Pestera. © *Simona Buretea*

Gathering wool and taking a break at a
shepherd camp. © *B&C Promberger*

Town side street in Zarnesti. Piatra Craiului is in the background. © *Kolja Zimmermann*

Paper mill, Zarnesti.
© *Alan E. Sparks*

Small open market of a type common throughout the region. © *Jürgen Sauer*

Zarnesti potato fields. © *Alan E. Sparks*

Road to the cabin. © *Alan E. Sparks*

Planting potatoes. © *Alan E. Sparks*

The edge of Zarnesti, with the Bucegi Mountains behind. © *Alan E. Sparks*

Bucegi Mountains. The Glajerie wolf pack's territory covers the forested slopes and the lower, rolling foothills, extending to the left, which is the core area (off the photo). © Peter Sürth

Zarnesti Gorge, with artificial snow left from movie filming.
© Alan E. Sparks

Piatra Craiului. © Alan E. Sparks

Eastern (Romanian) Orthodox
ceremony, April 23, 2005.
© Jürgen Sauer

Local man. © Jürgen Sauer

Enjoying Sunday afternoon.
© Jürgen Sauer

Traditional mountain home (Bran Castle museum). © *Alan E. Sparks*

Local transportation near wolf cabin.
© *Alan E. Sparks*

White stork *(Ciconia ciconia).* © *Jürgen Sauer*

Cabin yard protected by fence. © *Alan E. Sparks*

Curly in front of Piatra Craiului. © *Alan E. Sparks*

Roma man with child, and folks heading to the village (inset). © *Jürgen Sauer*

Haystacks with the Bucegi Mountains in the background.
© *Oana Vinatoru (istockphoto.com)*

A typical Roma village, this one in Slovakia. © *Jürgen Sauer*

Brasov central plaza. © Arpad Benedek (istockphoto.com)

Harvest of hay. © Jürgen Sauer

Bear at Racadau
containers, Brasov.
© B&C Promberger.

Rasnov Fortress (in the vicinity of Zarnesti). © *Gabriela Insuratelu (istockphoto.com)*

Brasov's old town center. The Black Church is on the left. Wolves and bears dwell in the forest to the city's edge.
© *Marcin Kaminski (istockphoto.com)*

Black Church, Brasov. © *Simona Buretea*

Sibui central plaza. © Alan E. Sparks

Monument of Decebal, a Dacian King, in the Almaj Mountains, Danube valley, Romania. This 40-meter-high statue was completed in 2004 and is the tallest rock sculpture in Europe. © Falk Kienas (istockphoto.com)

Sibiu Center with the Evangelical Cathedral. © Snezana Negovanovic (istockphoto.com)

Bran hills. © *Alan Grant*

Horses graze freely in the Barsa Valley,
near the wolf cabin. © Alan E. Sparks

Chamois (Rupicapra rupicapra).
© Peter Surth

Hills near Zarnesti. © B&C Promberger

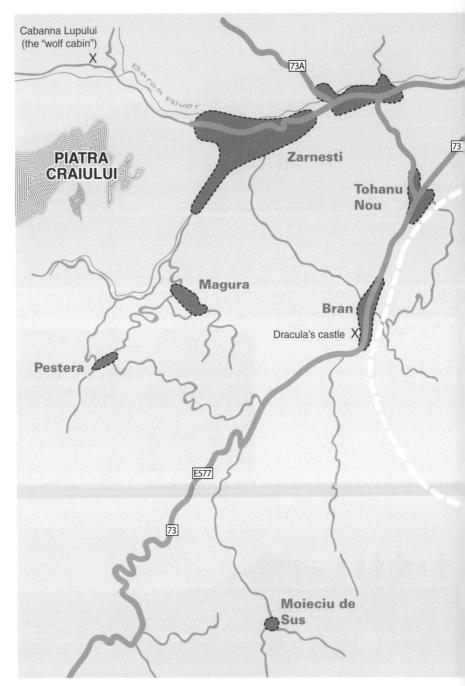

Map of Zarnesti area and Glajerie wolf pack territory.
© Alan E. Sparks

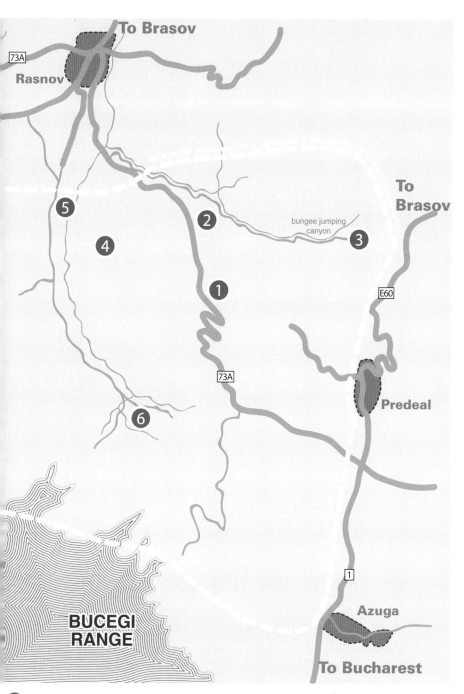

1 wild boar kill (1)   3 wild boar kill (2)   5 red deer kill
2 fox or small dog kill   4 roe deer kill (1)   6 roe deer kill (2)

An earlier CLCP wolf also named Crai at about five months old, in the hills near Pestera. Killed by a car in his first year. © B&C Promberger

routes that might be particularly intriguing or convenient for tour groups. Here in the lush forests of the Carpathians, vegetation grows on slopes that in Colorado would be bare, and more than once I was surprised to find nothing but slick rock under leaves where I had expected the softer ground of a viable forest floor to hold my foot. I began to slow my pace and watch my step, particularly since I was treading on a knee I had recently twisted while throwing my backpack into the rear seat of our pickup from the front (one of the doors doesn't open).

After regrouping for lunch on a pleasant, sunny meadow, we began our descent. We were soon confronted by a precipitous slope that had been recently clear-cut. The acutely slanting ground was hidden somewhere under tangles of thick brush and slippery trunks and limbs strewn every which way, but to find another route down would have required a considerable retreat back up the ridge. We slowly picked our way, tightrope walking the logs and hopping down from one to the next. We had to watch our feet and not each other, so we chose separate routes down the decline until we reached the orderly course of a stream that cut like a gash straight down the middle of the slope. The course of the cascading waterfall, which had been carved by tumbling water over the ages, was now scraped and gouged by the large logs that had recently been hauled down the slope, its route now decorated with fragrant branches, twigs, and fresh green needles. Overhead still stretched the thick, steel cable that was used in the operation, attached to a descending sequence of isolated trees left standing for the purpose. The slope had been devastated, but the clear-cut is relatively small, and plenty of vegetation remains to hold the soil, so the water still ran clear.

Although steep, the most expedient way down for water and logs also sufficed for us, and by stepping carefully onto the slippery rocks, and hopping from one side of the gully to the other when our path was blocked, we made our way down to the bottom of the slope, to a logging road, where we could finally release the grip of concentration required by our legs and feet and begin to marvel at the profusion of new life springing up around us. The rich, green, grassy banks of the road were luxuriant with yellow, purple, blue, and white blossoms, and the streamlet of snowmelt that trickled along the road's side was filled with newts and frogs and their countless eggs. The amphibians and their gelatin-encased progeny also thrived in the flowing runnels and tire ruts carved in the mud of the road, oblivious to the inevitable doom that would arrive with the next thundering truck.

Tuesday, April 30

The flat table of land lying on the outskirts of Zarnesti along the road to the cabin has rested quiet under a blanket of white throughout the winter. During the last few weeks the snow has gradually receded to reveal the rich brown soil of the cultivated fields. Today as I left the town behind me, expecting the usual long, placid walk to the cabin on this warm spring day, I was surprised to find that the peace and quiet of the fields had yielded to bounteous activity. The fertile scent of newly turned earth confirmed that I was witness to an ancient annual rite: the plowing and planting of the potato fields of Zarnesti. The mood was both earnest and festive, as men unloading sacks of seed potatoes from carts and carrying them along the road and into the fields shouted friendly greetings and observations and advice to each other, and as young children darted about the wagons, laughing and playing games. I wasn't certain whether the cheerful sentiment extended to the women and older children who were laboring in the fields, hoeing or bent over digging and planting potatoes by hand, but I saw no dreary or unhappy faces. Everyone seemed to know their role, and the entire community projected determination and efficiency at doing the work that had to be done.

Each family worked its own rectangular section of the large plots, delineated by what markings I could not tell. Older boys coaxed and guided reluctant horses, while their fathers grasped the weathered wooden handles of the plows, pushing and steering them through the stubborn earth. Neighbors helped neighbors carry heavy sacks and fix broken plows. On a couple of plots, presumably owned by wealthier farmers, ancient tractors supplanted horses, the black puffs of smoke and roaring noise they spewed being easily swallowed by the broad expanse of limpid spring air hanging over the valley. As I watched several men puzzling over one such clunker, I wondered which could be more stubborn, the tractors or the horses. Meanwhile, on the bright green terraces beyond and above the fields, horses occasionally paused in their romping and cows in their chomping to look out over the plain, as though to relish the spectacle of humans bent and toiling in the dusty croplands below.

For how many centuries has this beautiful and vibrant and sacred vernal scene unfolded on these rich fields splayed under the towering pinnacle of Piatra Craiului? Certainly it wasn't always potatoes planted here. The potato was originally developed by the indigenous horticulturists of the Americas and didn't arrive in Europe until late in the fifteenth century (when its relatively hardy, caloric, and vitamin-rich characteristics helped spur a population boom on the continent). But surely humans have been taking advantage of this flat, fertile land for as long as they've known how to plow, sow, and reap in this part of the world, regardless of the crop.

And how does it happen that everyone plants on the same day? Is the day set by tradition, or does it depend on the weather, or does everyone just wake up one spring morning and know that today is a good day to plant? And for how much longer will this venerable tradition continue? As I watched the people and animals at their focused toil, so near the source that sustains their existence, everything seemed natural, primal, *appropriate*. Yet this life must be hard. I haven't chosen to live it. So is it right to suggest, as I'm tempted to do, that no labor could more satisfying than that which directly, through our hands and feet and backs, provides for our fundamental sustenance? Is it part of human nature to prefer watching TV, or reading a book, or creating art, to working in these fields? Regardless, one can feel the inevitable approach of pesticides, modern machinery, and corporate farming that have already eliminated traditional rural life in much of Europe.[101] This seems unfortunate on several levels, not least of which is the fact that the potatoes I have eaten while in Romania are the best I have tasted in decades.

As I continued walking past the long, straight furrows lined with seed potatoes waiting to be covered, suddenly I recognized one of the farmers. He was a white-haired, smiling man of about fifty who had stopped by the cabin a few evenings ago in a group of five or six men. One of them could speak a little broken English and had translated as the group asked questions and I provided explanations. They seemed very friendly and genuinely interested in the wolves and the project, although they kept their distance from the enclosure. I remember wondering about the group, who they were exactly, for they were different from most of our visitors — neither foreign tourists nor curious local youngsters nor people from the city. So now I saw that they were local farmers, and I admired their respectful curiosity about a project that they could understandably view with suspicion.

This farmer was one of those using a tractor on his plot. Or trying to; his was the tractor that was broken down. Just as I was trying to decide whether to interrupt him and his companions with a greeting, he glanced my way. His smile widened and his eyes lit up. He immediately left the recalcitrant machine and came rushing to the roadside to exchange warm greetings and shake my hand. After our *buna ziuas*, we were at a momentary loss, but then I recalled the one word in Romanian I knew that seemed pertinent. *"Cartof!"* I pointed and swept my arm over the fields. *"Da! Da! Cartof!"* he laughed. I'm not sure why it felt appropriate to reciprocate with an English lesson, but I pointed over the fields again and offered the word "potato." Both very satisfied that we had established a connection, we shook hands again. But before we could exchange additional lessons, his friends at the tractor urgently requested his attention. I proceeded on my way to the cabin, waving and shouting *"La revedere!"*

Friday, May 2

I'm going home. Back to the States, that is. I bought a plane ticket to Boston today. I depart on May 24th. Negotiations with various local and national officials to obtain land for the Information Centre have been dragging on with no clear results. I hear bits and pieces. Apparently there was a deal with the Ministry of Defense for a large parcel of land in the hills just outside Zarnesti (in the same area of my first horseback ride), then there wasn't. Also apparently the mayor of Zarnesti is sometimes a CLCP ally and sometimes is not, lately saying that he wants the town to build a Centre of its own.

Anyway, it has become clear that any services I could provide for the Centre will not be needed for some time, six months minimum, and in the meantime I can probably accomplish more from the States. I can investigate museum exhibits there (such as the Boston Museum of Science), and with an Internet connection that actually works most of the time, and at something more than a snail's pace, I can better investigate technology options.

When I informed Christoph of my decision, he acknowledged there would probably be a lack of activity on the Centre throughout the summer, but added there is always plenty to do here and I can stay as long as I want. I was flattered by the offer, and I suppose there are always dead horses to get and fences to repair and ticks to remove and reports to edit and funds to solicit, and maybe even a pack of wolves to locate occasionally, but would there really be enough to keep me busy full-time throughout the summer? Anja will be guiding horseback tours, but somehow I don't see myself atop an eccentric steed guiding tourists who may have equestrian experience roping cattle in Patagonia and stalking Przewalski's wild horses in Mongolia. Maybe I could create other opportunities to contribute to the project, but I'm not certain, and when I began this adventure, I had resolved that boredom for more than short periods would be the one thing I would not tolerate.

Am I quitting too soon? After all, I'm still in an exotic land. Certainly there are plenty of new experiences to be had. Actually, I've barely seen Romania, having been totally occupied with the project during my stay in this small corner of Transylvania. But I didn't come here to be a tourist. And anyway, if things change and I'm really needed here again, I'll come back. I also have family and business matters pulling me to Maine. The stars are aligned; the time is now. Or three weeks from now. I will try to make the most of the time I have left.

Large, noisy trucks have been passing by the cabin on these hot, dry days, kicking up choking billows of dust that disperse slowly and mix with prior infusions forming a permanent haze that hangs over the entire valley. Other than those trucks bursting with logs that occasionally storm down from the wooded hills far up the valley, most of the vehicles are carrying full loads of gravel on the way in, and nothing on the way out, so there must be major construction going on somewhere up the road — something more than those new trophy homes, I suspect. I will miss many things when I leave the Barsa Valley, but not this infernal dust.

We finally modified a cabin tradition that we had been accepting with too little thought. Instead of going to all the trouble to burn the rotten animal parts and scat from the wolf enclosure, which would even further pollute the air of the valley, we've decided to make use of the Zarnesti dump. Surely the scrawny, feral dogs that eke out a living there, foraging through the stinking piles of rubbish while they breathe fire and dust and smoke and dodge rocks thrown at them, would make quick work of our offerings. So we donned our rubber gloves under our leather gloves (a system I had devised to effectively repel the putrid effuse while also preventing cuts to the rubber gloves and our skin) and picked up the decayed animal remains and stuffed them in double-lined garbage bags. I held my breath as much as possible throughout the operation, and gagged as little as possible, and, looking at Anja, who was trying not to laugh at my gags, I laughed at my gags, but it was a much quicker and cleaner operation than burning. On the drive up the hill to the dump we were amazed to see picnickers and sunbathers enjoying the day on the green, open slope just downwind from the smoking and reeking pit.

We had been told that Gypsies controlled the Zarnesti dump, whom the authorities were allegedly reluctant to challenge, so there was effectively no regulation over what kinds of materials ended up there. I treaded carefully on the dusty ground while trying to act as though it was our natural duty and right to toss the contents of our bags as far as possible onto the smoking heaps of refuse. The attendants were curious but gave us no trouble. We were happy to depart as the pathetic dogs slunk over to investigate our offerings.

Later, Barbara showed up at the cabin carrying yet another bag of foul content: the head of the wild boar we had found in March. Although it had been kept frozen, it was now thawing fast in the summer heat. And it was dripping. Barbara asked us to bury it somewhere on the cabin grounds so that the worms and other denizens of the soil would do the dirty work for us and strip the bones clean. Choosing a spot just off the path to our outhouse, I dug a hole about a half-meter deep and held my breath (I was becoming proficient at holding my breath) while I dumped the head into it. After filling the hole I covered the area with heavy rocks to prevent Curly and her visiting canine friends from retrieving the tasty prize.

Since the hot weather is causing our perishable food to quickly

198

spoil, I rigged up a "refrigerator" in the creek. I arranged rocks to form a box in the cold water that we cover with a flat rock to keep things submersed. The system works pretty well, provided the items are well sealed from the water, and provided we avoid the leeches when retrieving our food.

Sunday, May 4

A clear, sunny, and cooler (~20°C) day, which is a nice change from the oppressive (~30°C) humid heat of the past few days. I spent the morning at the office working out the high-level design of an educational computer game that Christoph conceived, which is intended for the Centre. In the afternoon I walked up the road that supposedly goes to the site where an illusory village was constructed for the set of *Cold Mountain*. I want to check it out someday, but my goal today was to determine whether there were any signs marking the trailheads that the project hopes to use for guided horseback riding tours in the summer. The picnic season is now in full swing and cars were parked everywhere, with music blaring from radios and people splashing in the river. I had been told that cars were not allowed on this road, but if so, the picnickers don't seem to know or care.

A new group of shepherd dogs has been visiting the cabin, once in the morning when their flock of sheep grazes slowly up the valley, and again in the evening when they drift back. This particular flock is usually attended by two boys, who, after we discovered them cautiously peering into the enclosure from the side one day, I invited over to see the wolves. As they gazed up the slope searching for the elusive predators, the boys were respectful and intrigued, but also appeared a little suspicious and guilty, as though they had been invited to stick their hands into the proverbial cookie jar.

Curiously, Curly has no interest in having convivial relations with one of the members of this new dog pack, a large, sly-looking, black dog with yellow, wolf-like eyes, which, also curiously, seems friendly towards me. Actually, maybe "friendly" isn't the right word. The dog shows absolutely no fear of me, nor, it seems, of anything else, and while not aggressive, it is difficult to drive off. Whenever I try, this strange dog doesn't budge and just looks at me as though it knows that I know its amity is a ruse, and I had better give it up.

If it approaches the cabin too closely, Curly attempts to attack, but the dog is no more afraid of her than of me, and Curly suddenly looks ridiculous trying to drive off a dog twice her size. Recently, Curly hasn't been finishing her food in the morning (perhaps she doesn't need as much nourishment in the warmer weather), and for two days running this mysterious dark visitor has stolen some of her leftovers. Yesterday morning, I watched Curly slink by the front corner of the cabin with a chunk of food in her mouth, and then, while I remained unobserved, she dug a hole, dropped the food into it, and carefully filled it in, using her snout to cover the evidence with leaves and dirt. This morning, again, Curly very deliberately, slyly, and effectively cached another chunk of her morning meal. In well over two months I had never before seen her cache her food. The Buddha dog must have started anticipating the arrival of this thief after it had stolen her food the previous two mornings, and decided to do something about it. I'm not sure how old Curly is, but she's definitely capable of learning new tricks.

A group from Four Paws, an Austrian-based animal welfare group, stopped by the cabin this afternoon. They had heard of a captive bear somewhere in the region, and wanted to know if we could rehab and release it. We had to inform them that a live bear, unfortunately, is a bit beyond our current means.

A rather long (around one meter) black snake has made its home along the path to our outhouse, which startled me the first time I ran into it. Actually, we believe it is of a poisonous variety, but it seems to be as happy avoiding us as we are avoiding it.

Monday, May 5
A group of horses has been left to roam freely in the valley, and today upon our return to the cabin we noticed that one of them — a large gray stallion — was no longer as free as its companions. A small log had been chained to this unlucky fellow. Maybe it was known to wander more than the others, which were mostly mares. In any case, the horse's legs had become entangled in the chain, and it could do no more than shuffle without serious risk of stumbling. Anja is a horse-lover, and upon seeing this horse and its predicament, she became incensed and stomped across the pasture to see

what she could do. I followed at a more measured pace, ready to offer my help, but having no idea what that might be. As Anja slowed to quietly approach the horse, it became frightened, confused, and finally antagonistic, and we couldn't do much more than watch and ponder. I was relieved to see this stallion later in the day, further down the valley, still dragging the log, but no longer entangled.

Tuesday, May 6

I finally got a bike from Hermann, the man who owns the eco-tourist business. Anja and I have only one vehicle, and sometimes different destinations. But now there will be no more walking seven kilometers to or from town, unless we want to. A bike is going to save us time. How natural it sounds to say something so unnatural! Is a bike a time machine that will allow me to experience, say two hours, while the rest of the world experiences only one?

Okay, the bike won't save us time, but it will get one of us to and from town more quickly so we can do other things besides walk. But why do we want to do other things besides walk? This eternal question presented itself most forcefully as I approached the shepherd's house on my first ride from the town to the cabin. I braced myself for the inevitable encounter. Would these shepherd dogs react to a cyclist the same way their likely relatives did on the trail above town a month ago? The answer was yes. But I wasn't about to make the same mistake twice, so now I peddled for all I was worth. The dogs charged, and I peddled harder (adrenaline can produce remarkable effects). The fastest dog, and unfortunately therefore the one most enraged, dashed along beside me for all it was worth. Thankfully, however, the shortest distance between two points is a straight line, a fact apparently known even by this determined dog, which couldn't divert any closer to intercept me without losing a centimeter or two. After it had charged along next to me for some indeterminate passage of time and space, marked by jarring bounces of my bike over some indeterminate number of holes in the road, the dog gave up for reasons of its own and I escaped, out of breath but unscathed. The bike saved me even more time than I had expected.

In the evening I joined Peter for a "walk," which turned out to be a trek at least halfway up Mt. Omu (2,506 m) in the Bucegi Mountain range. We hiked up to a ridge above tree line overlooking a sweeping cirque, where we scoped the silent slopes with binoculars, looking for any sign of wildlife in the fading gray light. We were hopeful for a glimpse of wolves or bears, or maybe even an elusive chamois, but other than a few small birds flittering nearby, the scene was eerily still. Alpine flowers were beginning to close for the night in a final shaft of orange glow as the sun departed behind Piatra Craiului, now a long black silhouette topped with orange-gray clouds hovering over the southwestern horizon. On our descent into the forest and the blackness of night, we caught the last hazy views of mountain villages, farms, and pastures scattered on the slopes of the rolling purple-blue-black hills piled between Piatra Craiului and us. Tiny yellow lights began to pierce the darkness like fireflies.

Last week some cows got into our yard, and since they left through a small opening on the east side of our driveway, across the stream and around the thicket of trees, and since no existing section of the fence was destroyed and the gate was closed, I assume that's how they got in. So I extracted another long, straight sapling from a clump of trees on the slopes, trimmed it, and stuck it through the trees in the thicket along the stream — no posts or nails required. With a piece of rope, I secured the far end of the rail to the short section of picket fence that runs along the eastern border of our property. I believe our lot is now finally livestock-proof (excepting the options I cited earlier that are always available to a determined animal).

This accomplishment is not without pleasing results. Our lot is lush indeed, as spring has settled fully into the valley. The moist earth of our yard around the little stream is completely hidden under a luxuriant cover of tall grasses and broad-leaf greens, and is sprinkled with yellow, white, and purple flowers, including many dandelions, some of which we intend to eat.

Wednesday, May 7

My third night alone at the cabin. Anja has been housesitting for the Prombergers. Last night a drunken picnicker was screaming for what seemed half the night. Or was it something entirely different?

In any case, perhaps some significant rain would do more good than simply reduce the dust.

While driving through the side streets of town this morning on our way to the hills for a hike, we were blocked by an unusual procession of flower-draped horses, carts, and people. One particularly elaborate cart wobbling solemnly past featured a man's large nose sticking up from a thick bed of flowers. For someone from America, where we sanitize, hide, and ignore death as much as possible, it took a moment for it to sink in: a dead man was passing. Here on these dusty streets death and life and love and grief were on beautiful and intimate display for the whole community to share. Even for strangers from a distant land.

While Anja and I sat and watched the people stroll past — the men and boys dressed in plain dark suits, the women in flowery dark dresses and wide-brimmed hats, and the little girls trailing at the end in purple and white dresses and carrying bouquets of flowers — I couldn't help wonder — was this man's life, or his death, suspect? Will these gentle folks, the dead man's former neighbors, friends, and family, pin his corpse to the ground with a stake through the heart, stuff garlic in its mouth, and put a scythe across its neck so it cannot rise up and still keep its head on its shoulders? Will they place sawdust or poppy seeds in the casket and along the path to town so the mysteriously animated corpse will spend the entire night compulsively counting, as mysteriously animated corpses are wont to do in these parts, instead of rampaging through the countryside looking for fresh blood, as they are also alleged to be so fond of?

Thanks especially to the famous novel already mentioned, along with all the ensuing adaptations, Transylvania is known the world over as the land of the undead, the land of the vampire. While legends of reanimated corpses drinking blood from living beings are widespread, occurring in one form or another at one time or another in most cultures throughout human history, the folklore of Eastern Europe provides the fascinating details that most people today associate with vampires.[102] The earliest of these legends significantly predates the icon of the genre, Vlad Dracula the Impaler, and indeed all of written history in these parts, and I wonder whether the stories could have had their genesis in early instances of wolves running amuck in the dead of night in pens full of vulnerable livestock. After all, vampires are not believed to limit their blood thirst to human victims, and in Romania the wolf is a form that may be taken by the roaming undead of night. The term "vampire" has Slavic roots (possibly deriving from an Indo-European root meaning "to fly"), but Romanians have other names for the many types of roving corpses. The most common is *strigoi*, derived from the Roman word *strix*, a nocturnal bird that fed on human flesh in Roman myths. The "dead" *strigoi* of Romania (there are also live versions — people who have not yet passed through the grave, but who consort with those who have) and the vampires of neighboring Slavic cultures have much in common, although the legends of the undead throughout Central and Eastern Europe seem to be much flavored by local details, as might be expected when folklore develops in the localized manner typical of traditional, pre-historic societies. As best as I can determine,[103] if this dead man whose nose we saw rolling past on a side street of Zarnesti had been a criminal, or a bastard, or a magician or sorcerer, or was unbaptized or excommunicated, or committed suicide, or had been particularly cruel or wicked in life, or had been born with certain features or defects such as teeth, a caul or a lot of hair, or had red hair and blue eyes, or was the seventh son of a seventh son [McNally and Florescu (1972)] or the seventh child of the same sex [Summers (2001)], then here in Transylvania precautions would be advised — and all the more so if he had been adverse to garlic in life. And should snake holes appear near the grave, or holes that look like snake holes, they should be filled immediately with water and kept filled to prevent the vampire from emerging from its earthy abode. And if family members and livestock start turning up dead, followed by neighbors, then the corpse should certainly be exhumed (during daylight of course, when it is sure to be there),[104] preferably while wearing garlic and wielding crosses made of wild rose thorns and carrying vials of holy water. And if the body appears somewhat robust for having been in the ground for a time, and the face has a ruddy complexion, or worst of all some blood around the mouth, there can be no doubt — the corpse must be pinned to the earth with a stake made of ash or aspen, preferably through the heart (ignoring as much as possible the consequent screams and yells), and then burned for good measure.

As I said, tonight is my third night alone at the cabin. I'm somehow comforted by the fact that the wild and powerful creatures living up the slope are my friends.[105]

Sunday, May 11

On Friday, Anja and I had completed another hike, this time through Zarnesti Gorge (where more plastic white flakes from of the filming of *Cold Mountain* lay scattered across the ground) and up onto the adjoining eastern ridges and spurs of Piatra Craiului, yet another mountain jaunt graced with spectacular vistas. We returned to the cabin in the late afternoon to find a woman dismantling our fence with an axe! I immediately leaped from the car and ran towards the culprit, a portly lady who I guessed to be in her fifties. Most of my laboriously planted posts and meticulously trimmed rails now lay in a heap on the pasture, and the boundary of our yard looked naked with about a third of the fence no longer standing. *"Nu! Nu!* Private!" I yelled.

The woman unbent herself and started ranting wildly, and once she realized I could not speak Romanian, loudly and wildly. Although she was here by horse-cart and was working the pasture with her husband (I assumed), who was busy across the road spreading manure from the cart, the woman was neatly and cleanly dressed and didn't appear to be an habitual worker of fields. Through yelling and gestures she made it completely clear that as far as she was concerned her land went all the way to the creek (from the road), and our fence, or at least the part that was now gone, had most definitely and obviously been on her property. I didn't know if it had or not, so I asked Anja for the phone and called Christoph. After explaining the basics, I handed the phone to the woman so she and Christoph could settle the matter while I would figure out how to restore the barrier, to which I have to say I had become emotionally attached and which now lay splayed about like the remains of a logging competition.

The woman was suspicious of the phone and held it uncertainly to her ear, but once she got going she and Christoph talked for quite some time. Or actually, while Christoph may have talked, the woman yelled, and when she handed me back the phone it was quite as heated as her emotions. Christoph explained that these people do own the pasture abutting the cabin's yard, but they continually dispute the boundary and a run-in or two with them happens every year. The parties have gone to court, where the project has prevailed, but on it goes.

While her man began to shout towards us — whether for her or at her was unclear — she now claimed with a little more precision, by more pointing and yelling, that her land extended to a wet depression running parallel and just prior to the stream. Thus she was now conceding a foot or so of her former claim. Our fence had curved away from this boggy ditch onto higher ground so the posts had a place to take hold, and I was reluctant to give up the turf. But Christoph had explained that no one really knows exactly where the boundary is, so via much gesticulation I agreed to move the fence as far as the ditch —a matter of a half meter in places, at most — if she would agree to desist in her destruction. She seemed to acquiesce, reluctantly, but then reverted to more verbal abuse. I decided to close the deal by walking away.

After not more than three steps, she pleaded with me to come back in a tone of exaggerated meekness. Taking a deep breath, I turned on my heels and faced the woman, who then, having got my attention, resumed railing at me. I reiterated the details of our agreement, but she had moved on to some other point, apparently related to the driveway.

I stood quietly until she finished, then indicated, with a shrug of my shoulders that I did not understand. More yelling. Another shrug. Christoph had suggested we go into the cabin and wait them out, so, after I was fairly sure I had made a strong enough impression that we would not tolerate any more destruction, we retreated.

We watched the woman's actions from the safety of our shelter until we saw her begin to rip up lush plants from around the stream — including from what she had just agreed was our property — and stuff them in a sack, presumably to provide as fodder for her livestock. Anja ran out, yelling in German, with me close behind. The woman began to laugh, but perhaps sensing our patience had finally reached its limit, she slowly strolled off to join her husband.

As this border war, or at least this particular battle, drew to a close, I wondered if our adversary was aware of the ironic fact that those precious plants, possibly the only ones of their kind left in the valley, had been protected from grazing by the very fence she sought to destroy.

It turned out that part of what had been demolished included the section of the fence that had been rebuilt last fall, which I hadn't yet bothered with, but which had been leaning in places and with which I hadn't been well satisfied. So I resolved to rebuild better and stronger than before, and that's what I've been doing over the past couple of days. Using large rocks to shore up the soggy soil, I've been carefully planting the posts at the very edge of the agreed-upon ditch — the edge most advantageous to the project's land claim, I have to admit.

Wednesday, May 14

Our new strategy for feeding the wolves is paying off. Which is a good thing, because in this warmer weather chunks of meat thrown into the enclosure morph into swarming balls of shiny metallic green-blue flies within minutes, and can be expected to remain as something resembling flesh for no more than two or three days. After that even the wolves don't care to go near it — not, at least, if they suspect a fresher morsel is likely to manifest soon.

We now give the wolves enough meat at a time so they can eat their fill over a couple of days, more or less. Then we wait two to four more days before feeding them again, depending on the voracity with which they devoured their prior portion, and on the intensity of Poiana's begging. (Crai hardly ever shows any outward signs of hunger.) In addition to reducing the accumulation of grotesque remains, we hope by this approach to more closely mimic conditions typically encountered by wolves in the wild.

Wild wolves tend to eat in sporadic binges, a pattern consistent with necessity, as wolves usually end up consuming a kill completely before another successful hunt can be achieved. In fact, because it may have been long since their previous meal, and because scavengers such as ravens, foxes, and bears are only too happy to share in the feast[106] — and because the wild world in general is so unpredictable — wolves usually voraciously consume as much as possible immediately following a kill (although possibly after a short rest on the part of the individuals most fatigued by the hunt). They will eat until their stomachs are full, with bellies and sides extended, or until the carcass is fully consumed, whichever comes first. Up to 10 kg (22 lbs) of food has been measured in the stomach of a newly fed wolf.

Wolves generally consume the nutrient-rich organs first, but if they have the opportunity they will munch down the entire carcass — organs, meat, fat, fascia, cartilage, bones — everything except the partially digested vegetation left in the intestinal tract – over a period of several days, if that's what it takes. Meat alone, without organs and bone, does not provide sufficient nutrition to sustain wolves over an extended period.

In winter, wolves can be more leisurely about their feast, both because the cold preserves the flesh, and because most scavengers have small mouths and cannot effectively tear into a frozen carcass (which, if it is too cold, can defeat even the efforts of wolves). Based on his research, Christoph has concluded that the average consumption per wolf after a kill is ten kilograms on the first day and six kilograms per day after that until the carcass is consumed. Other studies have shown that wolves will typically begin a second feeding four or five hours after their first engorgement, usually, especially in winter, after a nap. In spite of their aversion to the stomach contents of herbivores, wild wolves do sometimes eat vegetation, including berries, apples, and even grass (the latter possibly as a source of roughage to clean their guts).[107]

Poiana and Crai, now that we feed them this way, not being ones to contradict the intensive research into the dietary habits of their kind, both eagerly tear into their pieces of flesh immediately, which seems a healthier reaction than their previous apathy. Of course we've been keeping an eye on their weight, physical condition, and attitude to make sure they're not deprived. Poiana, at least, seems the picture of health. Crai, on the other hand, does not. He has been looking pathetic for weeks. He's shedding his winter coat, and looks haggard with irregular clumps of fur sticking haphazardly from his thinning hair. He's also visibly thin in his body, his legs look like fleshless sticks, and we can feel the bones of his shoulder blades protruding from his back. Yet the gaunt male wolf seems always serene, even regal (thus living up to his name) as he sits on his haunches up the slope and watches the world. Nevertheless, just to be sure, we asked both Barbara and Peter to look at him and give us their opinion. They assured us that Crai always looks thin and pathetic in the spring, when he does not usually have much of an appetite. Peter did suggest that we should give both wolves de-worming medication, which should be administered once a year in the spring as a precaution.

I've also been observing carefully to see whether Crai has been able to subvert Poiana's dictatorship when we open the gate to let them into the feeding pen, and I'm convinced he has. Previous to our new feeding strategy I hadn't actually seen him eat for weeks, but now, while Poiana still usually tries to chase him off his piece, and the wolves often end up swapping pieces as he goes for hers, Poiana is so occupied with satisfying her own craving that her threats are half-hearted and don't usually prevent Crai from satisfying his.

I awoke this morning to a mouse scampering over my bed.

Conditions have been a bit unpleasant at the cabin lately. Lots of pesky flies with mean bites, and lots of dust and noise from the heavy trucks. Police or military personnel were shooting again this morning. This isn't feeling like the remote, peaceful setting it was in the winter.

As I sit on the shelf that serves as a bench along the front side of the cabin and look westward towards the late afternoon sun, the sunlight illumes swarms of countless insects — tiny moving beings swimming in the air. They can be seen darting about independently of the air currents, which are traced by the inert dust. The atmosphere seems no less full of self-propelling life than the plankton-rich surface water of oceans.

Pairs of pale yellow butterflies are playing, dancing, and apparently courting, as by hooking up they occasionally confute the illusory randomness of their floating and fluttering in the breezes. Are these minute flying beings witnesses enough to resolve quantum questions, to collapse the fundamental constituents of the universe's matter and energy into particular quantum states? If not, perhaps the storks that have been hanging out in the meadows around the cabin can do the job — perhaps *they* can play the role of Schrödinger's cat.[108]

Thursday, May 15
Offers of dead animals have been arriving about one per week. I've

been adamant about not accepting anything more than we need and can handle, but now our freezer is down to half full. So when our cell phone rang last evening, I had already figured we'd have to take the next offer that came along. Sure enough it was Christoph, and sure enough he asked the question. Do we need a dead horse? Anja and I exchanged the usual resigned nods, although we knew about one more week would have been ideal.

"Yes. But ask them to cut it into small pieces. And no hide."

We had been having great difficulty prying and hacking the large, frozen pieces of the Pestera horse out of the freezer, as they had frozen into a solid block of ice, meat, and bone. Due to the humidity I had anticipated this problem and had put plastic trash bags between the pieces, but they didn't really help. The ice just sort of formed over and around and through the thin sheets of plastic until they were irrelevant. So from now on I wanted to store only smaller pieces of flesh, which should be easier to pry apart and which we should also be able to more tightly pack.

I knew we wouldn't have enough space for this new offering — half the freezer wouldn't hold half of a horse — but the supply of unmarketable dead animals is not a sure thing. Understandable when there is a market of probably one. We had been told that weeks can go by between offers, and that after one such dry spell the project was forced to purchase a live sheep for slaughter (the wolves had been given dog food, but they do not thrive on it over an extended time). This is not something we want to repeat, so it was agreed: small pieces, no hide, pick the horse up tomorrow in Rasnov at 4:30 p.m., and pay 2.5 million lei (about $75).

After experiencing three or four of these dead animal pickups, we can never be sure what to expect, so we grabbed our rubber-within-leather-gloves system, girded ourselves for whatever mess would be thrown at us, and drove in the afternoon to the town of Rasnov to get the horse. We followed the directions to a neat stucco house, which was on a quiet side street tucked among other neat stucco houses — probably the closest thing to a suburb-like residential neighborhood in these parts. Entering the gated drive-way on foot, I silently rehearsed my limited Romanian vocabulary. I could see the back yard and adjoining barn, but I saw no dead horse and no live people. I knocked on the door and announced our arrival. No response. I knocked and yelled *"buna ziua"* a little louder. A woman came to the door and I got the usual blank stare when I tried to explain our purpose. I stammered and signed until finally a glint of comprehension swept her countenance. She pointed over the fence to the yard next door. Easy mistake: same kind of house, same kind of yard, same kind of barn.

As we entered through the gate of the correct house and walked toward the back yard, several pounding moments passed before I could completely process what confronted our senses. There, lying on its side in the dust was the huge, black body of a horse. At first I thought it was motionless and therefore dead. A foul odor hanging in the hair seemed to confirm this conclusion. But as I watched the horse's ribcage slowly, almost imperceptibly rise, I realized I had been hearing at the boundary of my awareness the extremely low frequency sound of the horse's raspy, hollow breath, rolling like the rumble of thunder through the heavy air and even through the earth. I now realized I had even heard it from next door. The man had called yesterday. How long had this poor creature lay here suffering?

Anja and I immediately rushed from the horrid scene out into the street towards our pickup truck. Anja was livid. We stopped and faced each other.

"What are we going to do? The horse is going to continue suffering if we don't take it," I said.

"There is no way I'm going back in there!" Anja replied with tears in her eyes. She couldn't hold still and was pacing back and forth like a raging tiger in a cage.

I opened the gate and returned to the house, determined to do something, even if it was just to convey our rage. A small, dirty, nervous man, with no front teeth, came to the door and rushed out, as though wanting to escape from what was inside. The sound of the horse's death-struggle continued to pound in my consciousness.

"What the hell is going on!?" I yelled in English.

He didn't understand my words, but he understood my anger. Anja, who was observing from the street, had already started calling Barbara, and I went to get the phone.

"Ask him why the horse is not dead!" I bellowed into the little cell phone, redirecting my anger from the uncomprehending man towards my blameless friend as I calculated the probabilities. Likely he had kept the poor beast alive to keep it "fresh" so we'd be sure to pay the 2.5 million. Maybe he would even try negotiating for more. I handed him the phone and had to interrupt my rage to show him how to use it before he began a loud, animated conversation with Barbara. When I got the phone back, Barbara explained that someone else had offered him three million and now he wanted more money.

[Yeah, right! Who the hell else is buying dead horses?]

Anja told me that the man tried to grab my arm as I turned away to leave in disgust.

Later in the evening we drove to the Brasov train station to pick up Kolja, a former student from Germany who had worked at the project in the past and was visiting for a few days. On our way back to the cabin we stopped at the Prombergers' so Kolja could say hello and get reacquainted. Of course that unfortunate horse was still haunting our thoughts, and I asked Barbara whether the guy had called back yet.

"No."

"I thought he would call back. I don't think he really has another buyer, I think he was just trying to get more money."

"He hasn't called."

"Well, maybe I'm wrong…" But I didn't really think so.

Friday, May 16

Barbara called in the morning. "The guy wants to sell us the horse. Now he'll take two million."

"No way."

"The horse is still alive."

My God! I had felt sure that if the horse had not expired on its own, the man would have killed it by now. How could anyone live with that inconceivable suffering reverberating from their yard? We were at a loss once again, but reluctantly decided that however repugnant it was to give the guy money, if it was the quickest way to get the horse out of its misery, we better make a deal.

"Tell him the horse is to be dead and cut into pieces when we get there at 10:30 a.m. Make it clear that if our conditions aren't met, there is no deal."

The man agreed.

We drove to Rasnov with the hope that at least the horse would now be dead, but still wondering what we'd run into. We tried to take our minds off the possibilities by listening to Kolja's stories about his time on the project. Arriving at the house we walked through the gate and into the driveway. There was no one in sight so we continued around to the back yard. The huge, dark mass lay in the same place, in the same dust and the same heat. It was not cut up. I was not happy.

"Is it dead?" I heard Anja's voice synchronize perfectly with my own urgent question as I approached the horse.

"Yes," I answered, detecting no motion and seeing its open, dead eyes.

Then I began to hear the start of a deep rumble, just an instant before I saw the horse's massive side begin to rise. "No!!!!" I let out an anguished yell. We stepped back and stared at the horse in disbelief, watching while the air from its nostrils kicked up a feeble stream of dust from off of the dry ground.

We rushed to the street and piled into our truck. As I was turning the key, the man came running frantically out of the house. [No way. We're out of here.]

I was pulling into the street just as he reached our truck. He was screaming at us to wait, and then gestured desperately for the cell phone. I hesitated for a moment before turning off the engine. Anja and I looked at each other. Leaving was not going to help. Anja struggled to hold back tears as she dialed the phone.

He hadn't found anyone to butcher the horse. That is, until that moment. A wobbly wooden cart was approaching pulled by two red-tasseled horses. They were plodding along under the whips of two Gypsy men who were sitting on the front of the cart while another reclined leisurely in back. The owner of the not quite dead horse pointed at the men as though they were his saviors: the executioners had arrived. Colorfully attired in baggy orange, yellow, red, and brown clothes, the men hopped off the cart sporting bright, friendly smiles, and bright, sharp knives gleaming from their belts.

We still didn't want to deal. We didn't want to reward this man for his callousness, and I thought the horse was probably no longer conscious and beyond all suffering anyway. But we couldn't be sure, so we got out of the truck. The three parties — the owner of the horse, the Gypsies, and the foreigners — formed a triangle in the street and a heated "discussion" ensued. As Anja, Kolja, and I debated what to do, the Gypsy men seemed to realize their opportunity was in jeopardy. They were very animated and effective at expressing their enthusiasm for the task, and how dissatisfied they'd be if we backed out. Finally we decided that the interest of the horse superseded all principles. I asked in Romanian how long it would take. Their answer was intelligible immediately. "An hour... no, no, an hour and a half."

"Okay, we'll return in an hour and a half."

On the drive out of Rasnov to kill an hour and a half we called Barbara to fill her in.

"You don't have to return."

"What?"

"He violated our agreement twice. We're under no obligation. Don't go back if you don't want to."

We didn't want to. But we reminded ourselves that the time to decide had passed. The men who had arrived to butcher the horse had had no part in the deception and cruelty, and they were currently working hard at a grisly task. We shouldn't return dishonor for dishonor. We had an opportunity to set an example. We did discuss, however, the idea of not paying the full two million. Maybe we would only take part of the horse, since we probably wouldn't be able to fit all of it into the freezer, and just pay for what we'd take.

We drove the twelve kilometers to Zarnesti and went to the freezer in Moserel's barn to rearrange the old meat to make more room. That task complete and an hour passed, we headed back to the house in Rasnov to find what we would find. We had been surprised too many times to expect what we should expect.

The Gypsy men were just finishing their work as we walked into the yard. We were amazed at what we saw. The horse's hide had been cleanly removed and was piled in a heap off to the side, while on the ground directly in front of us were twenty or so chunks of meat neatly stacked like firewood on top of a plastic tarp. The meat was fresh and red and looked healthier dead than the horse had looked alive. The head of the unfortunate animal sat upright on the ground, its dead eyes looking no different than when the creature was lying on its side just a couple of hours ago. There was little blood, in stark contrast to the gory red mess we had witnessed in Pestera. These guys were obviously pros at killing and butchering livestock. I had heard stories about the Gypsies — about how there are gangs like the Mafia, and the police do not dare to go into their villages to enforce the law, so they have their own — and I wondered at what other tasks these three men were so adept with their flashy knives and bloodied axes.

Whatever they might be, these men were obviously eager to please us. They asked with gestures if we wanted any pieces cut smaller. We did, and they were quick and accurate in following our directions, continuously checking to be sure we were satisfied. We asked them to trim the meat from the ribs, because we didn't want the large rib cages and other pieces that were mostly bone,[109] nor the head, nor the stomach. The owner wasn't happy that we were leaving so much, but we didn't have much sympathy for him. We were impressed with the results, however, and since we were taking all the useful meat, we agreed to pay the two million lei.

The Gypsy leader was a long-nosed, narrow-faced fellow, around thirty years old. His facial expressions and gestures were jovial in an almost exaggerated manner, as though intentionally masking an inner graveness. It seemed his friendly demeanor could evaporate in a flash given the slightest provocation. By the time they had loaded all the pieces into our truck, I had already thought we should tip the men for their excellent work when the leader turned to me with a smile and an open hand and pleaded for *suta*. He pointed to himself and each of his companions. He was asking for 100,000 lei for them all (around $3). His knife flashed as he wiped it back and forth on his leg in a seemingly absent-minded manner, and an almost imperceptible shift of his eyes acknowledged that he noticed that I noticed.

But really I felt no serious threat from this man as he continued to plead with a cheerful, even humorous demeanor. It happened that I had only 50,000 lei notes, so I handed him one. He gestured profuse thanks (whereupon I momentarily worried for my hand), and the word *multsumesc* had barely escaped from his lips before he pointed at his two companions. Knowing I had only the 50,000 lei notes, I wondered if 150,000 would be too extravagant. While one should certainly be generous in a poor country, being overly so can distort economic decisions in inappropriate ways (e.g., it can lead to dependency, intolerable begging, or antagonistic competition). But I decided it was okay and handed 50,000 lei to each grateful man.

In the meantime the neighbor to whose house we had first gone showed up to check in on the strange goings on. She spoke German, so she translated a discussion between Anja and Kolja and the horse owner regarding the payment, and relayed the fact we were furious with the way he had treated the horse, and passed along our request that the Gypsy men be fairly paid according to the original terms, even though we had tipped them generously. The Gypsies, apparently, concurred about the treatment of the horse and joined in chastising the owner.

By tossing a couple of the old pieces, we managed to get almost all of the new pieces of meat into the freezer, and gave the rest to the appreciative wolves. At least none of that poor horse's body was going to waste. We were happy the whole sorry affair was over, and I knew it would be the last dead animal retrieval that I would have to contend with in Romania.

Sunday, May 18

Last evening, Anja, Kolja, and I took the extraordinary step of dining out at one of the two (as far as I know) regularly open restaurants in Zarnesti, the one located in the *pensiunea* at the foot of the road that leads into Zarnesti Gorge. This guesthouse appeared to be long established and may be the only tourist-related business in Zarnesti that doesn't have some relationship with the CLCP (as far as I know). I imagine it has long served tourists coming to see the spectacular gorge, including perhaps state officials of the socialist era, and perhaps Ceausescu himself (I've been told he sometimes hunted in the hills above the Barsa valley).

The only other patrons in the dark dining room were a boisterous group of young adults, or perhaps they were teenagers. As they heard us speaking English and struggling with the menu, a young man came over to help. Once he learned I was from America, he enthusiastically tried to engage me in a conversation about American foreign policy. I resisted. Since arriving in Romania, I have had no real news of the larger world. I believe it is enough for me to know what is happening in this small corner of Romania. For most of human existence people's worldviews have extended no further than the neighboring valley, not beyond the nearest raging river or wide lake or impassable mountain range, and what the shopkeepers, townsfolk, farmers, shepherds, dogs, wolves, and my friends are up to in this valley and in these hills and in this town holds enough fascination and mystery for me.

After we had finished eating, the man — or boy, really — again approached our table and asked Kolja if he would send them copies of the photos they had seen him taking in their direction. Kolja obliged by getting up and posing them for a group photo. After the flashes ceased, several *multsumescs* followed the photographer back to our table. Without really thinking about it, I took it upon myself to reply, *"Cuplacherie"* (You're welcome).

Whatever ice remained was broken and the entire group of seven or eight youths rushed over to our table and crowded around us, eager to hear this American who could speak Romanian. They could all speak English, and the girls, especially the two bravest who introduced themselves as Tatiana and Katya, excitedly asked Anja and I to repeat every word of Romanian we knew. They giggled with delight at every one. I suggested our botched pronunciations were the primary source of their mirth, but this they denied; they were simply delighted to hear foreigners speaking their native tongue. We learned they were high school seniors from Galatia on a three-day vacation to the mountains. When I asked what they planned to do after graduation, they all shrugged their shoulders, and seemed more curious about what we were doing in Zarnesti than in what their future would hold.

Monday, May 19

Moserel's black Cerberus no longer guards his gate. Did the beast meet its demise naturally, or did its one-dimensional personality become unbearable? And will it be replaced by the poor creature cowering in the dust just outside the barn, a puppy chained such that it can barely escape a permanently dark, lonely, and hot wooden box? Pitifully aggressive/submissive, the puppy's wrath immediately converts to pathetic groveling whenever it is approached with any hint of kindness. I have seen the same with many dogs here, and as I walk along the streets of Zarnesti, I see, or more often only hear, dogs chained to small, loveless spaces, which, due to their fear and anger at the cruel world for their luckless plight, bark at every passerby. Such is the lot of dogs kept and treated to be alarm systems and guards. There are dogs here that are loved and well cared for, but I wonder if the perpetually hungry and filthy strays are luckier than some.

Stakes have been placed in the ground about 150 meters up the valley from Cabanna Lupului, on the same side of the road, up the stream that is our water supply. The stakes appear to delineate the prospective boundaries of a house and driveway. This valley is changing, and the cabin will not be isolated much longer.

The woman with whom we had the border dispute showed up today. We had been worried that our truce was temporary, and watched anxiously as she approached our new barrier, ready for action if she attacked the fence. She carefully inspected the location of the posts, and as I walked over to give her the opportunity to express her judgment, she began to point and talk with an exaggerated skeptical demeanor. She thought I had taken liberties in the interpretation of our agreement by placing the posts a few centimeters from the center of the trough that we had agreed was the border. She was right. But I let her harvest some of the plants on our side of the fence, and she seemed satisfied. Her canvas bag bursting with the fragrant greenery, we even ended with a pleasant "conversation" in Romanian, although I only understood about 5 percent of what she said.

Wednesday, May 21

Yesterday, wanting to experience during my final days in Romania as much of the local life as possible, I set out on my own. I wanted to travel as local people travel, so at 9:00 a.m. I boarded a bus in the center of Zarnesti that was stuffed with morning commuters destined for Brasov. After the minor uncertainties and errors typical of such a journey in an unfamiliar land (i.e., not getting off at the right places to make the necessary connections), I eventually arrived at my intended destination: Brasov's "Centrum."

I walked first to the famous trash bins located at an apartment complex in the nearby Racadau neighborhood, where in the evenings people gather to watch the wild bears that come down from steep, forested slopes abutting the city's central district to feed from the garbage.[110] The site has become an informal but significant tourist venue for the city, where people pose for photos with the "Racadau bears" and sometimes try to feed them by hand. The CLCP has long been concerned about this situation and has been trying to educate the public about the risks of close encounters with wild European brown bears — whether in a remote mountain forest or at a dumpster near the center of a large city — and has been trying to convince the civic leaders of Brasov to institute a garbage management plan that will stop attracting the bears. The city administration, however, seems reluctant to inhibit a popular source of entertainment both for local residents and for tourists.

[In July 2004, two people were injured in an attack by a female bear at the garbage containers of Racadau. In October of the same year, a rabid bear attacked several people picking mushrooms in the nearby forest. One man was killed at the scene, and at least one other died subsequently (some reports state that two people died subsequently).[111] As a result, Brasov was put under a "rabies alert."]

The impressive Black Church, "the largest Gothic church between Vienna and Istanbul", dominates the central plaza of Brasov.[112] Built in the fourteenth century on the site of an earlier church, which was destroyed by Mongol invaders in 1242, the Black Church was originally Roman Catholic. It was converted to Lutheran during the Reformation. Its name derives from the blackening the walls suffered during a fire set by Hapsburg invaders in 1689. The church contains many beautiful and interesting art objects: statues, frescoes, and the largest mobile bell in Romania. Services are still conducted for the small German community residing in the city, and recitals performed on its immense organ are a famous tourist attraction.

Unfortunately the church was closed, so after circling the imposing stone structure, I walked around the plaza and along numerous side streets of the attractive city center, ate a quick lunch, and began to plot my return to Zarnesti. Instead of taking the trolley from the Centrum, I walked the two kilometers to the Bartolemeu bus stop, situated along the main drag on the northern side of the city, where I assumed a bus to Zarnesti would eventually pass, since it was the way I had come. As I stood in the oppressive midday heat amidst the dust and noise of heavy traffic, my feet feeling a little sore and my mouth a little dry, if I began to indulge thoughts of discomfort or inconvenience, I staved them off by imagining the immeasurably worse plight of scores of Brasov merchants and their families, who, 544 years ago, writhed on stakes on the bleak dusty hill just across the busy street, while Vlad the Impaler sat comfortably dining at his table and watched.[113] Known today as Timpa Hill, the knoll is barren of trees and covered only with scattered thorny weeds, an ignoble and ignored rise of earth that appears cursed by its inglorious past.

Having waited semi-patiently for about forty-five minutes, when the bus finally arrived I was standing near the front of the line, anxious to board and take a seat to relieve my road-weary feet. After the doors closed and the bus took off, I counted myself fortunate to be onboard. I had felt like a rock in the middle of a rushing mountain stream as my fellow prospective passengers swarmed around me and clambered for the narrow steps and door of the rusty old transport. By the time I finally managed to climb the steps and enter the hot, stuffy interior, I was the last one on, and the bus was full.

[The Romanian people are known to be devout, and perhaps they honor the truth that many who are first will be last, and the last first.[114]]

As I took my spot at the front of the aisle I consoled myself with the fact that I had a handrail overhead to hold onto to and a nice view out the front window. I could stand a bit longer — after all, there was no space to fall should my legs give out — and surely the crowded bus wouldn't stop for more people. It wouldn't be long to Zarnesti.

At the next stop I marveled at several stalwart and desperate souls who managed to cling to their positions in the aisle like seaweed in the surf as seven or eight more bodies squirmed on board and I was forced past them in a surge. Perhaps these folks holding their ground were fortified by the knowledge they would be among the next to depart. In any case, surely *now* the bus was full and my tiny little space was safe.

At the next stop, a few more people squeezed onboard. And a few more after that. Apparently, no prospective passenger was going to be denied, regardless of the conditions on the bus. Even though I had maneuvered so as to keep my face relatively clear of the armpit of the man hanging onto the rail in front of me (a condition several others could not avoid), I still could only manage short gasps as my need for oxygen competed with my reluctance to breathe the foul air.

As we approached Cristian, I was sustained by hopes that the inflection point had been passed, that from here to Zarnesti more people would be getting off than on. I was convinced it was physically impossible to squeeze any more human beings onto the bus. I was in need of further education. A couple of people did get off at the stop, but I was shoved even further back as about five more victims embarked. Likewise at Rasnov. I drew strength from the impaled at Timpa Hill, but I also wondered why someone wouldn't at least open the windows.

After a bumpy, swaying, sweltering ride of about fifteen more minutes, during which the primal necessity for oxygen and space, so often taken for granted as we bustle about our lives in the West, was forced into my awareness, we finally reached the outskirts of Zarnesti. Now I was certain there would be some relief. A few got off, but about the same number got on. Nevertheless, it was the first stop at which our condition hadn't worsened, and from this I extracted a glimmer of hope. At the next few stops more people got off, almost none got on, and our precious personal spaces began to expand, until finally, with about two kilometers to go before the center of town, I was actually able to plop down in a vacant seat.

Could this be the normal daily commute for most of these poor souls? The woman I was sitting next to did not appear to be Romanian. I glanced at the book she was reading. English. "Hello, I see you speak English?"

She explained she is from Britain and works helping children for a charity about fifty kilometers from Zarnesti, at a "really remote location in the sticks" (I think it was Save the Children – Romania). She's been here about eight years.

"Is the bus always this crowded?"

"This isn't really crowded. And at least one window is open a little. Romanians are afraid of draughts, and usually they won't open the windows at all…"

Thursday, May 22

My little excursion to Brasov yesterday was intended primarily as a dry run with the Romanian public transportation system in preparation for the trip I planned to take today by bus and train to the city of Sibiu, my one truly touristic experience in Romania before I leave in two days. I chose Sibiu because it is not too distant (perhaps 150 km, as the human rides), my time is limited, and I had heard it spoken of several times by several people. I had heard it is home to the "King of the Gypsies."

The use of the word "Gypsy" originated in the Middle Ages from the erroneous belief that this darker complexioned ethnic minority scattered throughout Europe, and possessing a distinct linguistic heritage, migrated from Egypt. The term has recently been discouraged, with the hope that a new label will not carry historical prejudices and pejorative connotations. The recommended word is now "Roma" (adjective,"Romani"), which derives from the peoples' own name for their traditional language, *Romanes*, as well as from the Romani word for a married Roma man, *Rom*.[115] In spite of the similarity, as far as I can determine, the words "Romanes," "Rom," and "Roma" bear no etymological relationship with the "Roman" heritage of Romania.[116]

According to an analysis of genetic evidence, the Roma (who recognize several subgroups among themselves) migrated from northern India some forty generations ago, perhaps as soldiers in the employ of, or as slaves captured by, Muslim armies from the west, and arrived in Wallachia as early as the twelfth century.[117] Once in Europe they were initially free, many working as metalsmiths and soldiers important to military forces, especially to the armies of Hungary and Slovakia, and many serving as musicians. Enslavement of Romani people is first recorded in the fourteenth century when princes in Wallachia and Moldavia captured them as they participated in Tartar-led raids. By the fifteenth century the enslavement of *Tsigani* (as they were called in the provinces) became more widespread, as the *robi* (as Tsigani slaves were called) were forced into service, especially as craftsmen and blacksmiths. Vlad Tepes reportedly was only too happy to participate in the oppression of the Tsigani, including those he captured in battles with the

Turks among the many victims of his atrocities. In Hungary, along with the Ottoman invasions of the fifteenth century came suspicion of the Tsigani, and even misidentification with the enemy, so restrictions were applied to their lifestyles and commerce, causing them to become increasingly nomadic.

During the fifteenth century in Wallachia and Moldavia, the restrictions and oppressions increased and the robi[118] were divided into occupational categories, the names of which are still used by Roma clans to this day. Over the next centuries the robi shared the desperate and deteriorating social and economic lot of the other oppressed classes of the region — the indentured peasants and serfs — albeit with extra indignities such as being kidnapped and forced into the slave trade by *ghazi* raiders from the south. In the eighteenth century a few small steps toward less harsh treatment of slaves and serfs in Wallachia and Moldavia were taken, as certain local leaders began to limit particularly offensive practices like removing Roma children from their parents to be sold. Some of the state robi (as opposed to privately owned slaves) were given "a few liberties,"[119] but nobles resisted major changes. The boyars probably didn't want to give up a convenient arrangement: almost all their cooks, craftsmen, and laborers were Roma slaves and therefore free of cost except what was required to keep them alive. Meanwhile, in Transylvania decrees by Joseph II (Holy Roman Emperor and King of Hungary) in 1784 and 1785 allowed serfs to marry, work at a trade, move freely, and sell property.

Episodes of Russian control in Wallachia and Moldavia during the 1800s brought the sympathies and reforms then sweeping Russia in the treatment of serfs and peasants, which led to the governor of Wallachia, Alexander Ghica, granting freedom to state slaves in 1837. The governor of Moldavia, Mihail Sturdza, followed suit in 1842, and finally, with the revolutionary spirit evolving in Europe and conditions spurred by another Russian occupation, the ownership of all human beings was outlawed in the two provinces by 1856. Full emancipation followed the unification of the provinces, when relief from feudal dues and tithes, relief from restrictions on movement, and the ability to buy the land they worked, was granted to all peasants by decree of the Prince of the Union of Principalities, Alexander Ioan Cuza, in 1864. (To achieve this, he had to dissolve the previous parliament and hold a national referendum in order to circumvent the resistance of the large landowners.)

The lot of most Roma did not improve much, if any, during the decades following emancipation. While a few Roma did eventually integrate into the dominant society, thousands chose to use their newly acquired freedom of movement to emigrate from the kingdom. Others continued living in their settlements of shanties and working for their previous owners, and still others, perhaps the majority, continued to live a nomadic lifestyle (to the chagrin of politicians and authorities who tried to stop the common practice of living in tents in the summer and underground hovels in the winter).

The nomadic Roma were considered skilled at stealing and cheating, even by other Roma, but the energy of Roma workers was respected and their abilities as metalworkers, blacksmiths, bricklayers, farmers, laborers, and musicians was appreciated, if not highly valued (i.e., paid). Some Roma musicians became famous and well-paid performers. (Indeed, musical traditions throughout Central and Eastern Europe and beyond have been richly influenced by Roma music and Roma musicians, from the traditional folk music of the region, to the bolero and flamenco of Spain, to European jazz, to classical works by composers such as Brahms and Liszt.) Nevertheless, throughout the twentieth century efforts were made to force the settlement and assimilation of the Romani people, while many faced discrimination, deplorable conditions of housing, nutrition, health, employment and education, and holocaust.

During Ceausescu's regime, and especially as the dictator's control tightened and his eccentricities worsened in the 1980s, conditions for the entire populace of Romania (excepting Ceausescu's cronies) deteriorated. The country became increasingly impoverished under inept central planning, to the point where the people finally revolted and overthrew the regime in 1989. Roma activists participated in the revolution and Roma political parties have since evolved, but many of the Roma communities in Romania have continued to struggle. Some have fared worse without the social net of the planned economy on which they relied.

Before I left for Sibiu I told Anja that if I was not back by the end of the day, she'd be welcome to try to find me tomorrow. My journey went smoothly enough, however, and was memorable primarily for the opportunity it gave me to see from the train window some of the verdant Romanian countryside of the northern foothills of the Fagaras range of the Transylvanian Alps, and to explore on foot a small part of a Romanian city founded by German settlers some 800 years ago.[120] The former consists of gently rolling hills covered with forests and meadows and croplands stretching for kilometer after kilometer, with very few human dwellings or other structures. The latter is a city of about 155,000 residents situated near the geographical center of Romania, perched on a plateau nestled in a depression between the Fagaras and Cindrel Mountains. Sibiu abounds with interesting architecture and possesses a distinctive old centre, which is being considered for UNESCO World Heritage Site status. If you find a photo of the city taken on a clear day with a prospect towards the south, you will see white towers, medieval walls and fortifications, and red-roofed Gothic and Baroque churches, cathedrals, and houses, with a backdrop of snow-capped peaks (in the right season). But this is a view I was denied on this cloudy day. I walked around the central plaza and adjoining narrow streets having no idea of the historical or cultural significance of the venerable and colorful old buildings, but wishing I had, while keeping a watchful eye out for the King of the Gypsies. After my short tour I grabbed a quick lunch from a tiny food stall, sat on one of the benches lining the plaza under sprinkles of rain to eat it, and began to plot my return to Zarnesti.

So what about the "King of the Gypsies"? I can't say I ever found him, or his residence, but that may have been due to my lack of time and knowledge. After emancipation, the nomadic Roma and those sedentary Roma who maintained traditional lifestyles —particularly the *Ursari* ("bear trainers") and *Laješi*, who had enjoyed freedom of movement during the enslavement period because of their occupations (for example, as musicians) — traveled or settled in family groups called *salas*, each of which was led by a *jude*. Groups of *judes*, in turn, elected leaders called *buljubašas* in dramatic outdoor ceremonies that featured thrice tossing the honored chief into the air from a blanket. These Roma buljubašas were the "Gypsy kings" of Roma clans. They rode horses and dressed dramatically, were paid tributes, and held considerable political and judicial power. The buljubašas chose a Grand *Voivode* who served as the final judicial authority for all the Roma in the country as well as their primary interface with the Romanian government. By the early twentieth century the buljubašas and their grand leader no longer held official political power, but they remained influential within the Roma communities, and are still symbolic of the unique and colorful culture of the Roma people.

When I was there, Sibiu, it turns out, was home to one Florin Cioaba, self-proclaimed "King of Roma Everywhere." The "position" was actually created by Mr. Cioaba's flamboyant father Ion Cioaba, originally the buljubaša of the "Nomadic Metalworking Gypsies." The elder Cioaba invented and adopted the title (at the time, it was "King of the Gypsies Everywhere") in a staged public coronation in 1992, in which he had a thirteen-pound gold crown placed on his head in front of 5,000 followers. With no precedent or unanimity among modern Roma regarding such a position (he was challenged by a rival several months later who declared himself "Emperor of All the Gypsies"), some regarded Cioaba as primarily a publicity hound, but he did have legitimate credentials as a political activist and advocate for Romani rights and recognition, dating from the Ceausescu era until he died in 1997.[121] In any case, upon his death Florin claimed his father's title.[122]

Today, unless they venture from the hotels of the cities, and away from the airports and train and bus stations, the most prevalent image of the Romani people the traveler to Romania is likely to get derives from aggressive begging common at travel depots. It does seem that certain Romani individuals (adults and children) have finely honed the skill to plead. Whenever I arrived at the Brasov depot I was usually immediately accosted by a woman or a child (or a woman carrying a child) spewing a strange, continuous, monotonic verbal stream, with hands held out or even grabbing at me. However, according to the official Romanian census, there are over 535,000 Roma people living in Romania,[123] and since I never witnessed more than four or five at a time working the busy Brasov train station, one can certainly conclude those few are not representative of an entire people. Unfortunately, however, the aggressive beggars do know how to cause significant discomfort for naïve western travelers, and therefore have a disproportionate effect on perceptions.

For those travelers who do make it to the countryside, the impoverished circumstances of many Roma is apparent in the distinctive "Gypsy villages," collections of tottering but colorful shacks and shanties strung along roads or nestled into small sections of larger towns. In spite of rumors about crime and gangs, and while many Roma in the countryside met me with intense stares, none gave me any trouble, and if the ice was broken, whether with a family riding along in a cart pulled by red-tasseled horses, or whether with three men butchering one of the same, they were usually pleasant and friendly, or, like the attendants at the Zarnesti dump, at first curious and then indifferent.

At the Sibiu train station I experienced again the curious dynamics of Romanian queues: whenever I got in a line (I initially did not get in the right one), the people who arrived after me invariably shifted to one side or the other of my position, diverting the "line" in such a way that I was no longer in it. When I finally maneuvered my way to the ticket window, the clerk dealt with me brusquely, taking an inordinately long time to examine my passport before reluctantly stamping, one at a time and with lots of significant pauses in between, the three or four paper tickets that look like they had been printed forty years ago and handled frequently since. I guess the stamps were the only assurance the tickets hadn't been simply picked up off the ground. Wondering whether I was being directed to Brasov or to Novosibirsk (Siberia), before yielding my spot at the window I repeated "Brasov?" again to ensure I'd end up on the one-hop train to my desired destination.

It seemed I had; at least the countryside looked the same. At one stop a young professional-looking woman entered my compartment and took a seat across from me. She was immediately followed by a rather scruffy-looking man who sat next to me and lit up a cigarette, ignoring the no smoking sign posted on the wall. As I was trying to decide whether I should try expressing my displeasure in Romanian or by gestures, the woman pointed to the sign and told the man, in no uncertain terms, to get lost — or so I assumed, since that is what he did. Grateful for her interdiction, I asked if she spoke English.

"Yes, a little."

Her English was quite good and we exchanged some small talk. She was curious about my presence in Romania, so I described the CLCP.

"I'm a volunteer there," I finished proudly.

She gave me a puzzled look, so I started to explain what "volunteer" means.

"Yes, yes. I know. You work for free. This is strange for us. People here are constantly struggling to get somewhere, and you work for free."

I detected a certain annoyance and wondered if she had a point. In spite of their best intentions, do volunteers actually contribute negatively by depriving Romanians of jobs that would otherwise pay? I felt a rush of guilt, but then silently reasoned that at a macro level, doing work for free must surely be a net positive for a relatively poor country. All the work contributed by volunteers at the CLCP has likely created benefits, and spared resources that have allowed the project to produce even more benefits (such as tourism), which in total must exceed the benefit of the wages that would otherwise have been paid to do what the volunteers do — mustn't it?

"We're trying to help," I offered.

Saturday, May 24

I'm on the Royal Dutch Airlines plane at Bucharest's Otenpeni Airport, on my way to Boston, about 6:30 a.m. As I depart this beautiful country, I regret how little of Romania I have seen.

Perhaps it is fitting that my final journey in Romania consisted of the most harrowing ride of my life.

I had no great concern with how adroitly the driver of the hired minivan I boarded in Brasov wove his way through the chaotic traffic of the city, keeping to the middle of what might pass for traffic lanes and remaining always alert for the clearest path to the highway. He may have startled a few of his fellow commuters, particularly the oncoming drivers whose lanes he temporarily borrowed, but given the pace of the city traffic, we were in no real bodily danger. Once we were on the highway, however, and especially once we were on the winding road passing through the Carpathian Mountains, it was clear our lives were in the hands of a madman.

Apparently, there was no situation too precarious, no visibility too limited to allow a slower moving vehicle in our lane to hinder our progress, even for a moment, and I'm fairly certain every vehicle in our lane for the 170 kilometers between Brasov and Bucharest was slower than ours. Our torsos and heads lurched back and forth as though we were bobsled riders while our fearless navigator played a game of chicken with the oncoming contestants. The middle of the road had become our own private lane — except for approaching drivers with the same idea, especially the other minivan operators, with whom our driver exchanged a casual nod and a smile as one or the other was forced aside.

But while our pilot vigorously worked the wheel and bounced in his seat with a swagger, he didn't neglect the two attractive young women he had placed in the front seat next to him. He chatted and laughed, occasionally glancing at the road, and after particularly harrowing maneuvers he stared an extra long time at his pretty companions, making sure they noticed his talent. The drivers of most of the private transport vans approaching us on the highway (and there were many, about one every ten minutes) also had one or more of these female assistants strategically placed in the front seat next to them, and I wondered if the competition between these road warriors transcended their vehicular maneuvers.

Justice prevailed, however, when our hero got pulled over by the police. After listening to the admonition of the officer and meekly accepting the little piece of paper, he pulled back onto the road and cussed and cursed and threw the ticket several times down onto the dashboard, finally crumpling it in exaggerated disgust. "Do you see, ladies, with what I must contend?" he seemed to ask as he threw a look to his right. He continued driving not a tad bit safer, although he may have kept his eyes slightly more on the road and the rear view mirror and slightly less on the legs next to him.

But my prayers were answered — no car or truck approached as we were passing on any of the blind curves — and by the mercy of God, I am sure, we finally made it to the outskirts of Bucharest, where the driver graciously dropped me off on the side of the busy highway near the airport and a hotel.

The plane lifts into the air and the city fades away into the flat plains of Wallachia. The fields seem planted in smaller crop patterns than in the Midwestern US, although the total cultivated plots seem of similar size. Here there are also some large patches of forest scattered about the plains. I see the rippled landscape of the Carpathians, and the plateau beyond, Transylvania. Somewhere down there I dwelt for a time.

[Will the women working in the shops of Zarnesti, who came to understand my few words of Romanian, and who smiled at my attempts to repeat the additional words they taught me, the words for bread and cheese and apples, will they wonder why I no longer appear at their counters? Will Turnu and her mate, as they hunt, now not only for themselves but also for their new litter of pups, will they sniff the air and wonder where went the familiar human scent? Will the shepherd, ambling past the cabin with his flock of sheep, will he look at the fence and think of me as just another interloper from a foreign land, like all the others, here one day and gone the next? And what of his dogs, will they finally feel satisfied at having driven me off, or will they miss the familiar challenge? And Poiana and Crai, looking out from their slope, will they watch for their human pack mate striding along the road with stick in hand? Will the wolves howl for my return?]

The Carpathian forestland is even more extensive and less developed than I had realized, as we fly for quite a time over the green, wrinkled landscape, with barely a sign of human presence for areas that span many dozens of miles. Here and there brownish highlands rise out of the verdant forest carpet, sprinkled with a few patches of snow — the high peaks of the Carpathian Mountains.

[I got to track wolves in the cold and the snow, somewhere in those lush forests below, which from here look so uniform and featureless. It was not a dream. But from here, high in the sky, I can no longer see the prints of wolves in the snow and mud, nor the spectacular stone ramparts of Piatra Craiului, nor the rail fence that protects the lush little garden at the wolf cabin, nor the storks that glide in circles to land on the pasture. I got to care for wolves, and even got to have wolves as friends, but I can no longer look into the yellow eyes of Poiana and Crai, nor feel their coarse hair. The barks and growls of the

diligent shepherd dogs and the yells and whistles of the shepherds will no longer reach my ears, and the smell of burning wood no longer permeate my being.]

Now flying over the plains of Transylvania, with its more open country of irregular fields, settlements, and smaller patches of forest, passing over a small hilly area amongst the Transylvanian plain, covered with a broken forest. Romanians seem reluctant to develop, or at least deforest, any land that is not flat. The Transylvania plain is largely cultivated, grazed, or settled with towns and villages, yet, wherever the land begins to slope upwards, human development ceases almost entirely, and the lush forest carpet takes over the landscape…

[Why do we need adventure? An answer, I think, is to create time. We experience the days and weeks and months and even years passing by like landscapes viewed from a plane, their features blended, obscured, and forgotten if they aren't colored by the unexpected. My three months in Romania seemed a lifetime. But it was a time of my life now finished.]

I assume we're over Hungary now. Similar pattern to Romania, but some of the hills are less forested.

[Must we travel to the ends of the earth to find adventure? Doesn't the unexpected occur everywhere and always, provided our minds and hearts are open to each moment? I seek to no longer ignore any thing or circumstance because I judge it as "familiar." I seek to be aware. I seek to notice.]

And what of the scene with which I opened this story? How did I find myself back in the heart of the Carpathian Mountains on the trail of wolves, working with The Way of the Wolf Expedition of 2005? While I looked down from my window seat on that flight back to the States, I thought my adventures with wolves in Eastern Europe were passing behind me forever, along with the lush green landscape of Romania. Little did I know I'd have more dreams of wolves come true.

Epilog

When I got home I discovered that I had lost fifteen pounds during my stay in Romania. I suppose it was weight I could stand to lose. In July of 2003, I received an email from Anja informing me that she had found Guardian. The rascally dog was alive, roped to a post in the backyard of a shepherd's house (not the house of the same shepherd from whence he came, but rather the house where I experienced my first encounter with Romanian shepherd dogs, on that still, snowy road so long ago). Since Anja would only be in Romania for a few more weeks, she had little choice but to leave him to his fate — a fate less pleasant, no doubt, than what he had experienced for a few short months at the wolf cabin. I wonder if he can make any sense of this crazy world.

A former CLCP volunteer gave Curly a new home in Munich, Germany. There the dog underwent surgery and the non-surgical thread that had been lodged in her hip was successfully removed. Her wound healed. But, Curly a city dog? Surely this will be a challenge to her Buddha-nature. No longer in physical agony, I don't wonder whether she misses the freedom and beauty of the Barsa Valley, and a way of life that will never be again. I know she does.

No sign of Yukai was ever found.

Due to bureaucratic hurdles and difficulty reaching an agreement on obtaining land, the Large Carnivore Information Centre which was to have been located in the vicinity of Zarnesti was never built. Christoph and Barbara have since moved on to the founding of the Sinca Noua Ecoregion Programme/Fundaţia Şinca Noua (Sinca Noua Foundation), dedicated to land conservation, the preservation and development of traditional agriculture, and the development of sustainable eco-tourism in the Sinca Noua (a village near Zarnesti) area. As this book goes to press, the Prombergers' vision has expanded further with the creation of the Conservation Carpathia Foundation, the goal of which is to establish through land purchases the largest forest wilderness in Europe, a 50,000 hectare forest reserve and park in the Piatra Craiului region.

Peter couldn't pull together his Way of the Wolf expedition for 2004. But on a September evening of that year, I turned off the evening news and went to my computer to check for email. There was a message from Peter. "Would you like to be on the backup team for the expedition? We will begin in April next year..." I glanced around my office, at the papers on my desk and at the books lining the shelves, and looked out my window at the familiar suburban yard, and then I turned and noticed my old beat-up backpack leaning against the wall in the closet behind me...

Postscript

Regular, long-term human occupation of the wolf cabin faded in the years following the termination of the CLCP, which left the wolves Poiana and Crai with decreasing human companionship. When I visited them at the start of The Way of the Wolf Expedition in late March 2005, they appeared very healthy.

Poiana died on May 1, 2008, a few days before her twelfth birthday. Peter Sürth became involved in creating Project Crai, the first wolf sanctuary in Romania (near Zarnesti), to provide a rich physical and social environment for Crai and other wolves to live out their remaining days.

Crai died on June 18, 2009, after spending his final months at the Project Crai wolf sanctuary. Although relatively old, he seemed healthy before he died and his death was unexpected by the people caring for him. In fact, the spring of 2009 was the first one in years in which Crai did not manifest his usual skin problems.

Crai's time at the sanctuary was reportedly pleasant and he shared the facility with another male wolf named Crock. But he never got to experience life in the larger, 1.5 hectare enclosure, which is still being built.

See Peter Sürth's website, which is listed in the Resources section of this book.

Notes

1. Metro-Goldwyn-Mayer, 1968.

2. DreamWorks, 1999.

3. NAI Entertainment, 1978.

4. The website of the International Wolf Center is an excellent resource for keeping up with the status of wolves throughout the world: www.wolf.org

5. Although there is some controversy, archeological and genetic evidence suggests the process began about 15,000 years ago (some sources suggest it was more like 100,000 years ago), probably from a single instance somewhere in East Asia (some sources suggest it was more like four instances, including a separate instance for the Irish wolfhound).

6. Some taxonomic systems classify domestic dogs as a separate species, *Canis familiaris,* rather than as a subspecies of wolf.

7. A brief summary of the theories of dog evolution is provided in Lange (2002), 2-1. More details can be found in Mech and Boitani (2003), 256–257.

8. Including: The Carpathian Wildlife Foundation (Romania), the Romanian National Forest Administration, the Romanian Forest Research and Management Institute ICAS, Piatra Craiului National Park, the World Wildlife Fund (UK and Switzerland), Jack Wolfskin Ltd. (Germany), Liz Claiborne & Art Ortenberg Foundation (USA), The Nando Peretti Foundation, People's Trust for Endangered Species (UK), Wildlife International e.V., and EURONATUR. The project was also a member of the Large Carnivore Initiative for Europe.

9. Actually, between 1998 and 2000, the United States ranked 24th in murders per capita with a rate of 0.043 per 1000 people, while Romania ranked 32nd at 0.025. There are several countries ranking higher than the US that might be considered to have more "traditional" societies. Data from the *7th Annual United Nations Survey of Crime Trends and Operations of Criminal Justice Systems, covering the period 1998–2000*, United Nations Office on Drugs and Crime, Centre for International Crime Prevention. . More recent data show both the US and Romania falling in the ranking (but maintaining their relative positions), as political, economic, and social upheavals have increased and shifted in the world, and as reporting accuracies have varied.

10. Travax Report Prepared for Worldwide Travel Medicine, Boulder, Colorado.

11. This was the Zarnesti paper mill, which once was a significant producer of paper and employer in the region, but was now barely operating — much like the paper mill in my hometown of Westbrook, Maine.

12. According to a ranking complied by Wikipedia using data from the United Nations World Population Prospects, 2006 Revision, Romania ranks as the 110th most densely populated country, just slightly more densely populated than Spain and a little less than Turkey. The United States ranks 180th. Population density data is for 2005, and is confirmed from the direct source. Wikipedia contributors, "List of countries by population density," *Wikipedia, The Free Encyclopedia,* http://en.wikipedia.org/w/index.php?title=List_of_countries_by_population_density&oldid=211450550 (accessed May 14, 2008).

13. The scattered farmers and shepherds and their families that do live in the countryside often rely on horse or mule-pulled carts for transportation, causing much angst for the nighttime drivers of cars on the unlit country roads (for there is a small but growing class of people wealthy enough to own automobiles). If they can't afford a beast of burden, then the country folks walk as well, or they ride on a neighbor's cart, or they hitchhike.

14. Though processed goods from the West carry western prices, local products are inexpensive. For example, a loaf of bread still warm from the oven costs about thirty cents.

15. The efficient land-use pattern of Romania is also partially a relic from the industrialization policies of the Ceausescu regime. Thousands of peasants were forced from the countryside to live in drab apartment block buildings and to work in dismal factories in the towns and cities. In some cases entire villages were destroyed.

16. Estimates of large carnivore populations in Romania in 2002. The numbers are not believed to have changed significantly through 2007. Hinrichsen (2007).

17. The European Brown Bear *(Ursus arctos arctos)* and North American Grizzly Bear *(Ursus arctos horribilis)* are both classified as subspecies of Brown Bear. Genetically there is little difference between the subspecies.

18. A spotted version of the tuft-eared feline genus, considerably larger than its North American cousins. The Eurasian lynx *(Lynx lynx)* is about twice the size of the Canadian Lynx *(Lynx canadensis).* The Canadian lynx, in turn, is somewhat larger than other North American lynx species, the Bobcat *(Lynx rufus).* (The largest male Canadian lynxes are about 20% larger than the largest male bobcats.)

19. This footage can be seen in the BBC documentary: Transylvania: Living With Predators.

20. When walking, an adult wolf's stride is up to 2 feet long; trotting, up to 3 feet long; running (galloping) up to almost 6 feet long. Elbroch (2003), 133.

21. See Halfpenny (1986) for an excellent description of gaits and other characteristics of mammal locomotion, and of the tracks they leave – including those of wolves.

22. Four to six pups is the average litter size across most wolf populations. Litter sizes average smaller in the high Arctic, and evidence suggests that litter sizes average larger where food resources are ample and where wolves face heavier exploitation by humans. The closest wolf population to Romania for which I could find litter size data is European Russia, where litter sizes average 5 – 5.2. Bibikov (1985), 606. In Poland the average pack size was found to be 4.7 [Kutal and Rigg (2008), citing Nowak et al (2005)].

23. While conflict between wolves and humans continues, including legal as well as illegal killing of wolves, as of 2007 the wolf population in Romania is stable. Ovidiu Ionescu, a wolf biologist with Romania's Forest and Wildlife Research Institute, believes there are currently (2007) too many wolves in the country, and that the optimum population, given the amount of habitat available and the degree of conflict with livestock and people, is "probably somewhere around 2,500." [Hinrichsen (2007)]. According to most experts, the greatest long-term threat to large carnivore populations in Romania is habitat destruction due to development. A report issued in 2001 states that "approximately 30% of standing forests are slated to be restituted to families of former landowners," and that up to 20% of restituted forests will be cleared [Hansen, 2001].

24. My sources for this very brief history of Zarnesti are informal and primarily oral. The reference to Zarnizis comes from the website of "Guesthouse Elena" in Zarnesti.

25. A question poignantly asked by Bill Bryson in his book, *A Walk in the Woods: Rediscovering America on the Appalachian Trail*. Bryson (1998).

26. All the known laws of physics are independent of the rate at which observers experience (or measure) time. In fact, according to Einstein's Special Theory of Relativity, observers moving relative to each other measure time at different rates (as defined by the motions of objects they perceive, such as the ticking of clocks).

27. 1959, Hammer Film Productions.

28. In 2002, average per capita income was $1850 per year, and more than 45% of the population lived below the poverty level (statistics from the World Bank). However, since 2000, Romania's business-friendly environment has turned its economy into one of the fastest growing in Europe. Inflation is low and unemployment has been falling. According to the US CIA World Factbook, 25% of the population lived below the poverty level in 2005. Economic data for Romania varies widely depending on source and year.

29. Data from 2004. Again, economic data for Romania changes rapidly (and varies by source). In 2007, the CIA World Factbook estimated that agriculture comprised 8% of the Romania economy.

30. On average. In the CLCP study area during 2002, wolves and bears killed 0.58% of sheep in the shepherd camps. A study by Kecskes et al in 2004 found an average flock loss of 1.12% to wolves in shepherd camps where some loss occurred during a season. Another study by the same team in 2007 found an average flock loss of 0.48% over an average period of 46 days [Kecskes in Kutal and Rigg (2008)].

31. According to Ionescu, as of 2007 poaching of wolves to protect livestock is diminishing, as attitudes towards wolves are gradually changing in Romania. Hinrichsen (2007).

32. See, for example, Lopez (1979).

33. See Quammen, *Monster of God* (2003), for a fascinating account of Ceaușescu's bear hunting and consequent wildlife management strategies.

34. In the Communist regime prior to Ceausescu's (which began in 1965), wolves were severely persecuted through the use of bounties, poison, and the killing of pups in dens, much like in the American West in the 1800s and early 1900s; their numbers had declined to about 1500 by the late 1960s.

35. 1992, Sony Pictures.

36. The core of almost all wolf packs is a breeding pair of wolves. In addition, packs may contain members from one or more generations of descendents (more recent descendents being more common), along with other relatives of the breeding pair such as siblings and parents, and, less commonly, nieces and nephews (depending on how the breeding pair came to be the breeding pair). Thus most wolf packs are families of various degrees of extension. As mentioned below, some wolf packs may also contain one or more wolves unrelated to the breeding pair, although this is not common. In the Carpathians, wolf packs seldom have more than seven members [Hinrichsen (2007)].

37. In the Carpathians, most wolf territories are 130 to 160 square kilometers in size [Hinrichsen] (for comparison, in western North America, wolf territories are usually larger; in Alaska and the Yukon Territory they may cover more than 1500 square kilometers [Mech and Boitani (2003), 172-175]).

38. Or, occasionally, to usurp the breeding position in an existing pack.

39. Unless an offspring takes over the breeding role left by a vacant parent, or usurps it. Based on genetic evidence, such inbreeding of parents with offspring, which occurs occasionally in captive wolves, is not common in the wild, where wolves not closely related to the pack more often fill available breeding roles.

40. For information about wolf dispersal, see Chapter 1, "Wolf Social Ecology", by L. David Mech and Luigi Boitani, in *Mech and Boitani* (2003). For information about pup rearing, see Chapter 2, "Wolf Beahvior: Reproductive, Social, and Intelligent," by Jane M. Packard, in the same book.

41. Most breeding pairs produce a litter each year if food resources are not too scarce and there aren't other hindrances. A study in Denali National Park in Alaska found that only about 15% of wolf packs did not produce a litter in a given year. Multiple female breeders in a pack is probably not likely unless food resources are plentiful, and may be more common when a male unrelated to the maturing females of the pack becomes available as a new breeding male (usurping the father, replacing a missing father, or managing to operate as an extra breeder).

42. Usually strange lone wolves that wander near or into the territory of a pack that already has a breeding pair are chased away or killed, but occasionally they are adopted into the pack. Most often such adoptees are male and no more than three years old. A strange wolf may also be accepted into a pack to replace a vacant breeding position, or it may create a vacant breeding position by managing to kill one of the breeders. In rare cases it may become an "extra" breeder within the pack.

43. In fact, according to Ovidiu Ionescu, a wolf biologist with Romania's Forest and Wildlife Research Institute, all "proper" wolf territories in Romania are currently occupied, and about thirty percent of the wolf population is killed each year by other wolves protecting their territories. Hinrichsen (2007).

44. This brief history of Turnu and Leasa comes from the wolf research section of the 2001 and 2002 Annual Reports of the Carpathian Large Carnivore Project, by Barbara Promberger-Fürpass, Peter Sürth, Christoph Promberger, Marius Scurtu, and Ovidiu Ionescu. No story of wolf pack formation can be called "typical," since the behavior of wolves is complex, varied, and adaptable, but this is one well-documented example.

45. Rigg and Findo (2000). See also Kecskes in Kutal and Rigg (2008).

46. The moose is the largest deer species. The North American elk is the second

largest, although in the Carpathians, red deer average about the same size as elk.

47. Based on the nutritional requirements of wolves living in a pack of six. 1999 Annual Report, Carpathian Large Carnivore Project.

48. Ginsberg and MacDonald (1990)

49. See for example: DelGiudice (1998).

50. See for example: Mech and Nelson (2000).

51. Points for a dead animal's quality, known as "CIC points," are assigned in Europe by the International Council for Game and Wildlife Conservation (CIC) (official French designation: Conseil International de la Chasse et de la Conservation du Gibier).

52. There are generally three categories of trophy fees: killed, wounded, and missed, plus "organizational fees," although not all categories apply to all game.

53. An estimate from a schedule of hunting fees (based on CIC points) by a private outfitter.

54. These numbers are approximate and vary by source and by year. The figures used here come from CLCP personnel in 2004 as rough averages. Quammen (*Atlantic Monthly*, 2003) cites a source in the Romania Forestry Department claiming that the quota for bears in a "recent year" was "seventy bears, or maybe seventy-two." According to an AVES Foundation for Wildlife & Nature Conservation in Romania report, in 2003–2004 the quota for bears was 74 in the Harghita district alone. Hinrichsen (2007), citing Ovidiu Ionescu, a wolf biologist with Romania's Forest and Wildlife Research Institute, reports that "300 or so" wolves are shot legally every year. Illegal poaching of carnivores and exotic animals such as the chamois in Romania is believed by some sources to be high (see for example, *Brown Bear Conservation in Romania*, Position Paper of the World Wildlife Fund, June 2004).

55. Rigg and Findo (2000).

56. As noted previously, some taxonomic systems classify domestic dogs as a separate species.

57. Heinrich (2006), 336.

58. Unless there are atomic or subatomic "seeds" buried in neurons somewhere that are capable of non-deterministically generating alternative neuro-electrical impulses by means of quantum mechanical fluctuations, a speculative possibility offered by some philosophers and physicists. As some neuro-electrical patterns that represent alternative choice models could thereby be "freely" (randomly) generated (using memory and sensory information to create likely candidates), and as such seeds could also cause "free" (random) selections from among the alternatives, the entire process of arriving at a choice, which would likely be iterative with feedback between the level(s) generating the alternatives and the level(s) choosing, could be considered "free" (so the thinking goes). In an uncertain world, it is impossible to always know the best alternative, and therefore making choices with the involvement of some random element, some chance, is a necessary adaptive strategy (for example, if our internal choice process fails to produce an alternative we like, we may "toss a coin" to break the impasse). For a discussion of these concepts, see for example: Tipler, F. (1995) Chapter VII.

59. Strictly speaking, the physical nature, or "state," of the fundamental particles of matter/energy can in theory be determined by anything that can interact with the particles (though never without some uncertainty). But such "detectors" are also made

of fundamental particles whose states are not determined until detected by something else. And thus on up a chain of detection. Whether something "conscious" is required to ultimately resolve the states of all things in the chain is unknown, and logically unknowable (for to know would require devising an experiment in which there is no one to perceive the results!).

60. See for example, Herman and Uyeyama (1999). The syntactic findings remain controversial. One finding of referential communication that also includes categorization involves an African Grey parrot that was taught the ability to use vocalizations to classify objects within the abstract categories of color, shape, and material. See Andrews (2008) for a discussion of this study (as presented in the book *The Alex Studies: Cognitive and Communicative Abilities of Grey Parrots*, by Pepperberg, 1999) as well as a general summary of animal intelligence and symbolic communication research.

61. The results of research by Dr. Con Slobodchikoff of Northern Arizona University, reported by various news media outlets. The quote is from Soussan, (2004).

62. Especially "A Raven Update," included as an addendum to the 2006 edition of *The Mind of the Raven* [Heinrich (2006)].

63. Christian Rutz, University of Oxford, as quoted in Schmid (2007).

64. It is not easy keeping up with the results of animal intelligence studies. More recent examples: Researchers observed chimpanzees in Senegal constructing and using primitive spears to hunt smaller primates [Pruetz, J.D. & Bertolani, P. (2007). "Savanna Chimpanzees, *Pan troglodytes verus*, Hunt with Tools." *Current Biology*, 17(5), 412-417]. Chimpanzees have been found to perform short-term memory tasks better than human college students [Inoue, S. & Matsuzawa, T. (2007). "Working memory of numerals in chimpanzees." *Current Biology*, 17(23), 1004-1005]. Researchers have found that macaque monkeys can perform nonverbal numerical addition as well as human college students [Cantlon, J. F. & Brannon, E. M. (2007). "Basic Math in Monkeys and College Students." *PLoS Biology* 5(12): e328]. A study found that dogs could locate food by only observing the behavior of another dog [Heberlein, M. & Turner, D. C. (2009). "Dogs, *Canis familiaris*, find hidden food by observing and interacting with a conspecific." *Animal Behavior* 78(2), 385-391]. Some capuchin monkeys likely use deceptive anti-predator calls to usurp food from their competitors [Wheeler, B.C. (2009). "Monkeys crying wolf? Tufted capuchin monkeys use anti-predator calls to usurp resources from conspecifics." *Proceedings of the Royal Society of Biological Science* 276(1669), 3013-3018]. As the first case of observation of what some scientists consider to be tool use in invertebrates, octopuses in their natural habitat were observed collecting, cleaning out, transporting, and assembling coconut shell halves to use as shelter/hiding places [Finn, J.K., Tregenza, T., Norman, M.D. (2009). "Defensive tool use in a coconut-carrying octopus." *Current Biology* 19(23), R1069-R1070].

65. There are scientists who are taking this approach. See Andrews (2008), Ristau (1991).

66. See footnote 108.

67. The fences ranged in height from 1 meter to 1.3 meters.

68. Wolf pairs are more efficient hunters per wolf than wolves in any other pack size, and are also likely to be more efficient than single wolves (again, per wolf), although the latter has not been proven. See Peterson and Ciucci in Mech and Boitani (2003) page 121.

69. All the facts regarding the tracks and other signs in this description are accurate. Some of the motivations and detailed actions are speculative, perhaps the most significant being the "relay running" in which the wolves swapped roles. Our tracking skills could not be that precise, but the tracks did indicate that after one wolf diverted to avoid a fence, one or the other resumed the direct pursuit. In any case, all speculations are consistent with existing knowledge of wolf hunting behavior as summarized in Chapter 4, "The Wolf as Carnivore," by Rolf. O. Peterson and Paolo Ciucci, in Mech and Boitani (2003). (With the caveat that "relay running" has been "claimed" by some researchers, but not conclusively proved.)

70. "Dracula's Castle" is the castle's popular, informal name. Its official name is "Bran Castle." It was never actually possessed by the historical Dracula, as explained below.

71. And free trade. Many of the merchants of Transylvania were Saxons who were trying to maintain a monopoly on trade in the region, which Dracula was eager to break.

72. Actually, from the point of view of less educated peasants of the Romanian Orthodox faith, Dracula's conversion to Catholicsim might have made him a candidate to become a vampire.

73. If that was his reason for converting, the device worked. He was let out of prison, married into the royal family (a second marriage for Dracula, his first wife having, according to legend, committed suicide by hurling herself from the tower of their castle into the Arges River to avoid capture by Turks), and regained Hungarian support in a successful bid to regain the throne of Wallachia for his third and final episode (which ended when he was killed in battle with the Turks in 1476).

74. A history of Vlad III Dracula is found in McNally and Florescu (1994). It should be noted that some details about the historical Dracula come from unverifiable local folklore (which tends to be complimentary of the Prince, in a Robin Hood-like fashion).

75. As of July 2007, the Romanian government leases the castle from the son of Princess Ileana, New York architect Archduke Dominic Habsburg, to whom it returned the property in 2006. The castle has been put up for sale by the Habsburg family.

76. During Vlad III Dracula's time the castle belonged to his sometimes ally and sometimes enemy John Hunyadi, Voivode (Governor) of Transylvania. Reports of the frequency and duration of Dracula's residency at the Bran Castle vary. According to McNally and Florescu (1994), Dracula "was undoubtedly a guest of Hunyadi at Bran and later a prisoner of his [Hunyadi's] son Matthias [King of Hungary]" (page 63).

77. An opinion I later found to be also expressed by McNally and Florescu (1994).

78. The bodies of some dracos were made of bronze with cloth streamers attached to the ends.

79. The persistence of the Romanized culture through these early invasions as been attributed to the fact that most of the existing inhabitants withdrew to relatively inaccessible mountainous territories, only gradually descending onto the plains after the 13th century.

80. While latter immigrants from the north and west may have been welcome for socio-economic and political reasons by certain of the ruling elite of Hungary (who

controlled Transylvania), they were not necessarily welcome by everyone in Transylvania and Wallachia, princes and peasants alike, especially when they tried to establish and perpetuate economic domination by monopolizing certain aspects of production and trade. There was friction and resistance, sometimes violent, as exemplified by Vlad the Impaler's rough dealings with the Saxon boyars and merchants of Wallachia and Transylvania.

81. The concept of "state" here, as elsewhere in Europe during medieval times, was relevant mostly to the power and privileges of ruling families and the noble estate. Of course, defense from external invasion, slaughter, religious persecution, and subjugation was of vital interest to the peasantry and the serfs, but one imagines their plight was only worsened by much of the constant warfare associated with dynastic power struggles within Europe and within their own provinces.

82. The set of books about Romanian history written in English and still in print is limited. See Keppler (2002). See also Wikipedia for a brief summary: Wikipedia contributors, "History of Romania," *Wikipedia, The Free Encyclopedia,* http://en.wikipedia.org/w/index.php?title=History_of_Romania&oldid=238731499 (accessed September 23, 2008).

83. According to the International Wolf Center, adult wolves have a biting power of about 1500 lbs per square inch (enough to break human bones), about twice the biting power of German shepherd dogs. There seems to be much emotion surrounding the issue of biting power in domestic dogs, especially pit bulls. I have found widely varying data, from sources that would seem to be respectable, including claims that there is no reliable data.

84. Additional details may be viewed on the park's website: www.pcrai.ro/engleza/parcul_istoric.html.

85. St. Vincent (2001). Updated editions are available.

86. Burford and Richardson (2001). Updated editions are available.

87. Linnell (2002).

88. A character in the TV series *Northern Exposure*, known for his domineering attitude and influence in a small town in Alaska.

89. This question about the simultaneity of consciousness was explored in the novel *October the First Is Too Late*, by Fred Hoyle (London: Heinemann, 1966). For a discussion of Hoyle's treatment and many other aspects of time, see Davies (1995).

90. And there would truly be nothing new under the sun. The information content of the universe would be fixed – in the whole, no new information could be created, and none could be destroyed. Our thoughts, our memories, and our dreams would be coded into the world from the beginning.

91. Einstein's Special Theory of Relativity already establishes that observers moving relative to each other do not experience a common "now." They do not agree about when events happen at different points in space, although the difference isn't noticeable at relative speeds much less than the speed of light.

92. More precisely, "everything **that has been observed** before now has been determined." Experiments have shown that unobserved quantum states in the "past" are not determined until some later effect is observed. It is possible, therefore, to take "now" completely out of the picture: everything observed is determined, everything unobserved is not. "Everything" in this context refers to the properties of the fundamental constituents of matter and energy that make up the world.

93. Actually, since signals relaying information about physical being – particularly about changes that effect other particles of matter transmitted by forces such as gravity and electromagnetism – travel at a finite speed, the speed of light, then the physical effects of choices made by others arrive at our location from just as far back in time as it takes light to travel from them to us. If everyone else happened to be conscious at just those points in time, the effects of their choices would arrive at our location just as we are making our choices. However, the effects of our choices wouldn't arrive at the location of everyone else until the time it takes light to travel from us to them, so our free wills would still act independently.

94. Rougier et al. (2007).

95. Miramax Films, 2003.

96. See for example Harber and Gill (2000).

97. Those measured in the CLCP study were: forest composition, forest density, altitude, slope inclination, and forest management practices. CLCP Annual Report 2000.

98. Ripple and Beschta (2004). Other biologists dispute a link has been proven, however, citing factors besides the presence of wolves for changes in vegetation, and citing the lack of controlled studies. A summary of the analysis is provided in Robbins (2004).

99. Romania has since issued a new currency, so the conversions of lei into dollars used in this book no longer apply.

100. This description is a simplification of a complex topic, described in Chapter 3, "Wolf Communication", by Fred H. Harrington and Cheryl S. Asa in Mech and Boitani (2003).

101. Romania entered the European Union on January 1, 2007, and in addition to market forces, EU regulations are adding pressures that are causing many small-scale family farms to go out of business.

102. While details vary by locale, the specifics described here were once common practices in Romania, especially during outbreaks of vampire hysteria that occurred periodically in centuries past. An especially strong episode occurred throughout Europe early in the 18th century, after a report appeared providing gory details about the features of the corpse of an alleged vampire named Peter Plogojowitz after it was disinterred in Serbia. Belief in vampires, and especially remedial actions as drastic as disinterring and staking corpses, have waned in more recent times; however, occasional reports of vampires and related exhumations continue to this day in remote Carpathian mountain villages (see for example, "Death rite unnerves Romanian EU bid," BBC News archive, March 5, 2004). McNally and Florescu (1972) include a couple of vampire stories reported by living villagers (one that occurred in 1939 and the other at an unspecified date), and the authors add, "belief in vampires is still prevalent in Dracula country particularly among the older generation" (page 121). Summers (2001), writing about the beliefs of villagers in Romania around 1929, reports that, "Although nowadays the appearance of a vampire may be regarded as exceptional, none the less it is a very distinct and a very terrible possibility…" (Page 301.) Summers goes on to relate several stories of belief in vampires, including disinterment and staking of corpses that occurred early in the 20th century. Barber (1988) also cites reports of anti-vampire measures being taken in Romanian villages in "recent times" (page 48).

103. Vampire/strigoi folklore in Romania is rich indeed, and the causes and characteristics of, and remedies for, vampirism vary by district and even by village. See Summers (2001). See also McNally and Florescu (1972). According to Summers, in Romanian vampire folklore can be found most of the essential aspects of beliefs that occur in Europe. The specifics described here are not a complete list. For detailed reports of some of the most famous cases of alleged vampirism in Europe, together with possible explanations for the ubiquity of vampire folklore and the common characteristics of vampires within it, see Barber (1988).

104. Or, in times and places where strigoi/vampire hysteria was particularly prevalent, a few years after burial — three if a child, four or five if a young person, seven if an adult — regardless of suspicious factors. Summers (2001), 301-302.

105. It is interesting to note that, according to Barber (1988), generally in Europe it was believed that "wolves and dogs were the enemies of vampires and attacked them on sight." This is a belief that contradicts Stoker's Dracula, who seemed to be on very friendly terms with the wolves lurking about his castle. Barber posits that this belief derived from the fact that dogs and wolves were occasionally observed consuming ("attacking") corpses that had been inadequately buried. In any case, were I to have trouble, Summers (2001) specifies remedies specific for Zarnesti, at least for female versions of revenants: drive large iron forks through the heart, eyes, and breasts, and rebury the body face downwards and very deeply.

106. In his research in the Yukon, Christoph determined that ravens alone can consume up to 37 kg a day from the carcass of a wolf kill, or up to 66% of a kill attended by a lone wolf (more like 10% when there is a pack of ten wolves). A CLCP study in 2001 concluded that foxes, ravens, other birds, and stray or shepherd dogs were the most significant scavengers at kill sites in Romania (CLCP Annual Report 2001).

107. Information derived from Chapter 4, "The Wolf as Carnivore", by Rolf. O. Peterson and Paolo Ciucci, in Mech and Boitani (2003).

108. Schrödinger's cat is a thought experiment used to illustrate a paradox that may result from the Copenhagen Interpretation of quantum mechanics, which assumes that each of the fundamental quanta of matter and energy that make up the universe exists in a combination of mutually exclusive states until it is observed, whereupon it resolves into a particular one of the states in a process called "wave function collapse" (or "reduction"). The paradox, which suggests that a cat placed in a box with a vial of poison gas that will be broken depending on the outcome of a wave function collapse is both dead and alive until observed, ignores the possibility that the cat itself might be able to detect whether it is dead or alive. An alternative interpretation of quantum mechanics, the Many Worlds Interpretation, posits that all the quantum states are realized at the moment of observation, but each is realized in a different "world": each act of observation splits the universe into multiple worlds.

109. On this point we were exhibiting some ignorance about wolf nutrition. As discussed above, following research I conducted after my Transylvania experience, at least some bones are important in the diet of wolves.

110. In the summer of 2001, CLCP observers counted a total of 37 bears (24 cubs, 2 yearlings, 11 adults) visiting the Racadau garbage bins, which were observed by an average of 7.6 people per night (CLCP Annual Report, 2001).

111. Robin Rigg, *Fatal Bear Attacks on Humans in Romania*, International Bear News, vol. 14, no. 1, February 2005.

112. Brasov Travel Guide: www.brasovtravelguide.ro/en/brasov/sightseeing/black-church.php

113. At least according to a German pamphlet published in Nuremberg in 1499, and as famously depicted in two woodcuts (1499 and 1500).

114. Mathew 19:30. The Holy Bible, English Standard Version.

115. Being an imprecise term, "Gypsy" is also sometimes used to refer to some groups of people who are not ethnically or traditionally "Roma."

116. Regardless of the advised shift in terminology, I have found that the word "Gypsy" is still current in literature for and about the Romani people, in documents wherein obviously no disrespect is intended and even wherein their interests are promoted. Often both "Gypsy" and "Roma" are used interchangeably, as though the writers aren't quite sure whether historical derogatory associations outweigh the rich cultural associations. In any case, it seems there are still Roma who use the term "Gypsy" to refer to themselves with pride. I have also found that "Gypsy" is still the label that most people, at least most non-Romani people, use conversationally in Central and Eastern Europe. So I admit to a bit of confusion regarding the current standing of these words, and before (and during) my sojourn in Romania, I had no knowledge that the term "Gypsy" might be pejorative, and next to no knowledge that it had been replaced. Thus, up to this point in my narrative, I have retained the word "Gypsy," both to stay true to my original conceptions (and journal notes), and to share with the reader my education.

117. Most of this information about the Roma from: Crowe, David M. *A History of the Gypsies of Eastern Europe and Russia*, New York: Palgrave Macmillan, 2007. See also Wikipedia: Wikipedia contributors, "Roma people," *Wikipedia, The Free Encyclopedia,* http://en.wikipedia.org/w/index.php?title=Roma_people&oldid=212242925.

118. During the Middle Ages of Europe there were many types of slaves, serfs, and indentured peasants, along with varied forms of institutionalized oppression specifically for each type.

119. For example, not selling Roma children without their parents.

120. At the time Ceausescu was deposed in 1989 there were over 350,000 ethnic Germans (descendents of 12th century settlers) living in Transylvania. Offered German citizenship, all but about 60,000 of them moved to Germany by 2002.

121. New York Times article by Robert Mcg. Thomas, Jr., February 27, 1997.

122. A few months after my visit to Sibiu, Florin Cioaba gained notoriety for marrying off his twelve-year-old daughter Ana Maria to a fifteen-year-old groom. Questions were raised about whether the girl was forced to marry (denied by Mr. Cioaba), and the event sparked controversy regarding the extent to which Roma tradition, as vigorously defended by Mr. Cioaba, should be accepted in modern society. Shortly after the wedding, child protection officials in Sibiu required that the couple live apart until Ana Maria reaches sixteen, the legal age for marriage in Romania.

123. Or, according to the United Nations Development Programme, something over 2,000,000, which illustrates the difficulty of counting them.

Acknowledgements

I express my sincere thanks and deepest appreciation to the following people:

My older brother Richard, for his encouragement, which was first and most consistent. I could not have written this book without his faith and support.

Christoph and Barbara Promberger, for the opportunity to change my life, for their friendship, and for much information about wolves and wildlife management in Romania.

Peter Sürth, for his friendship, for the opportunity to pursue further adventures in Central and Eastern Europe, and for much information about the ways of wolves and other wildlife in the Carpathian Mountains.

Titus and Vanessa, my first teachers at Cabanna Lupului, and, along with Joris and Silverine, my first family there.

Anja Kleeberg, my second family, my sister at Cabanna Lupului, whose positive spirit helped smooth many frustrating and heinous tasks.

Simona Buretea, my friend and resource in Romania, for patiently answering my many questions about local culture, history, and place.

My mother and father, Andrea Matheson, Richard Sparks, Steven Sparks, Jim McVey and the writing class at the University of Colorado, Todd Smith, and Dan Wages, for their faith, encouragement and valuable editorial input.

Jürgen Sauer, Thilo Brunner, Steffen Leiprecht, Stephan and Kathrin Merkel, Christa Schudeja, Kolja Zimmermann, Barbara and Christoph Promberger, and Simon Buretea, for graciously providing photographs.

David Hancock, publisher; Theresa Laviolette, editor; Ingrid Luters, production editor; and all the folks at Hancock House Publishers for editing, design, layout, and putting this book together. Maria Williams: None of this would have happened without your help, encouragement, and sage advice at the very beginning. Thank you Basia, Nancy, Maria, Holly, and Phil for your dependable and nurturing friendships — my primary sources of inspiration and strength.

My apologies to those I haven't mentioned: the many proximate contributors I've overlooked, and the innumerable other beings, human and non-human, who have enriched my life and made my journey possible in one way or another.

A portion of the text first appeared in the article "Wolves as Neighbors," in the winter 2005 edition of *Northern Woodlands* magazine, published by the Center for Woodlands Education, Inc., Corinth, Vermont, USA. I thank the editor, Steven Long.

References

Andrews, Kristin, "Animal Cognition", *The Stanford Encyclopedia of Philosophy (Winter 2008 Edition)*, Edward N. Zalta (ed.), URL = <http://plato.stanford.edu/archives/win2008/entries/cognition-animal/>

Barber, Paul.1988. *Vampires, Burial, and Death: Folklore and Reality.* New Haven: Yale University Press.

Bibikov, D.I. (ed.). 1985. *The Wolf. History, Systematics, Morphology, Ecology.* Nauka, Moskva, p 606.

Bryson, Bill. 1998. *A Walk in the Woods: Rediscovering America on the Appalachian Trail.* New York: Broadway Books.

Burford, Tim and Dan Richardson. 2001. *The Rough Guide to Romania.* London: Rough Guides, Ltd.

Carpathian Large Carnivore Project. Annual Report 1999.

————. Annual Report 2000.

————. Annual Report 2001.

————. Annual Report 2002.

Crowe, David M. 2007. *A History of the Gypsies of Eastern Europe and Russia.* New York: Palgrave Macmillan.

Davies, Paul. 1995. *About Time: Einstein's Unfinished Revolution.* London: Penguin Books.

DelGiudice, Glenn D. (prepared by). 1998. The Ecological Relationship Of Gray Wolves and White-Tailed Deer in Minnesota. Minnesota Department of Natural Resources, State of Minnesota (June).

Eisberg, Robert and Robert Resnick. 1985. *Quantum Physics of Atoms, Molecules, Solids, Nuclei, and Particles.* New York: John Wiley & Sons.

Elbroch, Mark. 2003. *Mammal Tracks & Sign, A Guide to North American Species.* Mechanicsburg, PA: Stackpole Books.

Feynman, Richard P., Robert B. Leighton, and Mathew Sands. 1965. *The Feynman Lectures on Physics.* Menlo Park, CA: Addison-Wesley.

Ginsberg, Joshua R. and D.W. MacDonald. 1990. Foxes, Wolves, Jackals, and Dogs: an action plan for the conservation of canids. International Union for the Conservation of Nature/Species Survival Commission, Canid Specialist Group.

Halfpenny, James. 1986. *A Field Guide to Mammal Tracking in North America*. Boulder: Johnson Books.

Hansen, John. 2001. *Biodiversity Assessment Report Romania 2001*. Submitted to USAID/ Romania.

Harber, Ralph and Robin Gill. 2000. Natural Regeneration in Broadleafed Woodlands: Deer Browsing and the Establishment of Advance Regeneration. Publication by the Forestry Commission of Great Britain: Edinburgh (July).

Heinrich, Bernd. 2006. *Mind of the Raven: Investigations and Adventures with Wolf-birds*. New York: HarperCollins.

Herman, L.M. and R.K. Uyeyama. 1999. The dolphin's grammatical competency: comments on Kako. *Animal Learning & Behavior* 27, no. 1:18–23.

Hinrichsen, Don. 2007. Romania's Wolves: In the Crosshairs of Conflict. *National Wildlife Magazine*, vol. 45 no. 4.

Klepper, Nicolae. 2002. *Romania: An Illustrated History*. New York: Hippocrene Book.

Kutal, Miroslav and Rigg, Robin, editors. 2008. *Perspectives of wolves in Central Europe, Proceedings from the conference held on 9th April 2008*. Olomouc, Czech Republic: Hnutí DUHA Olomouc.

Lange, Karen E. 2002. Wolf to Woof. *National Geographic Magazine*, vol. 201, No. 1:2–11.

Linnell, J.D.C., et al. 2002. The fear of wolves: A review of wolf attacks on humans. Norsk Institutt For Naturforskning, Trondheim (January).

Lopez, Barry. 1979. *Of Wolves and Men*. New York: Charles Scribner's Sons.

McNally, R.T. and R. Florescu. 1994. *In Search of Dracula: The History of Dracula and Vampires*. New York: Houghton Mifflin Co.

Mech, L. David. 1970. *The Wolf: The Ecology and Behavior of an Endangered Species*. Minneapolis: University of Minnesota Press.

——. 1991. *The Way of the Wolf*. Stillwater, MN: Voyageur Press.

—— and Luigi Boitani. 2003. *Wolves: Behavior, Ecology, and Conservation*. Chicago and London: University of Chicago Press.

—— and Michael E. Nelson. 2000. Do Wolves Affect White-Tailed Buck Harvest In Northeastern Minnesota? *Journal of Wildlife Management* 64, no.1:129–136.

Quammen, David. 2003. *Monster of God: The Man-Eating Predator in the Jungles of History and the Mind*. New York: W.W. Norton & Company.

——. 2003. The Bear Slayer. *Atlantic Monthly*, vol.292, No. 1:45–63.

——. 2000. The Post-Communist Wolf. *Outside Magazine* (December).

Rigg, Robin. 2005. Fatal Bear Attacks on Humans in Romania. *International Bear News* 14, no.1.

Rigg, R. and S. Findo. 2000. Wolves in the Western Carpathians: past, present and future. *Presentation at Beyond 2000: Realities of global wolf restoration symposium*. Duluth, Minnesota, 23–26 February.

Ripple, William J. & Robert L Beschta. 2004. Wolves and the ecology of fear: Can predation risk structure ecosystems? *Bioscience* 54, no. 8.

Ristau, Carolyn A. 1991. *Cognitive Ethology: the minds of other animals*. New Jersey: Lawrence Erlbaum Associates.

Robins, Jim. 2004. Lessons from the Wolf: Bringing the top predator back to Yellowstone has triggered a cascade of unanticipated changes in the park's ecosystem. *Scientific American Magazine* (May).

Rougier, Hélène, Ştefan Milota, Ricardo Rodrigo, Mircea Gherase, Laurenţiu Sarcină, Oana Moldovan, João Zilhão, Silviu Constantin, Robert G. Franciscus, Christoph P.E. Zollikofer, Marcia Ponce de León, and Erik Trinkaus. 2007. Peştera cu Oase 2 and the cranial morphology of early modern Europeans. *Proceedings of the National Academy of Sciences of the United States of America* 104, no. 4.

St. Vincent, David. 2001. *Lonely Planet Romania and Moldova (2nd Edition)*. Victoria, Australia: Lonely Planet Publications.

Schmid, Randolph E. 2007. Crows Bend Twigs Into Tools To Find Food. *Associated Press*, October 5.

Soussan,Tania. 2004. Language of Prairie Dogs Includes Words for Humans. *Associated Press*, December 6.

Summers, Montague. 2001. *The Vampire in Lore and Legend*, Mineola, NY: Dover Publications Inc. (originally published: New York: E.P.Dutton, 1929).

Stoker, Bram. 1897. *Dracula*. Great Britain: Archibald Constable and Company.

Thomas, Robert. 1997. Ion Cioaba, 62, of Romania, Self-Styled King of All Gypsies (Obituary). *New York Times*, February 27.

Tipler, Frank J. 1995. *The Physics of Immortality*. New York: Anchor Books.

Tipler, Paul A. 1969. *Foundations of Modern Physics*. New York: Worth Publishers.

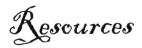

Resources

Websites of organizations and eco-tourism businesses of people mentioned in this book.

Environment

Sinca Noua Ecoregion Programme/Fundaţia Şinca Noua (Sinca Noua Foundation): www.fsn.ro/

Conservation Carpathia Foundation: http://www.conservationcarpathia.org/

Eco-tourism

Equus Silvania (specializing in horseback tours around Sinca Noua, Romania): www.equus-silvania.com/en/indexe.htm

Absolute Carpathian (eco-tours around Zarnesti and elsewhere in Romania): www.absolute-nature.ro/

Peter Sürth's The Way of the Wolf website (mostly in German, but some pages have English versions): www.thewayofthewolf.net/

This book

www.dreamingofwolves.com

Index

activity monitoring (of wolves), 84, 128
Alans, 121
Alaska, 21
Andrei (horse), 140-143, 144, 154, 168
animal behavior, 88-89
Anja (Kleeberg), 135, 138-140, 149, 155,
    158, 159, 160-161, 165-168, 171-174,
    176, 198, 200-201, 202-203, 205-206,
    210-214, 216-217, 224, 232
Atlantic Monthly, 66
Austria, 121-123, 140
Austrian Empire, 121
Avar Empire, 121

Banat, 123
Barsa River, 131, 171
Barsa Valley, 97, 123, 189, 197, 216, 232
Bath, Dr. Allistair, 147-148
Bavaria, 164
BBC, 44, 57, 66
Bern Convention, 65
Bessarabia, 123
Black Church, Brasov, 186, 219
Bran, Romania, 93, 96, 103, 105, 113,
    114, 162-163, 188
Bran Castle, 93, 96, 104, 183
Brasov, Romania, 26, 44, 67, 81, 84, 95,
    131, 136, 137, 138, 154, 185, 186, 218-
    220, 222, 226, 227, 228-229
Bucegi Mountain Range, 45, 70, 72, 99,
    102, 106, 127, 159, 162, 180, 181, 184,
    202
Bucharest, Romania, 26, 29, 31-32, 50,
    61, 133-134, 136, 176, 228-229
Bulgaria, 121

Bulgarian Emprire, 121
Buljubašas, 225-226
Bungee Canyon, 74, 78, 84, 163
Bureta, Simona, 67-68, 69, 137, 150-154,
    158, 160, 166, 167, 173- 175

Cabanna Lupului (Wolf Cabin), 10, 31,
    32, 34, 52, 53, 60, 68, 97, 98, 139, 152,
    164, 178, 183, 189, 218, 230, 232, 234
Canada, 21, 45, 124, 148, 169
Carmi, 32-33, 133
Carol I, first King of Romania, 123
Carpathian Large Carnivore Project. *See*
    CLCP
Carpathian Mountains, 9, 11-12, 43-44,
    81-83, 159, 164, 230
Carpathians. *See* Carpathian Mountains
Ceausescu, Nicolae, 64-65, 96, 216, 224
    bear hunting, 64-65
chamois *(Rupicapra rupicapera),* 81, 190
Cindrel Mountains, 225
Cioaba, Florin, 226
Cioaba, Ion, 226
CLCP, 23-26, 37, 40, 44, 48, 54, 55, 57,
    65-70, 73, 81, 93, 97, 115, 119, 124,
    131, 139, 148, 152, 154, 163-165, 196,
    216, 219, 228, 234
    conflict resolution, 26, 49
    conservation and management, 25-26,
        48, 119
    mission, 48
    predation studies, 49, 54, 68, 72, 73,
        93, 119
    public awareness, 25-26, 49, 67-68
    research (*see also* predation studies),

25-26, 49, 65-66, 119
rural development, 25-26, 49, 131,
  164-165
Cold Mountain, 163, 199, 205
Colorado, 9, 27, 43, 193
Coltii Chiliei (Rock Monastic Shelter),
  112, 158-159
consciousness, 53, 86-89, 134, 156-158
  and "now," 156-158
  and time, 53, 134
  neural basis, 86-87
  subjective nature, 87-89
Crai (male wolf), 37, 54, 60, 66, 89, 97,
  98, 108, 109, 116, 123-126, 133, 136,
  149, 152, 155, 161, 165, 167-168, 169,
  172, 191, 207-209, 234
Crisana, 123
Cristian, Romania, 129, 221
crows
  tool use, 89
cuckoo bird *(Cuculus canorus),* 176
Cumans, 122
Curly (dog), 36, 38-40, 60, 61-63, 69, 77,
  98, 100, 120, 126, 136-137, 138, 149-
  150, 155-158, 167, 175, 183, 198, 199-
  200, 232
Cuza, Alexander Ioan, 223

Dachian draco, 120-121, 123
Dacia
  automobile, 123
  Kingdom of, 121
Dacians, 120-121, 123
Djanga (Peter's dog), 74, 81, 90, 91, 124
dogs. *See also* shepherd dogs
  depredation by wolves, 72-73, 81
  evolution from wolves, 22-23
  tracks, compared to wolves, 46
dolphins
  language capabilities, 87
  self-recognition, 88
  tool use, 87
Dracula, 93-96, 203
Dracula (the novel), 22
Dracula's Castle. *See* Bran Castle

eco-tourism, 49, 69, 115, 164-165, 233

Einstein's Special Theory of Relativity,
  157-158
Einstein's Theories of Relativity, 157-158
electric fences, 26, 65
elephants
  tool use, 88
Emerald lizards, 126
Eurasian Lynx *(Lynx lynx),* 44, 105
Europe, 12, 21-22
  biodiversity goals (Bern Convention),
    65
  large carnivores in, 44
  oldest modern human fossil in, 159
  over-browsing by wild ungulates in,
    163
  Roma migration into, 222-223
European Brown Bears *(Ursus arctos
  arctos),* 25, 44, 82, 105, 219
European ravens *(Corvus corax),* 131
European Red Deer *(Cervus elaphus). See*
  red deer
European Roe Deer *(Capreolus capreolus).
  See* roe deer
European Union, 65

Fagaras Mountains, 176, 225
foxes *(Vulpes vulpes),* 81, 207
free will, 87, 157

gamekeepers, 82-83
Germany, 122,165
Ghica, Alexander, 223
Glajerie pack, 44, 47, 49, 71-74, 162
Gothic Empire, 121
Grand *Viovode,* 226
great apes
  language capabilities, 88
  self-recognition, 89
Guardian (dog), 36, 38-40, 43, 60, 61-62,
  69, 100, 114, 120, 126, 135-140, 232
Gypsies, 198, 213-216, 222-227
Gypsy "kings", 225-226
Gypsy villages, 227

hares *(Lepus europaeus),* 81, 116
Heinrich, Bernd, 86-87, 89
horseback riding, 139, 140-143, 165, 177

Hungarian Kingdom, 121
Hungary, 94, 121, 122, 222-223
Hunnish Empire, 121
hunting areas, 82-83
hunting in Romania. *See* Romania,
    hunting in
Hunyadi, John, 95

Ialomicioara cave, 159
intentions (animals knowing), 88-89
International Wolf Center, 148

Joris (eco-volunteer), 36, 37, 59, 61-62,
    68, 69, 100
Joseph II (Holy Roman Emperor, King
    of Hungary), 223

King, Stephen, 19
"King of the Gypsies", 222, 226
Kogălničeanu, Mihail, 123

language
capabilities in animals, 88
large carnivores, 12, 25-26, 44, 49, 63-65,
    67, 164-165
conflicts with livestock, 63-64
Leasa (female wild wolf), 70-74
livestock
    economic importance in Romania, 63
    as a source of conflict with wolves,
        49, 63-64
    depredation by wolves, 81, 83, 165
    protection of, 65
Lonely Planet, 136
Lord of the Wolves, 66

magazines, 43-44
Magyars, 122
Maine, 13, 19, 44, 130
Maramures, 123
Maria, 28-29
Marmot, 12
Mehmed II, Sultan, 95
memory, 86-87, 134
Metro
    supermarket, 67, 129
Michael the Brave, 122

Middle Ages, 11, 122, 222
Mind of the Raven, 86
Minnesota, 22
Mircea II (brother of Vlad III Dracula),
    95
Moieciu de Sus, Romania, 153
Moldavia, 122-123, 222-223
Moldova, 121
Monster of God, 66
Mt. Omu, 202
Munich, Germany, 54, 232

Nini, 29, 32-34, 133-134

observers
    in quantum mechanics, 88, 156-157,
        209
Order of the Dragon, 94
Otenpeni Airport, 228
Ottoman Empire, 93-95, 121-123, 223
Outside Magazine, 66

Peace Corps, 17-20
Pestera cu Oase (The Cave with Bones),
    159
Pestera, Romania, 112, 150-153, 159-160,
    172-175, 178, 191
Petchenegs, 122
Piatra Craiului, 35, 51, 97, 98, 106, 119,
    130, 135, 150, 151, 155, 158, 171, 176,
    179, 181, 183, 190, 195, 202, 205
Piatra Craiului Carthusian pink, 131
Piatra Craiului National Park, 130-131,
    171
Plaiul Foii, 130, 138, 171
Poiana (female wolf), 37, 54, 60, 66, 89,
    98, 102, 107, 108, 109, 116, 123-126,
    133, 136, 152, 154, 155, 159, 160-161,
    165, 168, 169, 207-209, 234
Poland, 122
Pope Pius II, 95
potato, 180, 194-196
prairie dogs
    vocalizations, 88
predation study. *See* CLCP, predation
    studies
Princess Ileana, 96

Project Crai, 234

Promberger, Barbara, 42, 49, 50, 57, 69, 100, 111, 117, 119, 125-126, 137, 140, 143, 145, 146, 148, 198, 208, 211-212, 214, 232

Promberger, Christoph, 25, 27, 40-42, 45-47, 50, 66, 69, 99, 119, 126, 137, 139, 140-143, 146, 148-149, 161, 163, 167-168, 172, 197, 199, 205-206, 208, 210, 232

Quammen, David, 66

quantum mechanics, 88, 157-158, 209

Racadau bears, 185, 219

Racadau neighborhood, 218

radio collar, 37, 55-56, 70, 119

radio telemetry, 54-56, 102, 113, 128, 162

Rasnov, Romania, 34, 186, 210, 213-214, 221

ravens. *See* European ravens

red deer, 72, 81, 84, 90-93, 103, 110, 116

Rietschen, Germany, 12

robi (Roma slaves), 222-223

roe deer, 81, 84, 85, 103, 110, 117-118

Roma people

a brief history in Romania, 222-227

Roman Empire, 121

Romania

economy of, 43-44, 63, 82, 93, 164

history of, 120-124, 222-227

hunting in, 63-64, 82-83

land use in, 44

Romanian Forestry Department, 83

(The) Rough Guide to Romania, 136

Russia, 21, 44, 122-123, 223

Russian Empire, 122

Sarmatians, 121

Saxons, 51, 94, 122

sea otters

tool use, 88

sheep

as a source of conflict with wolves, 63-64

depredation by wolves, 73

protection of, 65

shepherd dogs

role protecting livestock, 65-66

depredation by wolves, 81

shepherds

work and methods protecting livestock, 63-65

Sibiu, Romania, 187, 222, 224-227

Sigismund, King of Hungary, 94

Silverine (eco-volunteer), 36, 37, 38, 47, 53, 59-61, 100

Sinca Noua Foundation, 232, 248

Slovakia, 81, 83, 184, 222

Stephen the Great, 96

Stoker, Bram, 22, 69, 94, 96

strigoi, 204

Sturdza, Mihail, 223

Sürth, Peter, 9-12, 54, 57-59, 74-81, 84-86, 90-91, 93, 100, 102, 113-119, 120, 126, 136, 176, 201-202, 208-209, 233, 234, 248

Szeklers, 122

Tartars, 11, 122

Teutons, 122

Thoreau, Henry David, 21

Thurn, Valentin, 66

Timpa Hill, Brasov, 220-221

Titus (student volunteer), 36-38, 47, 49-50, 59, 60, 61-62, 69, 74, 77, 78, 84, 100, 114, 116-117, 119, 120, 127, 313-134, 135, 137-138

tools

use by animals, 88

Tohanu Nou, Romania, 162

Transylvania, 9, 22, 34, 43, 81, 82, 95, 121-123, 203-204, 222, 231

Transylvania — Living with Predators, 66

Transylvanian Alps, 33, 225

trophy fees, 82

Turkey, 122-123

Turnu (female wild wolf), 45, 47, 49, 70-74, 76, 162

Ukraine, 121

vampires, 95-96, 203-204

Vanessa (student volunteer), 36, 37, 40,

53, 59, 69, 70, 84, 100, 102, 119, 127-
128, 131, 133-134, 135, 137-138
Vlad III Dracula. *See* Dracula

Wallachia, 33, 82, 93-95, 122-123, 222-
223, 230
(The) Way of the Wolf
    expedition, 9-12, 115-116, 231, 234,
    248
wild boar *(Sus scrofa),*
    kill,
wild ungulates, 81
    hunting of, 81-83
    over-browsing by, 163-164
wildcats *(Felis sylvestris),* 81
Wolf Cabin. *See* Cabanna Lupului
wolf tracks, 9, 45-47, 56, 57, 74-76,
    79-80, 84-85, 90-91, 114, 116-118, 176
wolves
    biting force, 125 (*see* note 83)
    conflicts with human interests, 22, 64,
        81-82
    dispersal, 71
    ecotourism and, 49, 164-165
    ecological niche and early humans,
        21-22
    evolution of dogs from, 22-23
    feeding ecology, 81, 207-208

grooming in, 168
howling, 37, 39, 71, 98, 168-170
hunting by, 81, 91-93
hunting of, 83
nutritional requirements, 81
pack structure, 71 (*see* note 36)
paw size, 160
population in Romania, 44
pup rearing, 71-72
sexual activity, 47
tracks (*see* wolf tracks)
    characteristics of, 46
vocalizations, 169-170

Yellowstone National Park, 163
Yukai (Christoph's dog), 111, 124, 142-
144, 146, 232
Yukon Territory, Canada, 45

Zarnesti, 26, 34, 40-41, 50-51, 67, 68, 77,
    84, 128, 131, 153-154, 163, 164-165,
    179, 180, 189, 190, 194, 196, 198, 204,
    216-217, 218, 221, 230, 234
    economy, 164
    founding, 51
    potato fields, 180. 194-196
Zarnesti Gorge, 10, 181, 205, 215

About the Author

Alan E. Sparks is (or has been) an engineer, writer, actor, and teacher. He has a BS degree in Engineering Physics from the University of Maine, and an MS degree in Electrical Engineering from Stanford University. Alan has also completed post-secondary courses in philosophy, sociology, psychology, drawing, painting, acting, exercise physiology, film making, and writing at the University of Colorado, Merrimack College, and Naropa University. He was employed for over twenty years as a software engineer developing new technologies in the telecommunications industry, including over nineteen years at Bell Laboratories.

An avid walker, hiker, backcountry skier, and animal tracker, Alan has lived, worked, and trekked extensively in the wilds of Central and Eastern Europe. He is a voracious reader and enjoys studying the natural and cultural history of the places he visits. To supplement his indoor studies, he has completed courses in mountaineering with the Colorado Mountain Club, mountain ski touring/expedition leadership with the National Outdoor Leadership School, and winter ecology/animal tracking with renowned animal tracker Dr. James Halfpenny of A Naturalist's World.

Alan currently divides his time between Krakow, Poland and Boulder, Colorado. He continues to write (working on the sequel to Dreaming of Wolves about The Way Of The Wolf expedition) and teaches English (in Poland), and occasionally seizes an opportunity to perform as an actor or percussionist.